THE
JAY
TREATY

THE
JAY
TREATY

Political Battleground of
the Founding Fathers

JERALD A. COMBS

University of California Press
Berkeley, Los Angeles and London 1970

University of California Press
Berkeley and Los Angeles, California

University of California Press, Ltd.
London, England

Copyright © 1970 by
The Regents of the University of California

SBN 520–01573–8
Library of Congress Catalog Card Number: 70–84044
Printed in the United States of America

To Sara

CONTENTS

PREFACE

The treaty that John Jay negotiated with England in 1794 was one of the most crucial in United States history. It was also one of the most bitterly debated. People who were coalescing under the leadership of Thomas Jefferson and James Madison to form the Republican party called the treaty a surrender to Great Britain. The United States was powerful enough to have achieved a far better bargain, they claimed. Their opponents, who were coming to be called Federalists, asserted that the treaty was the best the United States could expect in the face of America's weakness and Great Britain's strength.

This story is well known. All historians of the Federalist era have related it, some at length. But they have differed as vociferously as Jay's contemporaries concerning the necessity and desirability of his treaty. Historians attached to the libertarian and humane domestic policies of the Republicans seem to have accepted without much investigation the sincerity and accuracy of Republican views in foreign affairs as well. They have argued, as Madison and Jefferson did, that America was powerful enough to have extorted more concessions from Britain than Jay obtained. They have regarded Federalist arguments to the contrary as cynical exaggerations of America's weakness, designed to cover other reasons for a quick, "appeasing" settlement with England. In the opinion of Claude Bowers, Federalists refused to stand against Britain because of their attachment to British aristocratic ideology. Charles Beard thought the primary reason for the Federalists' supine attitude was their desire to protect Hamilton's domestic financial system. William Appleman Williams claimed that their real motive was a dream of an Anglo-American economic empire. Joseph Charles said the Federalists were simply pursuing partisan political advantage. Even Alexander DeConde, who is more impartial than these historians, has doubted the sincerity of Federalist contentions that the United States was too weak to stand against Great Britain.

On the other hand, some historians have regarded Federalist contentions of American weakness as obvious truths and have doubted that Republicans believed their own public estimates of America's strength. The more rabid Federalist historians of the nineteenth century thought that the Republicans by these arguments were disguising an attempt to bring the United States into the war against England as allies of the French revolutionaries. This view is no longer taken seriously. But many authors, such as John C. Miller and Broadus Mitchell, still regard Republican policy as having been dangerous, unrealistic "pipe-dreaming," adopted on ideological, economic, and partisan grounds without much thought given to the power situation. Paul Varg has stated this theory well. After referring to Hamilton as a *realpolitiker* with a profound grasp of the importance of power in international affairs, he comments: "James Madison exemplifies the idealist in foreign policy. He spoke often of the rights of the republic and of what was just in international affairs but never felt it necessary to balance goals with the power available."

Contrary to all these views, this essay argues that Federalist and Republican leaders alike sought to "balance goals with the power available" and were sincere in their arguments regarding the relative power of the United States and Great Britain. The founding fathers disagreed over the Jay Treaty not because they ignored or purposely misrepresented the power situation, but because they had opposing domestic and foreign goals to balance with America's available power. In addition, they held opposing theories regarding the nature and extent of power necessary to enable America to stand against the might of the British Empire. Party politics and ideology rarely superseded power considerations in the foreign policies of men like George Washington, Alexander Hamilton, John Adams, John Jay, Thomas Jefferson, and James Madison.

If both Federalists and Republicans sought to balance goals with power, it is necessary to ascertain which party had the more accurate view of the power situation before one can decide which was the more "realistic" in its policies during the Jay Treaty controversy. This is a difficult and complicated task, for it involves not only the relative strength of England and the United States, but the ability and willingness of each side to use that strength. Only Samuel Flagg Bemis has made a thorough and concerted attempt to resolve the question by investigating both American and British records. His *Jay's Treaty* is an excellent work, but there are significant areas where Bemis is either incomplete, ambiguous, or mistaken. His evidence and presentation lead to the conclusion that America could have had a far better settlement with England than the Jay Treaty achieved, yet he concludes the contrary. The present study seeks to resolve this ambiguity, and to supplement his treatment by an extensive use of private papers in both England and the United States as well as the diplomatic archives which Bemis used so well.

Except where it might harm the meaning or flavor of a quotation, words abbreviated in the original text have been spelled out. Quotations from the Jay Papers are by permission of Columbia University, those from the Adams Papers are from the microfilm edition, by permission of the Massachusetts Historical Society.

In the course of writing this book I have accumulated many personal debts. Bradford Perkins of the University of Michigan suggested the project to me and provided much help in the early stages of my research on it. Page Smith, now provost of Cowell College at the University of California, Santa Cruz, was a patient and perceptive dissertation supervisor. The style and organization of this book would have been far more barbarous without his help. Professors Alexander De Conde and Wilbur Jacobs of the University of California at Santa Barbara, Joseph Illick and John Tricamo of San Francisco State College, and Keith Berwick of UCLA read the manuscript in various stages of its development and made many helpful criticisms. Robert Kelley of the University of California at Santa Barbara first stimulated my interest in the intellectual history of American diplomacy, and his influence is reflected in my whole approach to the subject of this book. Samuel Flagg Bemis helped me track down one particularly elusive document. Mrs. Evelyn Phillips typed most of the manuscript with some help from the members of the manuscript typing pool at San Francisco State. Robert Schoelkopf contributed his artistic talent and many hours to the creation of the dust jacket. To all of them I am deeply grateful. My greatest debt is to my wife Sara, my editor–critic–consoler-in-chief.

Part I
SEEDS OF DISCORD: ANGLO-AMERICAN RELATIONS, 1782-1789

1. GREAT BRITAIN: FROM CONCILIATION TO CONFRONTATION

By 1782, George III and many members of the British Parliament had concluded that the American colonies would have to be given their independence. But they had yet to decide whether America was to be treated as a potential rival or potential friend. Was independence to be given freely or grudgingly, with generous terms in hopes of attaching America to the British interest or with terms designed to circumscribe the power of a potential enemy? Britain had to choose between a policy of conciliation and one of confrontation.

Lord Shelburne, who had become head of the government in 1782, chose conciliation. Through his envoy, Richard Oswald, he negotiated and signed a very liberal provisional peace with the United States, and he planned further to offer a liberal commercial treaty based on the free trade principles of Adam Smith. He hoped to bind America to England once more, substituting for the colonial ties now severed the silken threads of commerce.

During the negotiations, Shelburne's conciliatory approach toward the colonies met with little opposition in England. Some of the London press did proclaim that it was mortifying for a country possessing 460 ships of war to acknowledge the independence of a country "whose Produce was the principle [sic] Source of our Naval Glory," and lamented that now "Yankies shall become High and Mighty Lords!"[1] One newspaper even proposed strengthening Canada to drain the population of the United States and "make them curse their Independence."[2] But the same newspapers commented on the potential strength of the United States and on the advantages to be derived from friendly relations and a prosperous trade with it.[3] There was surprisingly little anti-American sentiment being publicly expressed in Britain at this time. In fact, the London press was more critical of its own leaders than of the rebellious colonists. The *Public Advertiser*, which had vigorously supported the war, commented, "The more we reflect on the loss of our once flourishing Colonies . . . the more we execrate and loath those Men, who by their Folly and Ignorance caused them to be dismembered from the British Crown."[4] The same newspaper also blamed the British people for the loss of the colonies because they had refused to support the action necessary to keep them.[5]

When Shelburne's government announced the specific terms of the peace, however, the mood of Parliament and the press quickly changed. Many expressed astonishment that Britain should have sacrificed so much to the upstart colonists. Even the *Public Advertiser*, which had generally supported the Shelburne ministry, declared, "The terms granted to the Rebellious Colonies are hardly to be mentioned: our Language does not furnish Expressions adequate to so great a Disgrace."[6]

This announcement of opposition by the *Public Advertiser* was one of the first steps toward the reversal of Shelburne's policy of conciliation. The arguments that were now made against the concessions granted to the United States in the Peace Treaty of 1783 raised issues that were to help push England and the United States to the brink of war in 1794 and set the stage for negotiation of the Jay Treaty.

The portions of the treaty most bitterly assailed were those dealing with the British Loyalists in America and with Britain's Indian allies. Lord North told Parliament that the Loyalist Americans had been "sacrificed for their bravery and principles," being left to their enemies with only the stipulation that Congress recommend to the states the restoration of Loyalist property.[7] "Better . . . to have been totally silent upon the subject in the treaty," said Edmund Burke, "than to have consented to have set our hands to a gross libel on the national character, and in one flagitious article, plunged the dagger into the hearts of the loyalists, and manifested our own impotency, ingratitude, and disgrace."[8]

The Loyalists were not the only people abandoned to the tender mercies of the vengeful and barbarous Americans. "Twenty-five nations of Indians made over to the United States," mourned the earl of Carlisle in the House of Lords, "[and in return] not even that solitary stipulation which our honour should have made us insist upon, . . . a place of refuge for those miserable persons . . . , some haven for those shattered barks to have been laid up in quiet."[9] Instead, those Indians who had aided the British in their fight against the colonists were left to their fate, with no provision for their safety.

Opponents of the treaty also raged that the boundary drawn between Canada and the United States gave to the United States all the land between the Ohio and Mississippi rivers. The earl of Carlisle told the House of Lords that this border meant the loss of all Canada, for without that fertile triangle of land between the Ohio and Mississippi, Quebec and Montreal were merely ports without trade and would have to be supported from England.[10] Canadian merchants visited Shelburne and told him that the Grand Portage, the only route by which furs could be brought from the Indian country to Montreal, was now on the American side of the border, and as a consequence the fur trade was "totally destroyed." Shelburne could only express surprise and tell them that "it had not been foreseen that these consequences would follow from the boundaries agreed on."[11]

The fur trade was not all that was sacrificed by this border, continued Shelburne's critics; "all the forts which commanded the lakes [are] in their hands, and we [are] wholly defenceless, and at their mercy, in our navigation of the lakes," admonished Lord Stormont.[12] He was equally chagrined at the provision allowing the Americans liberal "rights" and "privileges" in the Newfoundland fisheries, out of which "Eternal jealousies would arise, and instead of securing a peace, we had, in truth, granted all this for the sake of involving the nation in a new war."[13]

Any treaty that acknowledges a nation's defeat is bound to be criticized by the opposition whether better terms were available or not. The criticism of Shelburne's peace is doubly suspect because much of it came from men like Edmund Burke and Charles James Fox, who in all probability would have accepted the same terms themselves had they been responsible for making the peace. Nevertheless, the criticism was not motivated simply by political expediency. There was real concern in England over the extent of the concessions to the Americans.[14] The issues of the Loyalists, the Indians, the fur trade, the Canadian border, the Great Lakes forts, and the fisheries would haunt Anglo-American relations for decades to come. These issues were deemed important enough in Parliament to result in the fall of Shelburne's government, as the followers of Fox and his old rival, Lord North, combined to bring him down.

Yet the fall of Shelburne did not result in an immediate reversal of his conciliatory policy toward the United States. George III hated Fox and fought frantically to keep him from forming a cabinet. Meanwhile, William Pitt the younger, a protégé of Shelburne, headed an interim government. From this position, Pitt made a half-hearted attempt to continue Shelburne's policies. He proposed to Parliament a liberal treatment of American trade. Temporarily, American ships would be treated like all other foreign ships, but American imports would receive special consideration, and Britain's remaining colonies in the western hemisphere, including the West Indies, would be thrown open to American ships and merchandise.

Only twenty-three years old when he headed the interim government, yet Pitt was self-assured to the point of arrogance. The speech with which he defended his temporary commercial measure therefore seems out of character. It was hesitant, deferential, and almost painfully unsure. He pointed to the insecure tenure of his position and the pressing need for some sort, any sort, of legislation that would reopen the American trade which had been closed during the war. He confessed his "little share of knowledge of commerce." He explained that he "was by no means tenacious of any part of the Bill then under consideration." The bill, he said, was an experiment, and worse, an experiment hazarded in great measure on conjecture. He disclaimed responsibility for the effects of the bill, saying that it was hastily thrown together and that he presented it only because somebody had to do it and take responsibility for it. It rested with the House to adopt, reject, or alter it, and "if the Bill passed into law, the legislature would then bear the responsibility of it."[15] This was hardly a speech that would inspire Parliament to throw over its mercantilist principles in favor of free trade and the conciliation of Britain's defected colonies.

Yet some of Pitt's hesitancy was understandable. The subject was indeed momentous. The heart of any trade bill that America would deem liberal involved the opening of the West Indies to American goods and ships. Since British trade to the East was still not fully developed and the United States was now independent, Britain's commercial relationship with the West Indies was the most important of all its colonial ties.[16] If Britain opened the West Indies to American ships and merchandise, it might call forth an American navy to challenge its own in an area where Britain was weak; America's proximity to the West Indies might well allow it to dominate the West Indian market to the exclusion of Britain's remaining colonies in North America and even Britain itself. On the other hand, if the British did not open the West Indies to American ships and merchandise, the West India planters might suffer, since before the war they had been largely dependent on the Americans for lumber and provisions. In addition, the United States would regard the closing of the West Indies to its ships as a hostile act, and Britain could conceivably thereby lose the great American market for her manufactures.

Pitt's bill received harsh treatment at the hands of Parliament. Although Burke and Fox gave grudging support to its principles, they roundly criticized many of its specific provisions. Their criticisms, added to the outright attacks of those who opposed *any* liberal trade treaty with America, were sufficient to induce Parliament to amend the bill all out of shape. Finally Pitt himself moved that the bill should stand over until the king appointed new ministers to replace Pitt's interim government, whereupon those ministers could either proceed with it or substitute another measure.[17]

During the debates on Pitt's American Intercourse Bill, opinion out of doors seems to have been as hesitant as that in Parliament. Copious extracts of the debates were printed, but few or no comments were made concerning it in the British press. Pitt was criticized for following "unwise policies" in general, but no specifics were given.[18] Many were evidently unsure of all the implications of a liberal trade policy toward the United States. These implications were quickly made clear, however, in a pamphlet war instigated by the publication of Lord Sheffield's *Observations on the Commerce of the American States.*[19] Sheffield aimed his remarks straight at Pitt's American Intercourse Bill: "In the youthful ardour for grasping the advantages of the American trade, a bill, still depending, was first introduced into parliament. Had it passed, it would have affected our most essential interests in every branch of commerce, and in every part of the world. . . . Fortunately, some delays have intervened, and if we diligently use the opportunity of inquiry and reflection, which the delays have afforded us, the future welfare of our Country may depend on this salutory pause."[20]

Sheffield's premonitions of all-encompassing disaster resulted from the provision of the bill that opened the trade of the West Indies to American ships. This measure, he asserted, would have benefited the West India merchants and the Americans but ruined Great Britain. The same measure had ruined the French trade and, if persisted in, would have destroyed their navy entirely.[21] Better to give up the islands altogether than to give up the carrying trade, he maintained. The islands cost a great deal to protect, and the cost was worth paying only if West Indian commerce performed its primary function, that of furnishing employment for British ships and seamen. Even small American vessels should be prohibited from trading with Britain's islands, asserted Sheffield. If they were allowed, the principal part of the business of those islands would be usurped by them, "there will be no end of smuggling, and we shall raise a most numerous marine on the coasts of the Southern States where there is none at present, at the expense of our own."[22]

What about American reaction to the closing of Britain's West Indian islands to U.S. ships? For this question Sheffield was only too ready with an answer. If the United States should retaliate by refusing to furnish lumber and provisions to British ships trading with the West Indies, the Americans would "compleatly do what the British Legislature ought to do, they would give the monopoly of the supply of our West-India Islands to the British dominions" of Canada, Nova Scotia, and New Brunswick. As for the effects on the American market for British manufactures, there was no need to worry. The United States could not furnish its own manufactures, for the West drained the East of manpower, thereby making labor costs prohibitive. Although Americans might try to purchase their manufactures in a country other than Britain, those of Britain were cheaper and of better quality, and only Britain could and would furnish that extensive credit which

Americans required to purchase anything overseas. In addition, he argued, Britain had little need of American products except coarse tobacco. "Britain only takes American naval stores, indigo, and other products, which may be gotten as good or better elsewhere, to enable America to purchase British manufactures with the foreign exchange so acquired. Thus we need have no fear of being deprived of American products if they should take action against a British monopolization of the carrying trade of the West Indies."[23]

In any case, it was unlikely that America could or would retaliate. "It will not be an easy matter to bring the American States to act as a nation," he asserted; "they are not to be feared by such as us." They could not agree on anything involving expense, for their climate, their staples, and their manners were different and their interests opposite. "It is impossible to name any material advantage the American States will, or can give us in return, more than we shall of course have. No treaty can be made with the American States that can be binding on the whole of them."[24]

Despite Sheffield's pamphlet, Charles Fox, who with Lord North had finally formed a government to replace Pitt's interim ministry, decided to continue Pitt's policy of offering liberal treatment to American commerce. He gave permission to the delegate negotiating a commercial treaty with the United States to open the British West Indies to all American ships. Meanwhile, thinking that a parliamentary statute on the American trade should await the outcome of these negotiations, he moved to put off consideration of Pitt's American Intercourse Bill for four weeks. In its place, he proposed a bill that would simply repeal the Prohibitory Acts and reopen Anglo-American trade on prewar terms. An opponent of a liberal policy toward American trade, however, offered an amendment to give the King-in-Council discretionary power to regulate trade between America and Great Britain for nine months. This meant that conceivably the King-in-Council could restrict trade with America rather than leaving it on the basis of the liberal prewar regulations. Nonetheless, Fox accepted the amendment, and the bill passed.[25]

Suddenly, on July 2, the policy vaguely implied by this amendment was put into effect. The government issued an order-in-council forbidding American vessels to trade with the West Indies. This shattered the commercial negotiations with the United States.[26] Fox had abandoned conciliatory attempts to reconcile British and American interests. He had decided instead to confront the United States with a policy based entirely on British interests and to dare the new nation to do anything about it.

Fox's shift may well have been the result of a growing movement opposed to conciliation of the United States. Sheffield's pamphlet evidently had struck a responsive chord with much of Parliament and the press. Perhaps it was a refreshing change from the hand-wringing self-criticism that had prevailed since the end of 1782. It must have been pleasant for many Britons to hear once again the power and virtues of England extolled, and to contemplate the reassertion of its power and rights against its presumptuous ex-colonies after the humiliating treaty of peace. In any case, the West India planters pleaded in vain that American provisions and lumber were necessary to their survival, and that it was nonsense to claim that these could be provided by Canada and Nova Scotia.[27] Such pleas were answered by more and more vitriolic pamphlet attacks on the United States which asserted that Americans were too deceitful and perfidious to keep commercial treaties in the face of self-interest and ought to be considered not only as aliens, but as potential rivals.[28] The newspapers began to print reports of American disunity and weakness and to imply that Britain ought to take advantage of this weakness to insure that the United States did not develop to its full potential as a rival. In January 1784, for instance, the *Morning Herald* reported that "The authority of Congress, to which [the states] submitted but from necessity during the war, they have now almost generally thrown off. . . . This cannot fail of being most consonant to the wishes and interests of the European powers and will therefore no doubt be encouraged, in preference to the establishment of one grand empire, which would in time become exceedingly alarming to all who have colonies in the western world."[29]

In 1784 William Pitt succeeded in overturning the Fox-North coalition and in winning a resounding vote of confidence. He found himself faced once again with the problem of American trade, and, like Fox, he reversed himself on the question. Instead of pushing through his American Intercourse Bill, Pitt decided to refer the question of West Indian trade to the newly constituted Committee of the Lords of the Privy Council on Trade and Plantations and to await its report. Prominent on this committee was David Jenkinson, soon to be Lord Hawkesbury, who was decidedly hostile to a liberal treatment of American commerce.[30]

The Committee on Trade heard many complaints from the West India planters. But their complaints were often contradicted by information from the governors of the various islands. The governors claimed that much of the planters' distress had resulted from their belief that no restrictions would be put on American trade. Thus they had not laid in supplies. The committee concluded that the planters' complaints were entirely unjustified. It reported that Canada and other British colonies in the western hemisphere could supply the West Indies with lumber and provisions, and that

9

elimination of American competition would induce these colonies to build their own ships. The committee concluded that the protection of the British islands depended on the augmentation of British naval strength in that theater and the corresponding diminution of that of "other countries." The committee expressed doubts that the United States could retaliate but advocated continuation of the West Indian policy in any case.[31]

On the basis of this report, Pitt abandoned his conciliatory trade policy toward the United States. In late July his government postponed the American Intercourse Bill on the grounds that the committee had deemed reports of the distress of the West Indies to be highly exaggerated.[32] On August 10, Henry Dundas "by order" moved in Parliament for a continuation of the law authorizing the King-in-Council to regulate the American trade.[33] Under that law the orders-in-council barring American ships from the West Indies along with all American products except tobacco, provisions, and naval stores were continued. Pitt still allowed American unmanufactured goods to be exported to England in American ships on terms more favorable than those given any other nation, but he knew that the United States would deem the closing of the West Indies to its shipping a mark of hostility. In the matter of American trade, Pitt had chosen a policy of confrontation rather than conciliation.

The new Pitt government found itself balancing between conciliation and confrontation in yet another matter—the northwestern posts. The Canadian boundary set by the Peace of 1783 gave to the United States not only the Grand Portage, but also seven of the eight frontier fortresses that controlled the navigation of the Great Lakes. Two of these fortresses, Detroit and Michilimachinack, also served as important entrepôts for the fur trade.

The frontier posts were thus invested with an importance far out of proportion to their size. They were vital strategically, for they controlled the possible routes for major military movements between Canada and the United States. They were vital commercially, for they dominated the routes followed by the fur trade. Since the Indians in the area were dependent on the trade and navigation which these posts commanded for the luxuries of civilization, the nation possessing the fortresses was in a position to control the Indians and their lands. As one experienced British officer wrote, "the Americans might as well (while we are in possession of these Posts) attempt to seduce our children and servants from their duty and allegiance" as to attempt to seduce the Indians.[34]

The allegiance of these Indians was as important as possession of the forts. Strategically, the Indians were a great threat to any military maneuvers in the Northwest, and their enmity was catastrophic for the tenuous frontier settlements on either side of the U.S.–Canadian boundary. Commercially, the Indians were the suppliers of pelts on which the prosperous fur trade of the Northwest was dependent, and their allegiance meant either prosperity or ruin for that enterprise.

The British may have decided to keep the posts very soon after they signed the provisional peace that officially gave them up. In 1783, orders went out to General Carlton, the commander of British forces in the United States, to evacuate New York. But none went out to evacuate the frontier posts. Certainly by April 8, 1784, the policy of withholding the posts was definite. On that date, Lord Sydney, the secretary of state for Home Affairs in Pitt's new government, wrote Governor Haldimand of Canada that Britain was justified in holding the posts at least temporarily, because there was no set time for evacuation of the posts and the Americans had not yet complied with even one article of the treaty.[35]

From this time forward, the British justified their policy by pointing to America's failure to abide by the Treaty of 1783 regarding British debts and the treatment of the British Loyalists. Yet the correspondence between the British Colonial Office and Canadian officials makes it clear that strategic and commercial considerations rather than American violations of the treaty were the real factors behind the decision to hold the posts.

Rumors of the impending peace terms had filtered to Governor Haldimand of Canada as early as September 1782, and his concern was immediate. He told General Carlton that Britain's Indian allies were "alarmed at the appearance of an accommodation so far short of what our Language, from the beginning has taught them to expect." This settlement, the Indians feared, would deprive them of their lands and leave them at the mercy of their American enemies. Haldimand reminded Carlton of the consequence of the Indians "to the Trade and Safety of this Province, the Expectations their services entitles them to from us," and of "the fatal consequences that might attend our abandoning them."[36] From this time until 1795, a constant theme of the British officials in Canada was that, if the Indians ever felt that Britain had abandoned them, they would turn on the sparse Canadian settlements and wreak death and destruction.[37]

When the peace terms were officially communicated to Haldimand, he told the home government that they constituted just such a betrayal as might turn the Indians against their former British allies. "It will be a difficult task, after what has happened," he wrote, "to convince them of our good faith."[38] Haldimand realized that by making peace without mentioning the Indians, Britain had in effect left them still at war with the United

States. He suspected, with reason, that the United States would claim that the Indians had forfeited all rights to their lands west of the Ohio River by warring with the United States, and that therefore new boundaries to these lands would have to be drawn. He knew full well that these boundaries would be as unfavorable to the Indians as America's power would allow them to be. Haldimand promised to attempt to reconcile the Indians and the Americans, bringing peace on terms that would protect the rights of the Indians, but he did not hold much hope for success.[39]

Meanwhile, the British tried to demonstrate their good faith to the Indians by asserting that their peace treaty with the United States had ceded to the Americans only the preemptive rights to Indian lands west of the Ohio River, not the lands themselves. This meant that the Indians maintained full title to the lands, with the United States holding the exclusive right against all other nations to purchase any lands in this area that the Indians might choose to sell.[40] But the Indians quickly saw that such legalisms were meaningless if the British refused to help them enforce this position against the Americans. So the British officials in Canada sought frantically to reassure the Indians that they would not be abandoned, promising them supplies, trade, and "all other Benefits in [the king's] Power to afford them."[41] They could not, however, promise the one thing that would reassure the Indians—military aid in defense of their lands west of the Ohio.*

This predicament was the primary influence in the recommendation of the Canadian officials and the decision of the home government to hold the posts; but the fur trade played some part in that decision as well.

The principal part of the fur trade was with Indians on the American side of the new border. Half of the furs were collected there, and even many of those collected on the Canadian side still had to be brought east over the Grand Portage, which was on the American side of the border. The United States was in a position to dominate at least half of the fur trade by monopolizing the trade on its side of the border, and more if furs collected in Canada and brought through the Grand Portage were diverted to Americans. By holding the posts, the British could forestall this. They would keep control of the routes by which furs were brought east and maintain the loyalty of the Indians who brought them. (See Appendix I.)

The conciliation of America, espoused at first by Shelburne and Pitt,

---

* However, before the definitive peace, the commander of the upper posts promised the Indians that if the United States quarreled wantonly with the Indians, "I, with all the King's Troops, should stand by them at all Risks whatever might be the consequences." Michigan Pioneer and Historical Society Collections and Researches, XX, 120.

had thus been turned by Britain's conception of her interests and by a widespread desire for a new reassertion of British power and prestige to a policy of hesitant confrontation. Slowly that policy became more resolute and settled. Continuing reports of American weakness and inability to retaliate confirmed the British in their course. The longer that policy was enforced, the more British prestige was attached to it and the more difficult it became for the government to retreat without loss of face. Pitt's ministry resolved to meet any possible American retaliation with even harsher measures rather than back down. The commanders of the frontier forts were instructed to repel by war any attempt by the United States to take the posts.[42] The Committee on Trade, which was now in control of British policy toward American commerce, determined to retaliate against any attempt by the United States to force the opening of the West Indies.

The United States was not long in finding that Britain meant to be intransigent about its frontier and trade policy. John Adams, sent as minister to England in 1785 to settle the problems surrounding the execution of the peace terms and to negotiate a trade treaty, was greeted with open hostility by some of the press. "An ambassador from America. Good heavens what a sound! . . . tis hard to say which can excite indignation most, the insolence of those who appoint the Character, or the meanness of those who receive it," wrote one newspaper.[43]

His official reception was little more enthusiastic. In reply to Adams' protestations that the United States desired a restoration of "esteem, confidence, and affection" between itself and England, King George replied that he would be the first to meet that friendship the moment he saw a "disposition to give this country the preference." Adams interpreted this remark to mean that the price Britain placed on its favorable treatment of the United States was some sort of special alliance directed against France. This was an impossible condition.[44]

In an interview with Pitt, Adams found that evacuation of the posts depended on the payment of debts to Britain along with the interest accumulated on them during the war. But several American states had passed laws inhibiting the payment of those debts, and Congress under the Articles of Confederation was powerless to compel a change. Sentiment in the country was decidedly against the payment of the interest accumulated during the war in any case. Therefore, Adams concluded that there was no chance the posts would be evacuated in the near future. In addition, despite Adams' threats of retaliation, he could get no answer from Pitt concerning a relaxation of the British trade policy in the West Indies.[45]

After his interviews with the king and the prime minister, Adams' presence was virtually ignored by the British government. What was worse, no minister was sent by England to the United States in return for the appointment of Adams. After three years, a mortified and angry Adams returned to the United States.

Americans had not expected such treatment. They considered their commerce so important to Britain that the British would be forced into a compliant posture.[46] After all, the American trade had constituted from one-third to one-sixth of that of the whole empire before the Revolution.[47] Yet Britain had refused to acknowledge this dependence and had adopted a hostile attitude toward the United States.

Nor was Great Britain the only foreign obstacle to realization of America's goals. Spain, too, had an interest in preventing the growth of American power and stability. Her occupation of Florida and Louisiana was threatened by America's growing and restless population. To combat this threat, Spain used her control of both banks of the lower reaches of the Mississippi to close the river to American navigation. She also claimed that the border of Florida reached as far north as the Ohio River, a claim designed to keep the Americans as far from the Mississippi as possible. Spain made alliances with the Indians along the southwestern border of the United States, hoping that the spectre of unfriendly Indians and the closure of the area's main supply route would prevent the growth of America's population there. Like Britain, Spain flirted with American secession movements later in the Confederation period. And, again like Britain, Spain closed her colonies to American trade.

France, on the other hand, with no major territorial interests in North America outside the West Indies, found herself much less in conflict with the interests of the United States. But even France adopted a harsher policy toward American trade than the United States had expected. She withdrew the wartime decree authorizing relatively free trade between the United States and the French West Indies. She then enforced the decree of 1767 which excluded imports of flour and other foodstuffs to the islands, permitted exports of rum and molasses only, and limited American entry to two ports.[48] France's alliance with Spain also raised questions as to her ultimate attitude toward the United States. America could not depend fully even on her wartime ally. The overt hostility of Great Britain and the uncertain attitude of the other major powers of Europe surprised the leaders of the United States and forced them to consider anew their nation's relationship with England and the rest of the international community.

2. THE UNITY OF THE AMERICAN RESPONSE

The nature of America's response to Europe's challenge was determined to a great extent by the actions and attitudes of six men, George Washington, John Adams, John Jay, Alexander Hamilton, Thomas Jefferson, and James Madison. During the Confederation period, John Jay as secretary for foreign affairs, John Adams as minister to England, and Thomas Jefferson as minister to France exchanged correspondence defining the problems faced by American foreign policy and suggesting solutions. They concluded that none of their plans could be implemented without a stronger federal government. Alexander Hamilton and James Madison as members of Congress took primary responsibility for securing greater national power, first in unsuccessful attempts to create a permanent federal revenue through a tax on imports and later by successfully convening the Constitutional Convention at Philadelphia. Under Hamilton's urging, Washington attended the Convention, lending his prestige to the efforts of Madison and Hamilton to create a government capable of a vigorous foreign policy. Finally, Hamilton, Jay, and Madison composed the Federalist Papers, explaining to the people the import of the Constitution and helping to secure its ratification.

Assuming the most important offices created by the Constitution, these same men after 1789 were able to act on the foreign policies they had only been able to discuss during the Confederation period. Washington was elected president, while Adams became vice-president and presiding officer of the Senate. Washington appointed Jefferson secretary of state and Hamilton secretary of the treasury. Madison was elected to the House of Representatives and quickly established himself as its most influential member. John Jay became the nation's first chief justice. Although he had no official responsibility for foreign policy, he remained a close adviser to Washington and Hamilton in these matters and ultimately negotiated the most important treaty of Washington's administration. Truly these were the decision-makers of postrevolutionary America. An analysis of their ideas on foreign policy will explain much about the diplomacy of this era.

Considering the ferocious disputes over foreign policy that took place during Washington's presidency, it is astounding to see how unified the future combatants were in their response to the challenge of Europe during the Confederation period. The pronouncements of future Federalist leaders like Alexander Hamilton, John Adams, John Jay, and Washington himself

15

gave little indication of profound opposition to the opinions on foreign policy expressed by future Republican leaders like Thomas Jefferson and James Madison. All of them agreed that the country's basic task was to recover from the postwar depression and maintain political stability while preserving the nation's independence and internal liberty. They further agreed on a foreign policy to help accomplish this task.

First, they sought to increase opportunities for foreign trade to help restore prosperity. These leaders hoped to secure free access for American ships and goods not only to the home ports of European countries, but to these nations' colonies in the western hemisphere as well. The founding fathers also agreed that the right to navigate the entire Mississippi River would be vital to America's prosperity. They also sought international respect for what Americans conceived to be their proper borders. This meant turning the Redcoats out of the northwest posts and thereby eliminating the major source of supply for hostile Indians on American territory. It also meant securing a firm and favorable border with Spanish Florida, giving the United States access to the Mississippi River, and hopefully ending Spanish intrigue with the Indians and frontier settlers on the American side of the border.

Finally, these men wanted to achieve their foreign policy goals without another major war. The expense, the chaos, and the powerful military establishment that were natural outgrowths of war would threaten America's political stability and internal liberty, not to mention the very existence of the new nation and its institutions. Peace, trade expansion, and favorable borders—these were the goals that united the decision-makers of post-revolutionary America.

But these leaders remained united only so long as they could avoid assigning priorities to their foreign policy goals. For most of the Confederation period they were able to do this. Since the Articles of Confederation left the United States without the power to achieve any of these goals, there was no need to choose between them. America's leaders could cite all of the goals as equally desirable and claim that all were attainable if the government was given sufficient power to make itself respectable in foreign affairs.

The only major exception to this trend of affairs was the Jay–Gardoqui incident. Despairing of an increase in federal power in the near future, Jay decided that the United States would have to seek aid abroad to achieve any of its goals. He might get British aid against Spain by giving up the frontier posts and the hope of trade with the British West Indies, or he might secure Spanish aid against British occupation of the Northwest by giving up the Mississippi. Reluctantly, Jay decided to use the Spanish against the British.

to the United States that in his opinion the alliance between the two countries no longer existed.[9]

Yet Jay's dislike of France did not make him pro-British at this time. His attempts to mold an anti-British alliance with Spain is ample evidence of that. To add insult to injury, Jay even proposed to Congress that a silver medal of each denomination of United States coins be sent to all the monarchs of Europe except the English king.[10] The British, he suspected, "wish to see our Difficulties of every kind increase and accumulate. Indeed I fear that other European Nations do not regard us entirely without Jealousy." On this account he was "happy in reflecting that there can be but little Clashing of Interests between us and France, and therefore that she will probably continue disposed to wish us well and do us good."[11]

John Adams shared Jay's desire for nonentanglement. He too distrusted all Europe and relied only hesitantly on France. Adams claimed that both Britain and France, though Britain to a greater degree, calculated their policy toward the United States on a principle "not so properly of enriching and strengthening herself at our expense, as of impoverishing and weakening us even at her own expense."[12] Upon this general hostility to both countries he founded his conception of a proper foreign policy for America. He wrote John Jay:

My system is a very simple one; let us preserve the friendship of France, Holland, and Spain, if we can, and in case of a war between France and England, let us preserve our neutrality, if possible. In order to preserve our friendship with France and Holland and Spain, it will be useful for us to avoid a war with England. . . . This reasoning and this system, you see, goes upon the supposition that we are independent of France, in point of moral and political obligation. But if the sentiments of America are otherwise and those principles are general, which you and I once heard delivered with great formality and energy, namely,—"That America ought to join France against England in two future wars; one to pay the debt of gratitude already contracted, and the other to show ourselves as generous as France had been"—I confess myself all wrong, and to be so totally ignorant of the rights, duties, and interests of my country, as to be altogether unfit for any share in their public affairs, foreign or domestic.[13]

Though Adams thus seems to have considered the Franco-American alliance null and void, his experience as minister to England led him for a time in 1785 to believe that an alliance with France both offensive and defensive might be justified.[14] This proposal, however, was the fruit of his temporary indignation with England. Two weeks later he had decided that a defensive alliance but not an offensive alliance should be considered, and even this should "not be hastily adopted, nor ever, without Canada and Nova Scotia to be admitted into our confederation, and one half at least of the best of the English West India Islands, besides stipulations for the admission of our produce freely to the French West India Islands, and some articles into France, duty free, with similar stipulations with Spain and Holland."[15] These terms were sufficiently exorbitant to guarantee that such an alliance would never be concluded, and afterward Adams spoke of the matter no longer, returning to his original system.

Thomas Jefferson's anti-British feelings were more intense than those of Hamilton, Jay, or Adams in the Confederation period. His dislike of the British seems to have been almost entirely the product of the Revolutionary War, for in 1775 he had written John Randolph that he "would rather be in dependence on Great Britain, properly limited, than on any nation upon earth, or than no nation."[16] The destruction of the South and his own estate by the Redcoats and his humiliating experience as war governor of Virginia were probably instrumental in changing his opinion of Britain.[17] He came to feel that the British were the only people on earth who wished the United States ill from the bottom of their souls, and he considered them his country's natural enemies.[18]

Jefferson's distaste for the British people contrasted sharply with his feelings for the French people. "I would not give the polite, self-denying, feeling, hospitable, good humoured people of this country and their amiability in every point of view . . . for ten such races of rich, proud, hectoring, swearing, squibbing, carnivorous animals" as the British, he wrote Abigail Adams.[19]

Despite Jefferson's love of the French, he disliked their form of government, and he kept a close eye on France's activities in the western hemisphere while he was the American minister in Paris. He suspected a French expedition to the South Pacific of seeking a colony on the western coast of America or of desiring to establish factories there for the fur trade. Although these French projects held little interest for America, he wrote Jay, it was necessary to know "whether they are perfectly weaned from the desire of possessing continental colonies in America. If they would desire a colony on the Western side of America, I should not be quite satisfied that they would refuse one which should offer itself on the Eastern side."[20]

Thus, Jefferson's love of the French people and his dislike of the British did not make him totally sanguine about France's foreign policy, nor did it alter his idea that America should be independent and friendly to all nations. "Our interest calls for a perfect equality in our conduct towards [England and France]; but no preferences anywhere," he wrote

Adams in 1784.[21] British conduct prevented that equality of treatment, however; and like the rest of the leaders of the new nation, he looked to France to counter the designs of Britain. France was "the only nation on whom we can solidly rely for assistance till we can stand on our own legs," he believed. But even this sentiment was not unmodified, for he also believed that "no circumstances of morality, honor, interest, or engagement are sufficient to authorize a secure reliance on any nation, at all times and in all positions."[22]

James Madison's preference for France also was overshadowed by his desire for independence and friendly relations with all nations. Madison's dislike of the British and attachment to the French alliance seem to have been even better known during the Confederation period than Jefferson's. During the Revolution he had been among the foremost to favor the instructions to the American commissioners putting them totally under the control of the French foreign minister. His hatred of the British was equal to Jefferson's and had much the same roots. "No description can give you an adequate idea of the barbarity with which the enemy have conducted the war in the Southern States," he wrote in 1781. "Every outrage which humanity could suffer has been committed by them. Desolation rather than conquest seems to have been their object."[23] He even proposed once to shoot British prisoners of war if the British should continue to burn American property.[24] These circumstances led to his characterization by the crusty Fisher Ames as a man of sense, reading, address, and integrity, but "very much Frenchified in his politics."[25]

Yet Madison valued the independence of America from the rest of the world far above his attachment to France. In an unsigned article, he asked that the people be taught,

as the first step to political wisdom, to discard a flattering delusion of their unsuspicious minds—They are persuaded that all the powers of the world are their Friends.—My Countrymen! thy tyrant and oppressor was the oppressor of mankind—it was *his* enemies you mistook for thy *friends*—it is time now you should be undeceived. . . . We have been too long accustomed to lean on the supporting arm of France. It is not only unwise and unsafe for one nation to calculate on the support of another; but support and protection are so nearly allied, and protection and dependence join each other by such imperceptible connexion, that it is hard to say where the one begins or the other ends—therefore to be truly *free*, we must depend only on ourselves.[26]

George Washington has come to symbolize a policy of independence and friendly impartiality toward the outside world. The very model of self-restraint, moderation, rectitude, and prudence, his correspondence does not ring with the passionate denunciations of France or Britain as does that of most of the other leaders of America's early nationhood. Still his opinions are clear. Like Hamilton, Adams, Jay, Jefferson, and Madison, he regarded Britain as America's most dangerous and hostile antagonist. Not only would she be willing to take advantage of any local insurrections in New England, he wrote Henry Knox, but "she is at this moment sowing the seeds of jealousy and discontent among the various tribes of Indians on our frontier. . . . And . . . she will improve every opportunity to foment the spirit of turbulence within the bowels of the United States, with a view of distracting our governments, and promoting divisions."[27] Washington was friendlier to the French connection than was Hamilton, Adams, or Jay, but still he kept a watchful eye on America's ally. During the Revolution he had opposed a joint attack on Canada for fear of putting a large body of French troops in possession of the capital of that province. With France on the north, her ally Spain in control of Louisiana, and seconded by the hordes of Indians, he thought these countries might give the law to the United States.[28]

Thus Hamilton, Adams, Jay, Washington, Jefferson, and Madison shared to a greater or lesser extent a distrust of Britain and a hesitant reliance on France in the period before 1789. Still, they hoped to remain unentangled with Europe and refused to permit the "perpetual" treaty of alliance with France to interfere with this goal. Even Jefferson, as minister to France, avoided any statement that might solidly commit the United States to live up to the clause mutually guaranteeing each country's possessions in the western hemisphere. He told the British ambassador in Paris that in case of war between England and France an attack on the French West Indies "might perhaps force us into the war," but he emphasized that America would hope to remain neutral.[29] Despite instructions from Jay as secretary for foreign affairs, Jefferson avoided sounding France on possible aid in removing the British from the frontier forts under the guarantee clause. He feared a reminder from France of the reciprocal nature of that obligation.[30]

Given the impotence of the United States, however, the founding fathers realized that they had little choice but to seek aid from abroad if the nation were attacked. They remembered the necessity of promising to make no separate peace to secure a treaty with France during the Revolution. Later, Jay made his offers of an alliance to Spain and considered using the French treaty against England. Hamilton counted on an efficient government and increasing American strength "fortified by foreign alliances, which her acknowledged independence will at all times command," to prevent British aggression.[31] Washington, Adams, and Jefferson expressed a willingness to use the French alliance again for America's protection if it should become necessary, though they still hoped to avoid their reciprocal obligation to protect the French West Indies.[32] Thus, they would accept political alliances in an emergency but would seek to maintain nonentanglement as long as possible.

It was obvious to them that if they wished to accomplish their goals without foreign assistance, the federal government would have to secure more power than the Articles of Confederation afforded it. Without greater power, Hamilton warned, the United States would be the "football of European politics."[33] Basic to that power, they all thought, was an abundant federal revenue and stronger national credit. They also wanted to give the federal government the power to enforce the treaties it made. This was essential to both America's honor and its interest.[34] Britain used American violations of the peace of 1783 to justify retention of the frontier posts.[35] In addition the British sarcastically asked the American commissioners negotiating a trade treaty with them in 1785 "whether you are merely commission'd by Congress, or whether you have receiv'd separate Powers from the respective States . . . , repeated experience having taught . . . how little the authority of Congress could avail in any respect, where the Interests of any one individual State was even concern'd."[36] Throughout Adams' stay, the British insinuated that they would treat with the United States only when it had a national government worthy of the name.[37]

With a strong national government, the United States could then begin to build a navy. This was a popular measure among the founding fathers; for while a navy would increase America's power in foreign affairs, it would not offer a great threat to internal liberties.[38] They wanted the navy first to fight the Barbary pirates, but they also rejoiced that it would be a "bridle . . . in the mouths of the West India powers," as Jefferson put it.[39]

Madison even wanted to use the frigates to force recalcitrant states to pay the assessments of the Confederation government.[40] Jefferson agreed. "There never will be money in the treasury till the confederacy shews it's teeth," he wrote Monroe. "The states must see the rod; perhaps it must be felt by some of them. . . . Every national citizen must wish to see an effective instrument of coercion, and should fear to see it on any other element but the water. A naval force can never endanger our liberties, nor occasion bloodshed; a land force would do both."[41]

The desperate expedient of relying on a navy for internal police is a measure of the antipathy Jefferson and Madison felt for the more obvious solution to the problem—an army. An irregular militia was less dangerous to liberty and totally adequate for America's defensive purposes, they thought.[42] The vast majority of Americans shared their fear of a standing army. Among the decision-makers of the postrevolutionary era, only Hamilton was ready to welcome a large standing force.[43]

But although a nascent navy, a militia, and the ability to conclude political alliances might be adequate to deter outright attacks on the United States, there was only one weapon in America's diplomatic arsenal that the founding fathers declared capable of being used offensively to improve the nation's position. That weapon was trade.

Washington, Adams, Hamilton, Jay, Jefferson, and Madison had much experience in the use of trade as a weapon. They had wielded it powerfully against England prior to the Revolution. Jefferson and Washington had signed the Virginia nonimportation act of 1770 in an attempt to force the repeal of the Townsend Acts. Four years later Jefferson had authored the Albemarle Resolution for the complete embargo of British trade.[44] John Adams had been a moving spirit in the Continental Congress for the Association of 1774, which barred imports from England during the dispute over the Intolerable Acts. John Jay was a reluctant signer of that instrument.[45] Madison had also favored the nonimportation act, and Hamilton as a college student had written two shrill tracts in support of it.[46]

Although Adams, Madison, and Jefferson preferred a system of free trade to a system of commercial restrictions, the apparent hostility of Europe and particularly Great Britain led them quickly to the conclusion that such a system was unattainable for the present. Thus they joined Washington, Hamilton, and Jay in demanding commercial retaliation against England as a means of achieving America's foreign policy goals. "If we cannot obtain reciprocal liberality we must adopt reciprocal prohibitions, exclusions, monopolies, and imposts," wrote John Adams.[47] He and Jefferson continually exchanged letters from their ministries in England and France asserting the need for such legislation; and their superior, Secretary for Foreign Affairs John Jay, had been considering such a navigation law as early as November 1783.[48] Madison thought the only answer to British restrictions was "Retaliating regulations,"[49] and Washington agreed.[50]

Despite Hamilton's later opinions to the contrary, he too was one of the leading exponents of commercial retaliation against Great Britain during the Confederation period.[51] In one of his contributions to *The Federalist* he wrote, "Suppose, for instance, we had a government in America, capable of excluding Great Britain (with whom we have at present no treaty of commerce) from all our ports, what would be the probable operation of this step upon her politics? Would it not enable us to negotiate with the fairest prospect of success for commercial privileges of the most valuable kind in the dominions of that kingdom?"[52] In an article written for the *Daily Advertiser* in 1787, he attacked the stagnation of commerce under the Confederation. This he claimed was a result of the restrictions placed on American trade by foreign nations, "while our government is incapable of making these defensive regulations, which would be likely to produce a greater reciprocity of privileges."[53]

Although Washington, Jefferson, Adams, Madison, and Jay might agree with Hamilton on a program of commercial retaliation against Great Britain, it was difficult to secure the assent of enough citizens and states to implement it. As Jefferson remarked, the people had had too full a taste of the comforts furnished by British manufactures to give them up lightly. In fact, close to 90 percent of American imports came from Great Britain.[54] As one authority has said, "England was making the goods which America wanted, and making them cheaply, and no other country disputed the field."[55] In addition Britain received almost half the value of all American exports. Above all, only England supplied the long term credit of which America had great need. Jefferson put the matter pungently when he told the newly appointed French minister to the United States that he would "find the affections of the Americans with France, but their habits with England, chained to that country by circumstances, embracing what they loathe, they realize the fable of the living and dead bound together."[56]

Though American interests might be bound up with the British trade, the leaders of the United States consoled themselves that British interest was equally bound up in the trade with America. If the United States could threaten that trade with retaliatory measures. England might well abandon its policy of confrontation. The United States was England's greatest single customer. Between 1788 and 1792 it took between 10 percent and 17 percent of Britain's exports. Even more significant, these exports to the United States were almost totally composed of manufactures, while much of the remainder of Britain's export trade consisted of re-exports of the products of other foreign nations.[57]

The leverage of America's weapon did not depend solely on the market it furnished to British manufactures. The United States supplied valuable naval stores to England. In addition American grain was often imported to make up for any deficit in the British harvest. In fact Great Britain imported more goods from America than from any other country except Russia.[58]

An even more effective blow might be aimed at Britain by limiting or eliminating the rights of its ships in American ports. Such a navigation act "would be laying an axe at the root of British commerce, revenue, and naval power, however slightly they may think of us," wrote Adams.[59] In support of this thesis Jefferson sent word from Dr. Richard Price, a British expert on commerce who was friendly to the United States, that by excluding British ships from American ports, Britain "may be ruined but I do not see that America would suffer in its true interest."[60]

The leaders of the United States also thought that the dependence of the British West Indies on American provisions and lumber would make retaliatory measures effective. Hamilton, born and raised in those islands, had written in 1774 that the "West-India plantations . . . could not possibly subsist without us. I am the more confident of this, because I have a pretty general acquaintance with their circumstances and dependencies."[61] Americans were convinced that this dependence was no less in the 1780s, Adams asserting that "Nothing is more extravagent than the confident pretensions of French and English merchants, that they can supply their own islands."[62]

At first many Americans were confident that a unified effort on the part of the states to restrict British trade and navigation would quickly force a change in Britain's policy toward the United States. Jay reported in 1783 that he doubted the English ministers themselves knew what they meant to do, and that if America adhered to exact reciprocity with all nations and were well united in it, the British "would yield to it."[63] Sheffield's pamphlet caused considerable stir in the United States, and its emphasis on the inability of America to retaliate led Americans to think that Britain's policy was premised almost entirely on confidence in America's weakness. They thought that if once the United States showed itself able to strike back, the whole policy of confrontation would crumble.[64] Repeated discouragements in Anglo-American negotiations, however, lessened the early confidence that American retaliation would bring British surrender rather than British counterretaliation.

Though British self-interest and reason dictated a policy of accommodation with America, Jefferson, for one, was not confident that these factors would triumph over her pride. "In spite of treaties, England is still our enemy," he told John Langdon. "Her hatred is deep-rooted and cordial, and nothing is wanting with her but the power to wipe us and the land we live on out of existence. Her interest, however, is her ruling passion. When they shall see decidedly that without it we shall suppress their commerce with us, they will be agitated by their avarice on one hand, and their hatred and their fear of us on the other. The result of this conflict of [dirty passions] is yet [to be] awaited."[65] Thus American retaliation might bring counter-retaliation despite the obvious interest of Great Britain in avoiding such measures.*

Jefferson was not the only one who worried about the reaction of Great Britain to American trade retaliation. John Jay observed, "It is manifestly as much their interest to be well with us as it is ours to be well with them; and yet the gratification of resentments, occasioned by disappointment, seems to take the lead of more elevated and useful principles of action."[66] John Adams, too, knew how difficult it would be to change British policy. As he wrote Jefferson, "John Bull don't see it, and if he don't see a Thing at first, you know it is a rule with him ever afterwards to swear that it don't exist, even when he does both see it and feel it."[67]

Despite some uneasiness over the possible British reaction to American reprisals, Washington, Adams, Jay, Hamilton, Madison, and Jefferson all expressed a strong desire for a central government able to retaliate commercially against England. British hostility was playing into their hands. "Great Britain, viewing with eyes of chagrin and jealousy the situation of this country, will not, for sometime yet if ever, pursue a liberal policy towards it; but unfortunately *for her* the conduct of her ministers defeat [sic] their own ends. Their restriction of our trade with them, will facilitate the enlargement of Congressional powers in commercial matters, more than half a century would otherwise have effected," wrote Washington.[68]

As Washington had predicted, British hostility was one of the major forces that brought about the growth of sentiment in the United States for a stronger central government. The impotence of the nation in the face of foreign hostility helped convince many that a new constitution was necessary. When Edmund Randolph introduced the Virginia plan to the resulting Constitutional Convention, he listed the need for a stronger foreign policy first among his reasons for proposing such a drastic increase in federal power.[69] The states' defiance of America's treaty obligations regarding the British debts and Loyalists and the resulting imbroglio with Great Britain convinced even the most ardent advocates of states' rights at the Conven-

---

* Jefferson to David Ross, May 8, 1786, *Papers* (Boyd), IX, 474. About the same time he wrote Elbridge Gerry, "I am quite at a loss what you will do with England. To leave her in possession of our posts seems unadmissible, and yet to take them brings on a state of things for which we seem not to be in readiness. Perhaps a total suppression of her trade, or an exclusion of her vessels from the carriage of our produce may have some effect; but I believe not very great. Their passions are too deeply and too universally engaged in opposition to us." May 7, 1786, *ibid.*, IX, 468.

tion that treaties should be the supreme law of the land.[70] The paralysis of Confederation foreign policy by congressional squabbles induced the Convention to place these affairs primarily in the hands of the executive.

Finally, the Convention provided for a stronger foreign policy by giving Congress the right to regulate foreign commerce. The South was wary of this, but in return for a constitutional guarantee against taxes on exports and a twenty-year moratorium on interference with the slave trade, they conceded to Congress the right to regulate imports by a simple majority. This paved the way for commercial retaliation against Great Britain. The need for such action was a primary tenet of *The Federalist*, which Hamilton, Madison, and Jay coauthored in support of the new Constitution. When these men, along with Adams, Jefferson, and Washington, were given the positions of greatest power in the new government, there seemed no doubt that Britain's commerce was about to be pinched.

Part II

THE DECISION-MAKERS DIVIDE:
AMERICA FACES
GREAT BRITAIN,
1789-1793

3. ALEXANDER HAMILTON AND THE HEROIC STATE

In 1789, shortly after ratification of the Constitution, James Madison rose to address the newly formed House of Representatives. The government was still unsettled. The executive had not yet appointed a cabinet. Congress was so unsure of its role that even the most minute of procedural matters required hours of debate. The House did not think itself ready to undertake measures of any great magnitude. Yet Madison was determined that the House should immediately consider a bill to establish a federal revenue, since that had been one of the primary reasons for the whole constitutional movement. So he introduced a tariff and tonnage bill designed to tax imported goods and the ships that carried them. As if this were not a vital and controversial enough issue to toss before the new Congress, Madison shaped his bill to serve two other important purposes. He would protect American shipping against foreign competition and retaliate particularly against Britain's hostile commercial policy. To do this, he stipulated that American ships would pay lower tonnage duties than foreign ships. In addition, ships of foreign nations that concluded trade treaties with the United States would pay lower duties than nations so unfriendly as to refuse to do so.* Great Britain being the greatest power without such a treaty, the measure was obviously aimed at her. Madison said so explicitly and claimed that once Britain saw that the United States had both the power and inclination to do itself justice, there would be no trouble in securing the kind of trade treaty the United States wanted.[1]

The House hotly debated the idea of taxing foreign ships at a higher rate than American vessels. But only one speaker opposed the idea of discriminating between ships of friendly and unfriendly foreign countries, and

---

* It may be important to note here that Bemis' *Jay's Treaty* is somewhat misleading on this point. Bemis writes that Madison's bill "called for a higher tariff on importations from countries having no treaties of commerce with the United States than from those having such treaties and for heavier tonnage duties on the ships of such nations entering American ports. . . . After a lively debate Madison succeeded in carrying only a part of his program through the House of Representatives. . . . Though the tonnage discriminations passed the House, Madison's original tariff discriminations were toned down to the innocuous provision for lighter duties on spiritous liquors imported from countries 'in alliance' as distinguished from other countries" (pp. 53–54). In fact, however, Madison's original bill called for no tariff discriminations at all, only tonnage discriminations. Instead of watering down these tariff discriminations, the House added the provision regarding spiritous liquors midway through the debate, as we shall see. For Madison's original bill, see Joseph Gales, comp., *Debates and Proceedings in the Congress of the United States, 1789–1824*, 42 vols. (Washington, 1834–1856), I, 102.

the Committee of the Whole quickly overrode his objections to pass that section of Madison's resolutions.[2]

This inspired Samuel Smith of Maryland to introduce discriminatory tariff as well as tonnage rates against nontreaty nations, specifically on spiritous liquors.[3] Madison supported him, commenting that "Discriminations, however small, may have a good political effect."[4] The House agreed, and in three separate votes concerning the principle of discrimination between treaty and nontreaty nations, Madison's resolutions steadily gained votes. In the final vote the opposition had dwindled to nine or ten against nearly forty.[5]

Even while the House was passing his resolutions, Madison feared that the portions designed to retaliate against Britain were in trouble in the Senate. His fears were justified.[6] The Senate passed a resolution that such measures were too weak, that they would anger Britain but not force her to accord better treatment to American trade. The upper house then appointed a committee to bring forward a plan that would not be liable to these objections. Meanwhile, it struck out the discriminatory portions of Madison's tariff and tonnage bill and sent the bill back to the House of Representatives. Madison induced the House to adhere to its position, but his majority had dwindled to two votes.[7] A joint conference attempted to resolve the two positions. The House delegation, of which Madison was a member, offered to give up the discriminatory duties on liquors if the tonnage duties were left intact. But the Senate refused. Finally, the House agreed 31 to 19 on a bill from which all traces of discrimination between treaty and nontreaty nations had been eliminated. One part of the bill that had been discriminatory was now almost insultingly worded: "On all distilled spirits of Jamaica proof, imported from any kingdom or country whatsover, per gallon, ten cents. . . ."[8] Fisher Ames, member of the House from Massachusetts and opponent of discrimination, rejoiced at the outcome: "The Senate, God bless them, as if designated by Providence to keep rash and frolicsome brats out of the fire, have demolished the absurd, impolitic, mad discrimination of foreigners in alliance from other foreigners."[9]

George Washington was not so elated. He wrote that "The opposition of the Senate to the discrimination in the Tonnage Bill, was so adverse to my ideas of justice and policy, that, I should have suffered it to have passed into Law without my signature, had I not been assured by some members of that body, that they were preparing another Bill which would answer the purpose more effectively without being liable to the objections, and to the consequences which they *feared* would have attended the discrimination which was proposed in the Tonnage Law."[10] The Senate did in fact receive from its committee an alternate plan for commercial retaliation against Britain, and the Senate adopted the report. But the committee appointed to bring in a bill based on this plan never reported back.[11]

At this time, probably neither Washington nor Madison suspected that Alexander Hamilton had had a hand in defeating their plan for commercial retaliation against Great Britain. After all, the necessity for just such a measure had been one of Hamilton's primary arguments in support of the Constitution. Now, however, he revealed to a British secret agent named George Beckwith that he had been "decidedly opposed to those discriminating clauses" in Madison's bill, and that he had taken pains to determine the opinions of the various mercantile bodies in New York on the subject.[12] Evidently his efforts were successful. Representative Lawrence of New York led the assault on the bill in the House, and his arguments bore a striking resemblance to those that Hamilton later advanced. In addition, two of Hamilton's closest associates, Rufus King and Oliver Ellsworth, were instrumental in killing the Senate's substitute plan for discrimination against Great Britain.[13]

Hamilton's defection from the cause of commercial retaliation against England was the first major breach in the unity of the men who had led the struggle for the Constitution. It heralded the emergence of disagreement among the founding fathers that had formerly been submerged beneath their common desire to extend greater power to the federal government. Even the men who supported Hamilton's policies often came to find that they did so for reasons quite different from those that motivated Hamilton. Where they sought domestic tranquility, Hamilton sought heroism. Where they sought individual liberty, Hamilton sought national glory. Where they sought respectability, Hamilton sought power.

Hamilton, like all men, judged the good of his nation and his fellow human beings by his own experience, ambitions, and impulses. He transmuted personal goals into national goals. His private life, his domestic political system, and his foreign policy were thoroughly intertwined. To understand Hamilton's part in the Jay Treaty controversy we must examine his basic philosophical assumptions, his domestic political system, and his foreign policy as they developed between 1789 and 1793.

Hamilton was born in the West Indies about 1755, the illegitimate son of an impecunious Scottish laird who deserted his family when Hamilton was just a boy. At the age of eleven, Hamilton took a job as a clerk in a counting house to support himself and his destitute family. The circumstances of his birth and early life instilled in him a fierce desire to succeed. At fourteen, he wrote a close friend, "to confess my weakness, Ned, my ambition is prevalent."[14] His ruthless ambition coupled with a profound intelligence and personal charm were the basic elements of his political success. Despite his small stature and slightness of build, his ambition took the form of desire for military glory. Even as a clerk in the West Indies, his main hope of escaping his fate had been a war that would enable him to join the army and leave the islands. Instead, a group of wealthy islanders who were impressed by his abilities sent him to King's College (later Columbia University) in New York to study medicine.

In New York Hamilton was quickly caught up by the revolutionary fervor. He wrote tracts supporting commercial retaliation against the British and went off gleefully to seek glory in the war that followed. After a stint as a captain of artillery, he became an aide to Washington. As such he had a chance to demonstrate his intelligence and literary ability, but he chafed at the lack of action. His thirst for military glory would not let him rest. It goaded him to challenge fellow officers to duels, and to call to the retreating General Lee at Monmouth to join him in a two-man suicide stand against the British. When finally given a field command, he needlessly marched his men on the parapets before Yorktown in full sight and range of the British infantry. Finally, he prevailed on Washington to let him lead the charge on one of the two major redoubts defending Yorktown, a duty he performed with ability and relish.[15]

Hamilton's thirst for glory had a profound effect on his domestic and foreign policies. He believed that the United States as a nation should seek the same glory, the same heroic stature, that he himself pursued throughout his life. He knew that the United States should avoid war for many years until the new nation could build the strength necessary to prosecute it successfully. But when a war with a weak opponent beckoned or when the naval power of Great Britain might join the United States in a more serious enterprise and give it a good chance for success, Hamilton could not restrain himself. After making formal gestures to save the peace with France in 1798, he welcomed the prospect of joining Britain in a war against the hated French Revolution. As the effectual commander of the American Army during the crisis, he actually considered joining the Latin-American revolutionary Miranda in a blow against Spain's Latin American colonies. He considered Julius Caesar to be the greatest man who had ever lived and obviously hoped to carve himself a similar reputation as a soldier–statesman.[16] He even went to his death in a duel he disapproved of, withholding his fire while Aaron Burr killed him, because he feared that his refusal to fight would so affront popular prejudice that his chance of returning to political leadership and saving the country from Jeffersonian imbecility would be lost.*

Alexander Hamilton dreamed of a United States "ascendant in the system of American affairs," with himself at the head of the ascendant nation.[17] He wrote in *The Federalist*:

The world may politically, as well as geographically, be divided into four parts, each having a distinct set of interests. Unhappily for the other three, Europe by her arms and by her negociations, by force and by fraud, has, in different degrees, extended her dominion over them all. Africa, Asia, and America have successively felt her domination. The superiority, she has long maintained, has tempted her to plume herself as the Mistress of the World, and to consider the rest of mankind as created for her benefit. . . . Facts have too long supported these arrogant pretensions of the European. It belongs to us to vindicate the honor of the human race, and to teach that assuming brother moderation.[18]

Although other Americans might also share the vision of a United States ascendant in the western hemisphere, they usually had in mind a much more pacific and informal supremacy. Hamilton's was a military and imperial vision. He demanded heroism, bloodshed, and a sacrifice of individual pleasures for national destiny. In fact, his whole domestic political system was designed to drag an unwilling populace onto his road to glory.

Hamilton started with the premise that the common people were decidedly unheroic. In fact he said, "men are ambitious, vindictive and rapacious."[19] They thought only of themselves, and almost never of the national interest, he claimed. "Take mankind as they are, and what are they governed by? their passions. . . . Our prevailing passions are ambition and interest."[20] Even if the people were well intentioned, they were not so intelligent nor well informed to know the national interest. "The people are turbulent and changing," he said; "they seldom judge or determine right."[21]

How then could a republic like the United States rise to national greatness and undertake a glorious foreign policy when governed by such a turbulent, self-interested, and rapacious people? Hamilton thought that in every government there might be "a few choice spirits, who may act from more worthy motives."[22] These "choice spirits" were the "rich and well-

* In explanation of his part in the duel, Hamilton wrote, "The ability to be in the future useful, whether in resisting mischief or in effecting good, in these crises of our public affairs which seem likely to happen, would probably be inseparable from a conformity with public prejudice in this particular." Richard B. Morris, ed., *Alexander Hamilton and the Founding of the Nation* (New York, 1957), p. 608.

born," and Hamilton's object was to concentrate the powers of government in their hands. "Give, therefore, to the [rich and well born] a distinct, permanent share in the government," he told the Constitutional Convention. "They will check the unsteadiness of the [populace], and, as they cannot receive any advantage by a change, they therefore will ever maintain good government. Can a democratic Assembly, who annually revolve in the mass of the people, be supposed steadily to pursue the public good? Nothing but a permanent body can check the imprudence of democracy."[23] He went on to recommend a senate and executive elected for life.

Hamilton had no compunctions about concentrating such power permanently in the hands of a few, for he thought power purified rather than corrupted. Members of Britain's House of Lords, "Having nothing to hope for by a change, and a sufficient interest by means of their property, in being faithful to the national interest, . . . form a permanent barrier against every pernicious innovation, whether attempted on the part of the crown or Commons," he maintained. The king, too, might follow the national interest, for "the hereditary interest of the King was so interwoven with that of the nation, and his personal emoluments so great, that he was placed above the danger of being corrupted."[24]

Since Hamilton believed that power purified, he was much less attached to the idea of checks and balances than the rest of the founding fathers. When confronted by a superior power, his impulse in both foreign and domestic affairs was not to check it, but to join it, augment it, and make use of it. He thus sought a government of consolidated rather than balanced powers. He urged the federal government to "swallow up the State power" and would have been happy to do away with the states entirely.[25] Throughout his career he sought to elevate the executive above the Congress, and the Senate above the House. The upper classes in control of these offices would maintain a stable, powerful, domestic system capable of a heroic foreign policy.*

Hamilton's original plan to give the rich and well born a permanent and dominant share in the government failed. The Constitutional Convention rejected the idea of an executive and Senate elected for life. As secretary

* Hamilton did believe in a minimal check on aristocrats by the majority of the people, however. He told the Constitutional Convention, "Give all power to the many, they will oppress the few. Give all power to the few, they will oppress the many. Both therefore, ought to have power, that each may defend itself against the other." Max Farrand, *Records of the Federal Convention of 1787,* 4 vols., rev. ed. (New Haven, 1966), I, 288. But Hamilton made clear that he was far more concerned with the few checking the many than vice versa.

of the treasury, however, Hamilton devised a system that might effectively substitute for his original plan. He would create by other means an aristocracy dedicated to the proper national interest, one composed of merchants and speculators. Hamilton's plans for funding the national debt at par, assuming the state debts, and establishing a national bank purposely concentrated great profits in the hands of the northern merchants and speculators who were the primary holders of the federal and state bonds and the major investors in the national bank. These wealthy and powerful men would now find it to their interest to support the federal taxing power necessary to pay the interest and principle on the bonds and to supply deposits for the national bank. As directors of the bank, they would lend prestige to this instrument of national policy and would be willing to loan bank assets to the federal government in time of national need. In addition these were men who would invest the capital that Hamilton had concentrated in their hands on trade and manufactures, economic enterprises whose augmentation Hamilton thought essential to national power. Left in the hands of ordinary men, this money would be invested instead in agriculture and slaves.

Certainly these merchants and speculators were something less than the "choice spirits" who would instinctively seek national greatness. But their avarice was a handle by which Hamilton could lead them to support the national interest. Hamilton hated "money-making men," but he was willing to reward their greed if it allowed him to further his hopes for national greatness. Perhaps he even hoped that a permanent and institutionalized financial influence in the government would ultimately purify these men, make them wealthy and powerful enough to be exempt from the corruption of private interests, and create of them an aristocracy worthy of the name. Then they might support national power and greatness out of instinct rather than avarice.

If the upper classes were to be won to the support of federal power by appealing to their immediate interests, how were the masses to be attracted to it?[26] In a republic, where the majority ultimately determined government policies, the answer to this question was vital to Hamilton's system. Hamilton in fact came up with several answers, all of which failed in the end. But at least they were logical answers, and all had great influence on his ideas about foreign policy.

First, Hamilton hoped that the lower classes would defer to the opinions of the ersatz aristocracy he was creating. While he was waiting for the aristocracy to achieve such a position of leadership, he made brilliant use of the deference paid to the opinions of George Washington. By securing Washington's support for his measures, Hamilton kept the people from blocking what was otherwise an intrinsically unpopular program. Temporarily, then, Washington served the function of the aristocracy, inducing in the people an habitual obedience to federal law.

Where habitual obedience failed, Hamilton hoped that persuasion might succeed. Since Hamilton had little faith in the reasoning ability of the people, he must not have counted too heavily on the success of this approach. Yet articles, pamphlets, and speeches poured from him as he sought to win the people to his ideas. He paid homage to his views of human nature not by abandoning persuasion, but by studding his remarks with condemnations of the turbulent populace and assertions as to the inability of the people to judge for themselves. Perhaps Hamilton thought that people able to read the pamphlets he wrote would consider themselves exempt from these strictures by virtue of their literacy. More likely, he thought that the people wanted to be led by patriots honest and courageous enough to defy popular prejudices and tell the people the truth about themselves. All Federalists, and Hamilton especially, loved to assume that pose. Hamilton even adopted the pen name of Phocion, the Greek senator whose only explanation for the unexpected popularity of one of his speeches was that he had said something wrong. Hamilton must have thought that the people were so imbued with the assumptions of the age of deference that, despite all the democratic cant to the contrary, they assumed their own inferiority and would vote for aristocrats courageous enough to defy the majority. This would go far to explain why he and the rest of the Federalists were so surprised and chagrined when the Jeffersonians removed them from office even though the Federalists' avowed philosophy of human nature should have prepared them for that eventuality.

In any case, Hamilton did not rely solely on deference and appeals to reason to attach the lower orders of society to the national interest; he was also ready to use deception. Three times he attempted to manipulate the balloting of the electoral college to humiliate or defeat John Adams. When Adams was president, he hinted to the cabinet that it should take the government into its own hands and eliminate Adams from power. He anonymously attacked political enemies such as George Clinton, Thomas Jefferson, and Aaron Burr in print. He secretly composed a violent attack on Adams for private circulation among Federalist leaders. In 1800, when the Republicans won a majority in New York's state legislature, Hamilton suggested to Governor Jay that the outgoing legislature transfer the power to select New York's presidential electors from the legislature to the people. His sordid affair with Mrs. Reynolds demonstrates that his duplicity extended even to his private life. As we shall see, deception also played a large part in his foreign policy.

If even deception failed to bring the people to support the true national interest, Hamilton had one last recourse—naked power. Though he once told Jefferson that in a republic force was out of the question, Jefferson never quite believed him. And rightly so. The alacrity with which Hamilton raised an army to suppress the Whiskey Rebellion and the relish with which he led it as political commissar provided solid grounds for Jefferson's suspicions.

In these ways, Hamilton would induce an unwilling and unheroic populace to work for national greatness. These same assumptions and techniques would also determine his conduct in foreign relations. His ideas on power, human nature, checks and balances, deception, and honor were as important to his foreign policy as they were to his domestic system. Perhaps these ideas will help to explain his puzzling reversal on the idea of commercial retaliation against Great Britain. Why did Hamilton start on the road to glory by counseling appeasement of England?

First of all, he was probably little influenced in this decision by ideological antipathy to the French Revolution. He did not express serious doubts about the course of events in France until late 1789, several months after he had opposed Madison's first plan for tonnage discriminations.[27] Explaining his stand on Madison's bill to the British agent Beckwith, Hamilton did not even mention the French Revolution.[28]

Hamilton did, however, base his decision somewhat on a pro-British bias. He told Beckwith in 1789, "I have always preferred a Connexion with you, to that of any other Country, *We think in English,* and have a similarity of prejudices, and of predilections."[29] Yet this could hardly have been the major reason for Hamilton's reversal of policy. Americans had thought in English prior to 1789, and yet Hamilton supported retaliation against the British at that time.

Or at least Hamilton pretended to support commercial retaliation prior to 1789. Perhaps he was only urging this policy to enlist the people's anti-British sentiments on the side of increased federal power. In the many pleas he made for giving the national government the right to control trade and thus to retaliate against the British, he never said that the government should restrict British trade once it had the power. He may have hoped that the mere ability to pass such legislation would be sufficient to bring Great Britain to a more favorable attitude toward American commerce, and that there would be no need to proceed to actual retaliation.[30]

Yet, perhaps it was only after 1789, when the government actually acquired the power to retaliate commercially against Great Britain, that Hamilton considered the serious implications of such a policy. In any case, by 1789 Hamilton had come to believe that commercial retaliation against England might destroy his entire dream of a heroic and powerful America. It was this analysis of the power situation rather than any ideological antipathy for the French Revolution or predilection for the British that underlay Hamilton's reversal of policy.

After all, there was a chance that Great Britain would retaliate in kind rather than give in to commercial pressure. This would have been disastrous for Hamilton's system. The nation's entire credit structure, the basis of Hamilton's plans for national power, rested on the revenue derived from the tariff and tonnage duties charged on imports. These duties netted over six million dollars annually in all the years except one between 1791 and 1796. The amount garnered from internal sources in that period only once rose above six hundred thousand dollars.[31] Since the annual interest alone on the nation's foreign and domestic debts was well above two million dollars and the expenses of the government totaled some six hundred thousand dollars, the income America derived from import duties was vital.[32] Ninety percent of these imports came from Great Britain. Thus, a commercial war that shut off British trade might well bankrupt the United States. As Hamilton wrote Jefferson, "My commercial system turns very much on giving a free course to trade, and cultivating good humor with all the world. And I feel a particular reluctance to hazard any thing, in the present state of our affairs, which may lead to a commercial warfare with any power."[33]

British trade supplied not only revenue but vital manufactures as well. This gave Hamilton yet another reason to oppose measures that might bring on a commercial war with Britain. "The extreme embarrassments of the United States during the late war, from an incapacity of supplying themselves, are still matter of keen recollection," he wrote; "a future war might be expected again to exemplify the mischiefs and dangers of a situation to which that incapacity is still, in too great a degree applicable."[34] Thus Hamilton reasoned that the United States was dependent on Britain for some basic elements of its internal stability and self-defense.

His solution was to avoid challenging Britain until the United States had developed internal sources of manufactures and revenue capable of sustaining the nation in an emergency. In his Report on Manufactures, he laid plans to develop those internal resources that would ultimately enable the United States to challenge England if it should become necessary.

Some historians have charged that Hamilton never contemplated true independence of England, but instead was driven by the image of himself "at the head of an American-British empire embracing most of the world."[35] According to this view the Anglo-American alliances periodically proposed by Hamilton were not intended to be temporary, as Hamilton claimed, but permanent. It has even been said that Hamilton never sought a balanced political economy which would render the United States economically independent of England. As one historian puts it, Hamilton "never pushed manufacturing as an integral part of the economy and in fact opposed the efforts of others to accelerate its development."[36]

This argument is based primarily on Hamilton's opposition to the efforts of Jefferson and Madison to raise the tariff and tonnage rates against the British. Only raising these rates would have provided adequate protection for nascent American manufactures against overwhelming competition from Great Britain, it is maintained. Hamilton's use of an excise tax in preference to higher tariffs against England is seen as tantamount to opposition to manufactures, a balanced economy, and true independence from Great Britain.[37]

This argument dismisses several vital facts. First, it is clear that Hamilton did favor protection for American manufactures. In 1790 he advised Congress to raise the duty on unwrought steel, which, in an oversight, had been set too low to provide protection for the industry rapidly growing in Pennsylvania.[38] The tariff of 1792, which realized the purposes of his Report on Manufactures, provided very adequate protection and at the same time lowered the duties on certain raw materials for America's manufactures.[39] Yet it is correct to say that Hamilton refused to push these duties to prohibitive heights. In Federalist No. 35, he had already outlined a few of his reasons for this; some persons imagined that raising tariffs

can never be carried to too great a length; since the higher they are, the more it is alleged they will tend to discourage an extravagant consumption, to produce a favourable balance of trade, and to promote domestic manufactures. But all extremes are pernicious in various ways. Exorbitant duties on imported articles would beget a general spirit of smuggling. . . . They tend to render other classes of the community tributary in an improper degree to the manufacturing classes to whom they give a premature monopoly of the markets: They sometimes force industry out of its more natural channels into others in which it flows with less advantage. And in the last place they oppress the merchant, who is often obliged to pay them himself without any retribution from the consumer.[40]

Hamilton had still other reasons for refusing to push for higher tariffs once the protective rates of 1792 had gone into effect. To develop its manufactures, the United States needed capital even more than protection. In his Report on Public Credit, Hamilton pointed out that a properly funded national debt would answer the purpose of money; for if people had confidence in its bonds, these bonds would pass in business transactions as specie, and trade, agriculture, and manufactures would be promoted by them.[41] This great source of capital for the development of manufactures was dependent on the revenue derived from customs to support it. Higher duties indeed might have protected America's manufactures against competition; but by inducing British retaliation, they might also have destroyed the major source of capital on which those manufactures relied. A more subtle way to encourage manufactures without endangering the course of Anglo-American trade, Hamilton thought, was for the national government to furnish bounties rather than enact prohibitive tariffs.[42] Bounties would run little risk of triggering retaliatory duties, yet would enable American manufacturers to compete with the British. Though Congress did not accept the idea, it was a billiant way for the United States to have its cake and eat it too. Hamilton offered a means of supplying large amounts of revenue and manufactures while developing America's internal sources of these commodities. Ultimately, this would render America economically self-sufficient. Meanwhile, Great Britain would be helping to develop the resources that would enable the United States to challenge her for supremacy in the western hemisphere.

Thus Hamilton thought that a commercial war would threaten his entire system, and he believed such a commercial war would be very likely if the United States enacted legislation discriminating against the British. Others might argue that since Great Britain was so dependent on American trade, she would give in without a fight. But if Hamilton had any hopes of this, they were dissolved in October 1789 when Beckwith relayed to him a message from the British cabinet that Britain would retaliate. Beckwith said that the British ministers had had as their first purpose since the Revolutionary War "to hold the Nation high, in the opinion of the world. . . . You cannot suppose, that those who follow up such a system will be influenced by compulsory measures. Upon such minds their tendency must be diametrically opposite. The purposes of National glory are best attained by a close adherence to National honour, alike prepared to meet foreign friendship, and to repel foreign hostility."[43] Those were sentiments Hamilton could understand. He told Beckwith that "before I came into office and since, I have acted under that impression."[44]

A commercial war would be bad enough if it undermined the revenue and manufactures so desperately needed by the United States. But, Hamilton said, commercial warfare was also "productive . . . of dispositions tending to a worse kind of warfare."[45] He thought that if Jefferson and Madison were allowed to pursue their course of commercial retaliation, "there would be, in less than six months, an open war between the United States and Great Britain."[46] Great Britain, with its fleet and provinces bordering the United States, was capable of destroying America's commerce, drying up its sources of revenue and manufactures, mounting and supplying land attacks either from Canada or the sea, and bombarding America's port cities. At the very least, such a war would destroy the power base that Hamilton was building.

So Hamilton advocated great moderation to avoid war with Great Britain. Yet he also supported preparations for war. In *The Federalist* he had warned his countrymen,

Let us recollect, that peace or war, will not always be left to our option; that however moderate or unambitious we may be, we cannot count upon the moderation, or hope to extinguish the ambition of others. . . . To judge from the history of mankind, we shall be compelled to conclude, that the fiery and destructive passions of war, reign in the human breast, with much more powerful sway, than the mild and beneficent sentiments of peace; and, that to model our political systems upon speculations of lasting tranquility, is to calculate on the weaker springs of the human character.[47]

Thus, nothing America could do would insure peace. Peaceful intentions and treaties of friendship were as straw. History gave "an instructive but afflicting lesson to mankind how little dependence is to be placed on treaties which have no other sanction than the obligations of good faith; and which oppose general considerations of peace and justice to the impulse of any immediate interest and passion."[48] Some might argue that republics were exempt from the ambitions of monarchs that had caused previous wars, and that as the world became more republican, it would become more peaceful as well; Hamilton, however, laughed at the idea. "Have republics in practice been less addicted to war than monarchies?" he asked. "Are not the former administered by *men* as well as the latter? Are there not aversions, predilections, rivalships and desires of unjust acquisition that affect nations as well as kings? Are not popular assemblies frequently subject to the impulses of rage, resentment, jealousy, avarice, and of other irregular and violent propensities?"[49]

Hamilton had equal scorn for those who hoped that commerce would breed peace and that nations would hesitate to fight such a valuable customer as the United States for fear of losing trade: "Has commerce hitherto done any thing more than change the objects of war? Is not the love of wealth as domineering and enterprising a passion as that of power or glory? Have there not been as many wars founded upon commercial motives, since that has become the prevailing system of nations, as were before occasioned b[y] the cupidity of territory and dominion?"[50]

Since relations between nations were as subject to passion and interest as relations between individuals within a nation, so the solution was the same for both—power. And by power, Hamilton meant military power. He had little more confidence in commercial retaliation as a substitute for war than he had in commerce as a guarantor of peace. Joined to military power, commercial weapons might be useful in certain situations.[51] However, Hamilton thought trade's major function was to support the true instruments of power, an army and a navy.

The major purpose of a navy, as Hamilton saw it, was to protect America's trade. To do this, the navy had to be an offensive one, with large ships capable of ranging throughout the world. He despised the idea of a defensive navy composed of gunboats to protect America's coast and privateers to harass foreign shipping. Such a navy would be incapable of protecting America's own commerce. It was a "novel and absurd experiment in politics, [to tie] up the hands of Government from offensive war" if America expected to be a commercial people, he said.[52] Without a navy, "our commerce would be a prey to the wanton untermeddlings of all nations at war with each other; who, having nothing to fear from us, would with little scruple or remorse supply their wants by depredations on our property, as often as it fell in their way. The rights of neutrality will only be respected, when they are defended by an adequate power. A nation, despicable by its weakness, forfeits even the privilege of being neutral."[53]

Obviously the United States was unable to build a navy that in a short time "could vie with those of the great maritime powers."[54] But it could soon build one that "would at least be of respectable weight, if thrown into the scale of either of two contending parties. This would be more particularly the case in relation to operations in the West-Indies. A few ships of the line sent opportunely to the reinforcement of either side, would often be sufficient to decide the fate of a campaign, on the event of which interests of the greatest magnitude were suspended."[55] Thus America could hope "ere long to become the Arbiter of Europe in America; and to be able to incline the ballance of European competitions in this part of the world as our interest may dictate."[56] From there the United States could move on to the point where it no longer merely inclined the balance of European competitions, but maintained "an ascendant in the system of American affairs."

Then the United States would "dictate the terms of the connection between the old and the new world."[57]

Such a plan, however, would require a regular army as well as a navy. Though most Americans feared a standing army as a threat to internal liberty, Hamilton regarded it as a necessity for the defense of the nation: "The steady operations of war against a regular and disciplined army, can only be successfully conducted by a force of the same kind."[58] Besides, regular armies,

> though they bear a malignant aspect to liberty and oeconomy, . . . [render] sudden conquests impracticable, and . . . [prevent] that rapid desolation, which used to mark the progress of war, prior to their introduction. The art of fortification has contributed to the same ends. . . . Campaigns are wasted in reducing two or three frontier garrisons, to gain admittance into an enemy's country. Similar impediments occur at every step, to exhaust the strength and delay the progress of an invader. . . . Formerly an invading army would penetrate into the heart of a neighbouring country, almost as soon as intelligence of its approach could be received; but now a comparatively small force of disciplined troops, acting on the defensive with the aid of posts, is able to impede and finally to frustrate the enterprises of one much more considerable. The history of war [in Europe] is no longer a history of nations subdued and empires overturned, but of towns taken and retaken, of battles that decide nothing, of retreats more beneficial than victories, of much effort and little acquisition.[59]

Hamilton admitted that even without a regular army, America's geographical isolation and its great expanse of territory probably rendered it secure from total conquest by a European nation, so long as the country was united behind the war.[60] But an invasion of the United States under such conditions would destroy the power base Hamilton was attempting to erect. "The want of fortifications leaving the frontiers . . . open . . . would facilitate inroads. . . . Conquests would be as easy to be made, as difficult to be retained. War therefore would be desultory and predatory. PLUNDER and devastation ever march in the train of irregulars."[61]

Under such conditions, lack of a standing army might actually be more conducive to tyranny than the absence of one. "Safety from external danger is the most powerful director of national conduct," he warned. "Even the ardent love of liberty will, after a time, give way to its dictates. . . . To be more safe they, at length, become willing to run the risk of being less free."[62]

Thus, Hamilton planned the development of power and greatness for the United States. With an army, a navy, internal sources of revenue and manufactures, a unified federal government, and leaders seeking the glory that was America's true national interest, the United States would become

45

the leader of the western hemisphere, able to bid defiance to the rest of the world. But what for the present? The United States was dependent on British trade for the revenue and manufactures so necessary to build a military establishment. Hamilton told Beckwith it might be as much as fifty years before the United States had developed its military forces and internal resources sufficiently to attempt to incline the balance between European powers contending in America, let alone dictate terms between the old world and the new.[63] Allowing for diplomatic exaggeration, this would leave America forced to follow a foreign policy of appeasement for the rest of Hamilton's life. Where would be the glory and greatness he sought so desperately for himself?

4. HAMILTON, WASHINGTON, ADAMS, AND JAY: HEROISM VERSUS RESPECTABILITY

Alexander Hamilton could conceive of only one means by which the United States could undertake a glorious foreign policy in the immediate future without endangering the growth of the nation's domestic power base. That was to secure aid from the British; and from 1789 on Alexander Hamilton tried to maneuver the United States into an alliance with Great Britain. Such an alliance would not only guarantee peace with the one nation capable of seriously threatening America's growing power, but would enable the United States to undertake immediately the kind of exploits of which Hamilton dreamed.

Just what sort of alliance Hamilton wanted to make with Great Britain is difficult to ascertain. He said different things to different people. In 1800 he claimed, "I never advised any connection with Great Britain other than a commercial one." Then he qualified this statement in a footnote by saying, "I mean a lasting connection. From what I recollect of the train of my ideas, it is possible I may at some time have suggested a temporary connection for the purpose of co-operating against France, in the event of a definitive rupture; but of this I am not certain, as I well remember that the expediency of the measure was always problematical in my mind, and that I have occasionally discouraged it."[1]

Certainly this statement minimized his desire for a British alliance. He had sought political connections with England more often than that. But given his desire for American hegemony in the western hemisphere and his plans to render the United States powerful and self-sufficient, it seems likely that he intended the alliance to be temporary, allowing the United States to accomplish its foreign policy goals until it achieved power enough to challenge Britain herself. A temporary alliance would help guarantee British friendship and the continuance of the commercial connection that Hamilton thought vital to the growth of American power. In addition, it would allow the United States to carry on diplomatic and military operations against the Spanish colonies in North America. Here would be Hamilton's opportunity for glory. Finally, an Anglo-American alliance would forestall the possibility of an Anglo-Spanish alliance directed against the United States.

Hamilton greatly feared this last possibility.[2] Both England and Spain possessed colonies on America's flanks. Both were great mercantile powers whose trade was vital to the United States. Both had allied themselves with

Indians on American borders who were hostile to the United States. Both controlled the most important North American trade routes, Britain the Great Lakes–St. Lawrence system and Spain the Mississippi. Both had an interest in discouraging America's desire for westward expansion. An alliance between these two nations directed against the United States might be disastrous. One way to make sure this did not happen was to ally the United States with one against the other. Hamilton hesitated not at all in his choice. John Jay might choose Spain, but not him. Hamilton considered the navigation of the Mississippi far more important than anything to be gained from the British on this continent. Excepting the Great Lakes posts, he thought it would never be to America's interest to expand northward.[3] Besides, Great Britain was the stronger of the two nations. Some might regard that as reason to ally with the weaker nation to check the overweening British power. Hamilton saw it as a reason to join Great Britain. As he had preferred consolidated government to checks and balances internally, he preferred joining the stronger side to maintaining a balance of power in foreign affairs.

Hamilton's plan in 1798 for joining the Latin American revolutionary Francisco de Miranda and the British navy in a joint assault on Spain's American colonies was only the last in a series of similar proposals that he made throughout his career in government. An account of these proposals and the circumstances under which they were made between 1789 and 1793 illustrates many of the tendencies of Hamilton's ideas on foreign policy that we have discussed so far.

Hamilton first mentioned his thoughts on a political alliance with England during a secret meeting with a British agent. Major George Beckwith, an intelligence officer for the British during the American Revolution, was sent to the United States several times after the war by Lord Dorchester of Canada to gather information. In 1789, Beckwith arrived in New York directly from England. Lord Grenville, then British secretary for home affairs, had instructed him to sound warnings among his influential friends in the United States that Great Britain would retaliate if Madison's plan for discriminating against British trade were passed by Congress. One of the men Beckwith contacted was Phillip Schuyler, Hamilton's father-in-law. Schuyler relayed Beckwith's message to Hamilton, then in line to become secretary of the treasury under the recently elected Washington. Hamilton asked to see Beckwith, and in October 1789 he and Beckwith held the first of what was to be a series of clandestine meetings. It was then that Hamilton originally mentioned a political alliance with England.[4]

However, Hamilton merely mentioned the possibility of a political

all of the discriminatory provisions except two. Noting that there was a majority against these two also and that they would be defeated if brought to a vote, Madison substituted for them resolutions designed to retaliate against Britain in a different way. Instead of enacting discriminatory duties, he suggested treating the shipping of each foreign country in precisely the way that nation treated American shipping. But Congress adjourned without acting on Madison's substitute resolutions.[18] Again, Madison had seen his original majority dwindle mysteriously. Undoubtedly, Hamilton had helped to bring this about.

But Hamilton's ideas soon faced another crisis—the Nootka Sound incident. This erupted when England challenged Spain's claim to unilateral control of the Pacific Ocean, threatening war between the United States's two closest neighbors. Such a war offered both opportunity and danger to the United States. The belligerents might be willing to make concessions in trade, borders, posts, or navigation of the Mississippi to ensure that the United States did not join the opposing side. On the other hand, Great Britain might demand the right to cross American soil and attack the Spanish colonies. If the United States refused, it might bring war with England; if she acceded, it might mean war with Spain. Hamilton, of course, was determined to avoid war with England at all costs.

Thus he must have been happy and relieved when Beckwith arrived with instructions from Governor Dorchester indicating that England also wanted friendly relations with the United States. These instructions, which Beckwith allowed Hamilton to read, expressed hope

that neither the appearance of a War with Spain nor its actually taking place will make any alterations in the good disposition of the United States to establish a firm friendship and Alliance with Great Britain to the Mutual advantage of both Countries: I am persuaded it can make none on the part of Great Britain, whose liberal treatment of the United States in point of Commerce sufficiently evinces her friendly disposition, notwithstanding the non execution of the treaty on their part. . . . I think the interests of the United States, in case of a war, may be more effectually served by a junction with Great Britain, than otherwise.[19]

Hamilton regarded this message as so important that for the first time he revealed one of his contacts with Beckwith to Washington. He reported that Beckwith had first spoken of the content and meaning of the British instructions before showing them to him. According to Hamilton, Beckwith had said that Governor Dorchester "had reason to believe that the Cabinet of Great Britain entertained a disposition not only towards a friendly intercourse but towards an alliance with the United States," and "That it was therefore presumed, should a war take place, that the United States would find it to be their interest to take part with Great Britain rather than with Spain."[20] The letter that Beckwith then produced contained ideas similar to those he had already stated, though in more guarded terms and without allusions to instructions from the British cabinet, Hamilton reported.[21]

For half a century, historians have accepted Hamilton's report as an accurate representation of the instructions Dorchester had given Beckwith. Recently, however, Julian Boyd has pointed out that Dorchester's instructions, if read carefully, did not say that the British sought an alliance, but that they wished the United States to continue to seek one. On this basis, Boyd charges that Hamilton deliberately distorted his report to Washington to make the president think that England wanted an alliance with the United States. According to Boyd, Hamilton did this to forestall any attempt to revive the movement for commercial retaliation against England. Hamilton had good reason to think that Madison's proposals might actually be implemented this time. The promised embroilment of Spain and England over the Nootka incident would add leverage to Madison's commercial weapons. In addition, Washington had just received word from Gouverneur Morris, whom he had sent on a personal mission to London, that England had no intention of voluntarily changing its hostile policy toward the United States despite the Nootka crisis.[22] As a result, Boyd charges, Hamilton lied to Washington about Britain's desire for an alliance to make the president think that commercial retaliation was unnecessary to bring about a friendlier policy on the part of Great Britain. Then, according to Boyd, Hamilton fabricated rumors about Morris to discredit Morris' accurate reports of continued British hostility.[23]

Boyd's charges may be correct. But if historians could misinterpret Dorchester's instructions for fifty years, isn't it possible that an impetuous man like Hamilton, who wanted so desperately to believe that the British would be friendly if they were not threatened, could misinterpret them also? The instructions may even have been written with an intent to deceive. Dorchester and Beckwith had every reason for doing this. Dorchester feared that the United States would attack the frontier posts and perhaps even attempt to conquer all of Canada. Canadian defenses were weak. The population of the United States was far greater than that of Canada, the frontier posts occupied by the British were decayed and undermanned, and the Canadian militia was composed largely of Frenchmen whose loyalties were unreliable. Canada depended on a few scattered British regulars and the unstable Northwest Indian Confederacy for the bulk of its protection.

Under these circumstances, both Dorchester and Beckwith advised the cabinet to follow a friendlier policy toward the United States.[24] But the ministry made no move in this direction despite the threat of war with Spain which provided an excellent opportunity for the Americans to attack the posts. Dorchester was instructed simply to guard his posts, to profess friendship for the United States, and to attempt to turn America's attention southward toward Spanish possessions.[25] With no promise of material concessions, Dorchester knew his professions would ring hollow. Why not raise hopes in the United States by wording the offer of friendship ambiguously? Hamilton could be counted on to seize the most favorable construction possible, and his report of a major softening of British policy might succeed in diverting the Americans southward. The instructions from the cabinet indicated some desire for a closer connection with the United States if proper terms could be had, especially if there were a war between Spain and England. This could be emphasized in conversations with the Americans without actually violating the cabinet's instructions.* So, in a secret dispatch, Dorchester told Beckwith that in addition to showing his less secret instructions to men of importance, he might "assert it as your own opinion, that in case of a War with Spain you see no reason why we should not assist in forwarding whatever their interests may require."[26] In pursuit of these instructions, Beckwith could easily have prefaced Dorchester's letter with remarks justifying Hamilton's report that the British "entertained a disposition not only towards a friendly intercourse but towards an alliance with the United States."

If this is what happened, then it is unlikely that Hamilton "fabricated rumors" about Gouverneur Morris to destroy the credibility of his reports. Boyd's charge in this instance is based on the assumption that Hamilton was lying about British intentions and therefore thought it necessary to discredit Morris' reports of British hostility even though he knew Morris was right. Consequently, Hamilton created and spread rumors that Gouverneur Morris had been indiscreetly in the company of the French minister La Luzerne and the opposition leader Charles Fox during his negotiations in London, and that this was responsible for the cabinet's rejection of his proposals.

* Lord Grenville wrote Dorchester that the mission of Gouveneur Morris to England indicated a wish of the United States to cultivate a closer connection with Britain and said that in the first instance it had been necessary to firmly inform the Americans of British grievances. This implied that such language might not be held in the second instance, and although Grenville said only that the British should establish a greater "interest" in America, he went on to say that in case of war with Spain, the United States could gain more by joining England than by joining Spain. Grenville to Dorchester, May 6, 1790, printed in Julian Boyd, *Number 7: Alexander Hamilton's Secret Attempts to Control American Foreign Policy* (Princeton, 1964), pp. 140–141.

Then, in an interview with Beckwith, Hamilton himself brought up the subject of these rumors, and in turn reported to Washington that Beckwith had come to see him for the sole purpose of reporting that the cabinet's attitude toward Morris might have been the result of Morris' own conduct.

Again, Boyd's charges are derived from discrepancies between the reports of Beckwith and Hamilton concerning their conversation.[27] Because in Beckwith's account, Hamilton appears to have been the first to bring up the subject of Morris' conduct and to express disapproval of it and connect it with the ministry's coldness, Boyd concludes that Hamilton himself had fabricated these rumors, put them in Beckwith's mouth, and then reported them to Washington as having come from the British secret agent. Yet this is not necessarily the case. Beckwith's account is clearly fragmentary. Hamilton's discussion of Morris is almost certainly a continuation of a subject previously raised, and which Beckwith might well have initiated.* At the very least, by Beckwith's own account, the British agent was the first to suggest that Morris' conduct had stemmed from French influence, and that Morris had been seen in the company of Fox as well as La Luzerne while conducting the negotiations. In addition, Beckwith strongly implied agreement when Hamilton said that Morris' indiscretion might have occasioned the cabinet's coolness toward him.[28]

This raises several important questions concerning Boyd's whole case. By allowing Hamilton to believe that the coolness of the cabinet toward Morris' proposals had been the product of Morris' own conduct, was Beckwith not contributing to the impression of British friendliness and willingness to conclude an agreement with the United States? Would he have allowed this impression to remain if, as Boyd suggests, he was at pains to impress Hamilton with the firmness of the British position? Does this not suggest that indeed Beckwith and Dorchester were attempting to make Hamilton believe that the British were softening their policy? And if Hamilton believed that the British were now seeking a friendly agreement with the United States, is it not possible that he also believed that Morris' conduct truly had been responsible for his inability to secure an agreement in London? If so, it is entirely conceivable that he was convinced of the essential truth of his

---

* Beckwith's account begins with Hamilton saying that "23 [Beckwith's code number for Morris] is a man of capacity, but apt at particular times to give himself up too much to the impressions of his own mind. From the Duke of Leed's reply to 23's first application I confess I did not think favorably of the prospect, although it was far from being conclusive." The subject of Morris seems already to have been raised. Hamilton's reference to a "prospect" without further specification indicates that the conversation has been going on before Beckwith's account takes it up. "Extract of Report by Major George Beckwith . . . ," printed in Boyd, *Number 7*, p. 156.

communications and that he did not lie to Washington concerning the attitudes of a foreign power nor fabricate rumors to discredit Gouverneur Morris.

Of course, it is also possible that Boyd is right. Hamilton's desire for a commercial and political treaty with England and his opposition to commercial retaliation gave him ample motives to do what Boyd says he did. Even if Hamilton did not misrepresent Beckwith's communications concerning a British alliance and the conduct of Gouverneur Morris, there is no doubt that Hamilton put the best face possible on Beckwith's words. Also, he deliberately omitted one very important part of his conversation. After reporting to the cabinet Beckwith's claim that England sought an alliance with the United States, Hamilton was instructed to find out all he could concerning the terms the British might offer while leaving America totally uncommitted to such an agreement. Hamilton followed these instructions, but told Beckwith that if negotiations for an Anglo-American alliance were undertaken, Jefferson's prejudices might frustrate them. Therefore, Hamilton recommended that the British keep him fully informed on the progress of the negotiations so that he might counter such prejudices by "clarifying" the information that the President might receive from the secretary of state.[29]

Obviously, Hamilton was not above lying or fabricating rumors. He considered statesmen exempt from the ordinary rules of honesty. He thought Talleyrand "the greatest of modern statesmen, because he had well known it was necessary both to suffer wrong to be done and to do it."[30] More than once he warned his allies that "in times like these in which we live, it will not do to be over-scrupulous. *It is easy to sacrifice the substantial interests of Society by a strict adherence to ordinary rules.*"[31] Such a code could conceivably allow Hamilton to do almost anything of which Boyd accuses him. Still I doubt that Hamilton deliberately lied about Morris and the British alliance. The fabric of deception Boyd describes seems too intricate and too difficult to rationalize to be a product of Hamilton's code of honor and pattern of action. For Hamilton did have a code of honor. He scorned many opportunities for personal profit and was a paragon of financial integrity. In many conflicts he disdained trickiness or even discretion, as at Yorktown. In the duel that was to cost him his life, he refused to fire at his antagonist.

Hamilton seems to have had a dual code of ethics, one for his inferiors and one for his equals. In a duel, in a war, in diplomatic contacts with foreign nations, in any struggle with an equal, Hamilton's sense of honor was punctilious. But with inferiors, in a good cause, no holds were barred. And for him almost all his political enemies were inferiors. They had no sense of military honor; they were sly, secretive, devious, and demagogic politicians who would lead the people away from the national interest, emasculate the federal government, and destroy America's chance for glory and greatness by opposing Hamilton's policies and falsely impugning his honor. Unpleasant as it might be, they must be met on their own ground and destroyed at all costs. Since they were not men of honor, he need not treat them honorably. Thus, domestic politics were for him a low business, rarely involving matters of honor. They were to be manipulated so that the honor of the United States was maintained where it really mattered, in foreign relations. For in relations between powerful nations, Hamilton would be dealing with men like himself, men with a proper notion of national glory and greatness.

Still, Hamilton, with all his chivalric ambitions, must have despised deception. Perhaps that is why he was such a clumsy conspirator. His duplicity was always more heavy handed than that with which Boyd credits him. He anonymously attacked Clinton and Jefferson in the newspapers, yet he must have known that the authorship of these pieces could not long remain unknown because his style was so distinctive. He printed a distorted version of one of Jefferson's letters to discredit him, yet must have known that Jefferson could easily destroy his case by printing the actual letter in its entirety. He printed his vicious attack on John Adams for private circulation, yet must have known that it could not stay private. In fact he seemed happy when Aaron Burr made it public. Hamilton's attempts to manipulate the electoral college were exceedingly clumsy, and he must have known that at least one person he contacted would spread the news of what he was doing. Even in the case of Mrs. Reynolds, he seemed precipitately anxious to confess publicly the smallest detail of this sordid affair.

Obviously, deception was not Hamilton's element. His pride in his own actions and opinions, his disdain for those who opposed him, his impetuous nature, and his contempt for anything but a direct, frontal attack made it nearly impossible for him to carry on an effective conspiracy. He seemed almost happy to be exposed and then to boldly avow his true opinions, exhibiting his political courage and his disdain for popular opinion. At no other time in his life did he exhibit the subtle duplicity with which Boyd credits him in the Nootka affair.

In any case, the Nootka crisis still was not ended. In August 1790 Washington became concerned that if the Nootka Sound controversy did erupt into war, Great Britain might request permission to cross American territory to attack Spanish New Orleans. He asked his cabinet for advice in case this should come about. Hamilton's answer further illustrated his attitude toward a British alliance, the balance of power, and the nature of relations between nations. He argued that the United States should agree to allow the British to march across its territory because the new nation had no power to enforce a negative answer. "The consequence . . . of refusal, if not effectual, must be absolute disgrace or immediate war," he wrote.[32] War would be suicidal. By destroying America's revenue and credit, it "would be fatal to the means of prosecuting it." Though British acquisition of New Orleans or Florida would be a great evil for the United States, he said, the consequences of war would be worse.[33] The best course, then, was to grant the British request if it should be made. Perhaps the attack on New Orleans would fail. Even if it succeeded, America's cooperation might lead the British to revise their attitudes toward their former colonies.[34] It might even be to America's interest to join the British expedition, he hinted.[35] Certainly that was better than refusing passage and risking a war in which the United States would be fighting on the weaker side.[36] Yet if the United States did refuse passage and the British marched in defiance of that refusal, America must fight. A nation "had better hazard any calamities than submit tamely to absolute disgrace."[37]

Here was Hamilton's policy in a nutshell. He would avoid war with England, protect America's credit, and seek his goals and his glory not by balancing superior power, but by joining it. Yet when faced by a direct challenge he reverted to the *code duello*. If he saw disgrace or war as his only alternatives, he would choose war even if it meant the extinction of his hopes. Others might counsel evading an answer, but Hamilton rejected the idea. "An evasive conduct . . . is never dignified—seldom politic," he wrote.[38] Thus the code of honor asserted itself. The realist became the romantic, the Machiavellian became the knight errant. Since glory was America's goal, the nation could accept everything but disgrace while readying itself for glorious exploits. The United States should do everything possible to stay out of situations where it could not win, but when the challenge was unavoidable, it must fight even if it meant national extinction.

The fact that Great Britain never asked to cross American territory for an attack on Spanish colonies saved Hamilton from his choice between acquiescence, disgrace, or death. But it did not save him from further battles with Madison's proposals for commercial retaliation.

Evidently, sympathy for action against Britain had been growing since the defeat of Madison's measures in 1790. Beckwith's assurances of British friendliness during the Nootka crisis had done nothing to stop them.[39] In January 1791 Hamilton despaired of stopping the movement, telling Beckwith that Congress would enact a navigation law aimed at British shipping during the course of the present session.[40] But when rumors arrived by private letters of the intention of the British government to appoint a minister to the United States, Hamilton told Beckwith, "I think I can assure you that nothing will take place during the present Session, to the injury of your trade."[41]

Hamilton had to work diligently to make his prediction come true. Washington submitted a report to Congress drawn up by Jefferson and based on the dispatches from Gouverneur Morris. The indications of British hostility contained in that report revived the movement for restrictions on British trade. Jefferson told Congress that it was now clear that the British government would not give up the posts, would set the amount of debts owed by United States citizens to British subjects at so high a figure as to preclude agreement, and would not negotiate a commercial treaty unless a political alliance were joined to it. Jefferson also concluded that England would not send a minister to the United States.[42] His message to this effect was referred by the House of Representatives to a committee that included James Madison. From it emerged, not surprisingly, an American navigation act such as that offered by Madison in 1790 as a substitute for discriminatory duties. The opponents of the measure succeeded by parliamentary devices in putting off action on Madison's proposal, finally delaying it indefinitely by getting the House to refer the problem to Jefferson for a report to Congress on the general state of American trade, to be delivered to the next session of Congress.[43] The success of Madison's opponents was undoubtedly aided by Hamilton's influence and the rumors of an impending appointment of a British minister.

While Hamilton staved off Congress with one hand, he had to defend himself against Beckwith with the other. Beckwith accused Washington of submitting Jefferson's report with the intention of inspiring the retaliatory legislation that had resulted. This of course contradicted Hamilton's assertions that Washington had a predilection for Great Britain. Hamilton denied Beckwith's charges. He asserted "That the President's mind is the least influenced by any sort of prejudices whatever; he indeed is of opinion from Mr. Morris's letters, *that no commercial treaty is attainable with England*, but I am sure he is not led to make these communications to the Legislature at this time, from any idea of assimilating this with other questions. . . ." Hamilton admitted that others in the government might have intended otherwise. But he again assured Beckwith that the retaliatory legislation would be defeated. In addition, he tried again to tempt the English to conclude a commercial treaty by dangling the hope of a political alliance before them; he said,

In the present state of things, nothing has happened between us and France, to give a colorable pretence, for breaking of our treaty of Alliance with that Power, and immediately forming one with you, a regard for National decorum, puts such a decisive step as this, out of our Reach, but I tell you candidly as an individual, that I think the formation of a treaty of commerce, would by degrees have led to this measure, which undoubtedly that Party with us, whose remaining animosities and French partialities influence their whole political conduct, regard with dissatisfaction.[44]

In December 1791 Jefferson reopened his debate with Hamilton by informing the cabinet that the report which Congress had requested of him would recommend commercial retaliation against Britain. Hamilton opposed it strongly, arguing that commencing a commercial war with Britain would destroy any chance to obtain the posts from Britain through negotiations with the newly arrived minister from that country, George Hammond. Jefferson was struck by this argument, agreeing it would be imprudent to retaliate if there was a chance to obtain the posts peacefully. He said he would therefore postpone his report until the next session of Congress if he gleaned the slightest hope from Hammond that Britain meant to surrender the posts.[45] Despite the fact that Jefferson never did receive any such indication from the British minister, the length of time consumed by his negotiations with Hammond delayed Jefferson's report until Congress adjourned.

Finally, in 1792, when war again threatened between Spain and the United States, Hamilton directly proposed to Washington's cabinet a defensive alliance with Great Britain. This, said Hamilton, would involve British ships and American troops in a joint assault on Spanish control of the Mississippi. Washington summarily dismissed Hamilton's cure as worse than the disease.[46]

So Hamilton failed to convince Washington and the other leaders of the government that the United States should seek its fortune in alliance with Great Britain. But at least he had secured the acquiescence of Washington, Adams, and Jay to his policy of avoiding a direct commercial challenge to England. This in itself was no mean feat. These men had been lusty advocates of commercial retaliation before ratification of the Constitution. Washington had even protested the first defeat of Madison's discriminatory tonnage bill. But after Hamilton took office as secretary of the treasury, Washington, Jay, and Adams fell silent on the matter, allowing Hamilton's policy of pacifying Great Britain to triumph. Thus, they accepted part of Hamilton's prescription for building national power; but they balked at swallowing the whole dose. This was primarily because they did not share

Hamilton's thirst for glory. Their demands for national power were based instead on their desire for dignity and respectability. They wanted to be statesmen rather than heroes.

Washington, Adams, and Jay had been stridently ambitious as young men, perhaps almost as ambitious as Hamilton. But time, character, and success had moderated their ambition somewhat and allowed them to control it in a way that Hamilton could not. In them it took the form of an obsessive concern for reputation rather than a passion for military exploits. John Adams even concluded that a concern for reputation, or "emulation" as he called it, was the primary motive of all men's conduct.[47]

For Adams, Washington, and Jay, reputation was dependent on character, restraint, and moderation as well as power. The possession of these attributes would make a man or a nation dignified and respectable in the eyes of the world. Such attributes would also provide an atmosphere of peace and regularity in which other individuals might achieve power, dignity, and respectability. This, in fact, was their definition of liberty. Power was indeed an essential tool for achieving their goals, but they thought power had to be matched with restraint and moderation. They even regarded a great increase in federal power as something of a necessary evil rather than a positive good. Jay, Washington, and Adams feared that a weak government would invite anarchy, which in turn would induce people to exchange their liberty for the order provided by a man on horseback. They hoped that extensive national power granted immediately would forestall dictatorial power later. Hamilton often made the same argument, but his line between dictatorial power and the power necessary to forestall its coming seems rather hazy in retrospect. Washington, Jay, and Adams, on the other hand, demonstrated their willingness as president or state governor to accept strict limitations on their authority.[48]

Washington, Adams, and Jay all favored a system of checks and balances as a necessary restraint on power. They did not seem as confident as Hamilton that power itself purified the intentions and actions of its holders. Adams, for instance, feared that power and prosperity would ultimately so inflame the American people that at some time in the future only a hereditary executive and senate would be able to maintain order.[49] To check excessive concentration of strength in the federal government, Adams, Washington, and Jay strongly supported the separation of powers in the form of a strong federal court system and a division of the national legislature into two houses. They never dreamed, as Hamilton did, of destroying all powers of the states that might stand in the way of federal hegemony. As we shall see, this support for internal checks and balances was matched by a greater concern for maintaining an external balance of power than Hamilton manifested.

Yet important as internal checks and balances may have been to Washington, Adams, and Jay, these men were even more desirous of the unity, order, and power necessary to sustain national dignity and respectability. They were desperately afraid of factional quarrels, and their support for the separation of powers was at least as much designed to prevent the supremacy of any one faction as to protect individual liberty from the federal government. Washington despaired at the growth of parties, and Adams thought the growth of factions in America might ultimately require a monarchy to control them.[50] Thus Washington, Adams, and Jay thought it essential to attach the people to something beyond personal and factional interest, to unite them in a common cause. They looked to the federal government, and particularly the executive, to furnish this unifying force and to suppress factional excesses if necessary. "For my own part I am convinced that a national government, as strong as may be compatible with liberty, is necessary to give us national security and respectability," said Jay.[51] "Nothing but Force and Power and Strength" could restrain the partisan passions of the people, Adams thought.[52]

The chief executive was the person to exercise such authority, as far as Jay, Washington, and Adams were concerned. A separation of powers might check the interests and passions of legislative factions, but there was still need for a superintending power to guide the balance in a proper direction. This required a man above factional quarrels, beyond corruption by wealth and power, a man of an "all-seeing eye," as Adams put it. The chief executive was more likely than any legislator to be such a man, not only because of the virtue, ability, and status he would necessarily possess to be elected, but also because he would be continually in the public eye. Too little honor or blame attached itself to the actions of individual legislators to affect their conduct.[53] To this extent, Jay, Washington, and Adams would accept Hamilton's dictum that power purified.

Washington, Adams, and Jay, in search of national liberty, dignity, and respectability, found their vision largely compatible with Hamilton's desire to strengthen the national government against the states, establish America's financial credit, and build its defensive capabilities. So Washington supported and signed the legislation based on Hamilton's reports to Congress; Jay met with and advised Hamilton during this period; and Adams expressed approbation of Hamilton's policies, although he objected to the extent of commercial paper that circulated as a result of them.[54] Washington even moved toward acceptance of a standing army. Giving up hope that Congress would provide for adequate training of militia, he supported enlistment of troops for terms of three years to man America's garrisons.[55]

In accepting Hamilton's domestic policies, Washington, Adams, and Jay also demonstrated agreement with him that the United States was a weak nation which should seek to avoid the danger of war with Great Britain until America's power had been considerably agumented. During the Nootka Sound crisis, Jay and Adams submitted position papers to Washington that were much in line with Hamilton's. Jay said that a refusal to allow British troops to cross American territory might well be defied, and that this would necessitate a war for which the United States was unprepared. Therefore he, like Hamilton, advised Washington to grant the permission if it were requested.[56] Adams sought to maintain the peace in another way. He advised refusing permission, but said if the British marched in defiance of the refusal, the United States should remonstrate and negotiate rather than fight.[57]

How such sentiments affected the attitudes of Jay, Adams, and Washington toward commercial retaliation between 1789 and 1792 is difficult to say. They did not intervene or comment on the struggles between Madison, Jefferson, and Hamilton in Congress so far as one can tell from their writings. But this abstention itself was important to Hamilton. Had they intervened on Madison's side, no doubt the policy of commercial retaliation would have triumphed. Hamilton must have regaled them with the consequences for his system of a commercial war with Britain. In addition, the progressive disillusionment of Washington, Adams, and Jay with the course of the French Revolution after 1789 gave them less and less cause to reward France by fighting a commercial war with Great Britain. Finally, they were probably influenced in their decision to abandon commercial retaliation by the return of the nation's prosperity following the severe depression that had coincided with the Confederation period. Now there seemed to be less reason to risk America's economic well being in an attempt to force an increase of trade with Britain and its colonies. This returning prosperity probably had an effect on the sentiments of the people as well as those of their leaders.

During the Confederation period, the primary source of agitation for policies of commercial discrimination had been New England. But the Yankees had supported such legislation as a means of capturing trade for American ships and ending the nation's depressed financial condition rather than indulging resentment against Great Britain. Thus they supported tariffs directed at all foreign nations instead of duties designed to discriminate particularly against England. John Adams wrote to Jefferson in 1785, "I should be sorry to adopt a Monopoly. But, driven to the necessity of it, I would not do Business by the Halves. The French deserve it of us as much as the English; for they are as much Enemies to our Ships and Mariners. Their Navigation Acts are not quite so severe as those of Spain, Portugal, and England, as they relate to their colonies I mean. But they are not much less so. And they discover as strong a Lust to annihilate our navigation as anybody."[58]

Adams' philosophy was taken up by the legislatures of Massachusetts and New Hampshire. They passed navigation acts imposing double duties on all goods imported in ships not owned by American citizens. Jefferson reacted immediately; he wrote Adams that the "European nations [will be] in general commercial war against us. They can do too well without our commodities except tobacco, and we cannot find elsewhere markets for them. The selfishness of England alone will not justify our hazarding a contest of this kind against all Europe. Spain, Portugal, and France have not yet shut their doors against us: it will be time enough when they do to take up the commercial hatchet. I hope therefore those states will repeal their navigation clauses except as against Great Britain and other nations not treating with us."[59]

By the time Adams had received this letter, he had already abandoned his idea of retaliating against all Europe. Speaking with the Portuguese envoy to the Court of St. James, he mentioned that England's conduct might oblige America to pass a navigation act. The Portuguese minister replied unequivocally that any nation so doing would have its ships barred from Portugal. Adams must have seen the handwriting on the wall, for he "clarified" his statement by saying that he had meant a navigation law against England only. This the Portuguese minister found perfectly justified.[60] Massachusetts and New Hampshire also retreated and repealed their acts. But they did not give up the idea of an impartial navigation law directed against all European nations for the benefit of American shipping. Fisher Ames, representative from Massachusetts, said that the northern representatives had voted for Madison's discriminatory measures of 1789 because they would bring higher duties, and in spite of rather than because of the fact that they discriminated against Great Britain.[61]

As prosperity returned and trade increased, the nothern states became unwilling to risk a commercial war and the destruction of their trade in an attempt to coerce further concessions from the British. By 1791 Hamilton regarded the northern states as his primary allies in the battle against commercial discrimination.[62] With Massachusetts in the lead of this movement,

Adams had good political reason to follow his original instincts and avoid particular discrimination against Great Britain. With New York also a center of opposition to Madison's bill, John Jay had as good a reason as Adams to follow suit.

But if Adams, Jay, and Washington came to accept much of Hamilton's foreign policy, Jefferson and Madison certainly did not.

5. JEFFERSON AND MADISON: A FOREIGN POLICY IN PURSUIT OF HAPPINESS

A certain serenity of spirit set Jefferson and Madison apart from the rest of the founding fathers. The two Virginians had a pacific temperament, and their foreign and domestic policies reflected it. They were ambitious, but they were never driven by the intense, gnawing anxieties that dominated a man like Hamilton. Hamilton relished conflict; Jefferson and Madison hated it. Jefferson thought "social harmony the first of human felicities," while Madison longed for a government of "reason, benevolence, and brotherly affection."[1] Hamilton was dashing and arrogant; Jefferson and Madison were calm and deferential. Hamilton was a dandy; Jefferson was careless of personal appearance, and Madison wore little but black. Hamilton strutted; Madison stooped and Jefferson shambled. Hamilton was the total public man; his goals were public and he considered all private interests subordinate to them. Jefferson and Madison were essentially private men; for them the purpose of government was not national glory, but the protection of individuals in the pursuit of legitimate private interests. Jefferson and Madison thought the United States should seek not wealth but simplicity, not power but liberty, not national glory but domestic tranquillity, not heroism but happiness.

Hamilton's search for glory subordinated domestic to foreign policy. At home he sought merely to build a power base for the ultimate source of national greatness—foreign affairs. The pursuit of national happiness undertaken by Jefferson and Madison reversed these priorities. Their domestic system would provide the essentials of happiness, such as liberty, justice, and domestic tranquillity; foreign policy would simply defend this system from foreign interference and supply the minimum of foreign trade and territory that might aid its purposes.

Jefferson and Madison both recognized the necessity of national power to deal with foreign affairs. But both feared the effects of power on internal liberty. Jefferson considered that government best which governed least. Madison qualified this proposition with the observation that, when government power dipped below a certain degree of "energy and independence, . . . the direct tendency is to further degrees of relaxation, until the abuses of liberty beget a sudden transition to an undue degree of power. . . . It is a melancholy reflection that liberty should be equally exposed to danger whether the Government have too much or too little power."[2] Consequently, he advocated a stronger central government than Jefferson did, a fact vividly illustrated by Jefferson's reluctance to accept the Constitution that Madison had done so much to create. Even as late as 1798 Madison was forced to restrain Jefferson from claiming in the Kentucky Resolutions the right of a state to secede from the union.

Madison may have approved of greater federal power than Jefferson did, but he was still far from approving of Hamilton's ideas on the subject. Even when he was collaborating with Hamilton on *The Federalist*, Madison's distrust of power showed itself. He warned that "power is of an encroaching nature, and ought to be effectually restrained from passing the limits assigned to it," a possibility which did not worry Hamilton much.[3] Madison insisted that national safety and happiness were "the objects at which all political institutions aim," while Hamilton spoke of safety alone as the first goal of government.[4] Hamilton's policies as secretary of the treasury accentuated Madison's distrust of power, and by 1792 the Virginian was claiming that between the evils of governmental consolidation and political schism, the former was by far the worse evil.[5] "What a perversion of the natural order of things! to make *power* the primary and central object of the social system, and *Liberty* but its sattelite," he wrote.[6]

Jefferson and Madison saw two ways to restrain federal authority. They would separate and balance its component powers, and subordinate the whole to the will of the people. Jefferson and Madison were willing to trust the people with the ultimate power of society partly because they trusted human nature more than Hamilton. Yet that trust was not so encompassing as their critics have often asserted. Jefferson said that the people were "the most honest and safe, although not the most wise depository of the public interests."[7] Madison agreed that "as there is a degree of depravity in mankind which requires a certain degree of circumspection and distrust: So there are other qualities in human nature, which justify a certain portion of esteem and confidence. . . . Were the pictures which have been drawn by the political jealousy of some among us, faithful likenesses of the human character, the inference would be that there is not sufficient virtue among men for self-government; and that nothing less than the chains of despotism can restrain them from destroying and devouring one another."[8]

Jefferson and Madison were somewhat more enthusiastic about the nature of the American character than about human nature in general. This was not because they believed Americans to be exempt from the ordinary selfishness of humanity. "Human nature is the same on every side of the Atlantic, and will be alike influenced by the same causes," said Jefferson.[9] But Americans were almost all farmers, and this made them more virtuous than their European cousins. Where Hamilton looked to power and wealth to raise man above the worst aspects of his nature, Jefferson and Madison looked to agriculture. Madison claimed that health, virtue, profound intelligence, and competency were all more compatible with agriculture than with any other occupation.[10] Jefferson said that "those who labor in the earth are the chosen people of God . . . whose breasts He has made His peculiar deposit for substantial and genuine virtue. . . . Corruption of morals in the mass of cultivators is a phenomenon of which no age nor nation has furnished an example."[11]

Jefferson and Madison thought agrarians particularly virtuous because their occupation gave them little reason to deprive others of their livelihoods or liberties. This allowed them to wield political power with reason and justice. "The moderate and sure income of husbandry begets permanent improvement, quiet life, and orderly conduct both public and private," said Jefferson.[12] The promise of quick wealth in many other occupations produced a spirit of speculation and avarice, encouraging little respect for the rights of neighbors or the public good.[13]

Another factor contributing to the virtue of agrarians was their economic independence. Farmers looked to nothing but "heaven, . . . their own soil and industry" for their sustenance.[14] This enabled them to resist the pressures of those whose ambition or avarice would destroy the rights and liberties of the people. Merchants, manufacturers, and laborers, no matter how wealthy, could not be equally independent. Their livelihood was at the mercy of their customers or employers. They were not to be trusted, for "dependence begets subservience and venality, suffocates the germ of virtue, and prepares fit fools for the design of ambition."[15] Laborers, particularly, were "the panders of vice and the instruments by which the liberties of a country are generally overturned," according to Jefferson.[16]

Jefferson and Madison counted on relative economic equality as well as agriculture to keep the people respectful of the rights of others and capable of self-government. Great gulfs between rich and poor led to animosities which had overturned more than one republic, according to Jefferson.[17] Madison proposed that "the silent operation of the laws" should help maintain equality by diminishing the holdings of the rich and augmenting those of the poor as far as could be done without gross violations of property rights.[18]

Finally, Jefferson and Madison hoped that education would further augment the virtue of the American people by teaching them that their greatest happiness "does not depend on the condition of life in which chance has placed them, but is always the result of good conscience, good health, occupation, and freedom in all just pursuits."[19] Those who resisted this teaching and remained avaricious could be shown that their economic interest as well as their happiness coincided with a virtuous regard for the rights and interests of others. Jefferson believed that "A wise man, if nature has not formed him honest, will yet act as if he were honest: because he will find it the most advantageous and wise part in the long run."[20]

Yet Jefferson and Madison continued to fear power even when it was concentrated in the hands of a virtuous people. They were convinced that power corrupted, and consequently they always sought to balance it with a countervailing power. Where Hamilton's instinct was to augment and join superior strength, Jefferson and Madison usually tried to check it. Jefferson said that to concentrate all powers in one branch of government, even in a popularly elected legislature, was "precisely the definition of despotic government. It will be no alleviation that those powers will be exercised by a plurality of hands, and not by a single one. One hundred and seventy-three despots would surely be as oppressive as one."[21] His solution was to constitutionally restrict the federal government, separate and balance its remaining powers, and encourage the states to protect their rights against federal encroachments.

Madison accepted all these means of avoiding the concentration of political power in the United States, but he was not as strong an advocate of states' rights as Jefferson. He devised another system of checks and balances which he thought less dangerous to liberty than state sovereignty. He predicted that the masses would inevitably divide themselves into interests and factions as they happened to be creditors or debtors, rich or poor, farmers or merchants, and followers of different political leaders and religious sects. He believed it equally inevitable that, if one of these factions gained a majority in a republican government, it would use its power to suppress all competitors. This he thought more likely to happen in the states than in the federal government. In a smaller area there were likely to be few interests, making it possible for one to achieve a majority and suppress the others. In an extensive area, there would be many competing interests and correspondingly less likelihood of one gaining a majority.[22]

Far more important than the differences between Jefferson and Madison concerning states' rights, however, was their instinctive agreement to balance power rather than to unify and augment it. Madison's whole idea that an extensive country with a multiplicity of interests could be a stable republic was designed to counter Hamilton's claim that only a strong, unified government with an executive wielding monarchical power was capable of ruling a large nation.[23] Nor did Jefferson and Madison accept the idea that it was necessary and possible to have someone above the factional quarrels to moderate and direct them toward the true national interest. They doubted that anyone could really be above personal and factional interests, and that included Washington, who came as close to this ideal as humanly possible. A will independent of factional interests "may as well espouse the unjust views of the major as the rightful interests, of the minor party, and may possibly be turned against both parties," said Madison.[24] Too strong an executive might be corrupted by his power and pursue his own interests rather than the happiness of the people. He could easily manipulate the dependent merchants, manufacturers, and laborers to that end.

For Jefferson and Madison, the national good was not above or outside the balance of power. It was the product of the balance itself. The purpose of government was to balance interests and passions against one another, leaving reason free to arbitrate between them and arrive at a just solution.[25] This reason would not be embodied in an executive outside the balance. It would be exercised by men whose short-term interests had been checked, leaving them more likely to remember that their long-term interests were best served by respecting the rights of others and the good of the whole community. If a republic failed to check and balance power and the majority was able to suppress the minority, it would mean the ruin of the nation. "Justice is the end of government," said Madison; "It has and ever will be pursued until it is obtained, or until liberty be lost in the pursuit."[26]

The foreign policy of Jefferson and Madison was essentially a reflection of their domestic policy. It too was dictated by a preference for happiness over heroism, simplicity over wealth, liberty over power, tranquillity over glory, and justice over reasons of state. Underlying it were the same principles that supported their domestic policy—popular control of government, balance of power, beneficence of agriculture, necessity of economic independence, relative virtue of human nature, and belief that self-interest as well as happiness was promoted by honesty and a respect for others. These preferences and principles determined a foreign policy far different from that of Alexander Hamilton.

Jefferson and Madison decided that the best protection foreign policy could offer to their domestic goals was "to cultivate the peace and friendship of every nation."[27] Their prescription for virtue in individuals also became a basic premise of their foreign policy. "I have but one system of ethics for men and for nations," said Jefferson. "To be grateful, to be faithful to all engagements and under all circumstances, to be open and generous." As in domestic affairs, Jefferson was convinced that to be virtuous "promotes in the long run even the interests of [nations]: and I am sure it promotes their happiness."[28] Madison agreed that the United States should act with "justice, good faith, honor, [and] gratitude."[29]

Jefferson and Madison used the same techniques they had devised for their domestic policy to ensure that American foreign policy was virtuous and peaceful—popular control, checks and balances, and legal limitations on governmental power. First, they were happy to see the Constitution give an "effectual check to the Dog of war" by transferring "the power of letting him loose from the executive to the Legislative body, from those who are to spend to those who are to pay."[30] To further ensure that the cost of war would give pause to the people of the United States, Jefferson and Madison proposed that the legislature prohibit government debts exceeding the present generation's capacity to pay. The generation that declared and fought the war would then have to pay for it without passing its cost on to their children and grandchildren. "Were a nation to impose such restraints on itself, avarice would be sure to calculate the expences of ambition; in the equipoise of these passions, reason would be free to decide for the public good," declared Madison.[31]

Still they realized that "The justest dispositions possible in ourselves will not secure us against [war]. It would be necessary that all other nations were just also. Justice indeed on our part will save us from those wars which would have been produced by a contrary disposition. But how to prevent those produced by the wrongs of other nations?"[32]

The question was not just an academic one. Both Great Britain and Spain had responded to America's offers of friendly and peaceful relations with what Jefferson and Madison regarded as downright hostility. Could the United States resist the wrongs of other nations while preserving happiness, liberty, justice, and tranquillity at home? Jefferson and Madison thought it could and must.

Jefferson and Madison were convinced that passive acceptance of aggression was more dangerous than resistance. "A coward is much more exposed to quarrels than a man of spirit," Jefferson claimed.[33] "Weakness provokes insult and injury, while a condition to punish it often prevents it. . . . I think it to our interest to punis[h] the first insult: because an insult unpunished is the parent of many oth[ers]."[34] Madison agreed that preparedness and resistance to injustice were more likely to maintain peace than appeasement: "being prepared to repel danger, is the most likely way to avoid it."[35]

Jefferson and Madison were particularly convinced of the necessity to resist the policies of Great Britain. To a large extent this attitude was a result of adapting their ideas about human nature to the nature of relations between states. Hamilton, who regarded nations and individuals as instinctively selfish, was not particularly surprised or chagrined at Britain's policies. In his opinion, these policies were the result of natural selfishness and a mistaken view of British interests, rather than any fixed hatred of the United States. If England could be made to see that its true interests lay in conciliating rather than opposing the United States, its policy would change. Retaliation, however, *would* induce hostility; and then appeals to reason and self-interest would be useless, for men were ruled more by passion than by reason.

Jefferson and Madison were not so worried about the effects of retaliation upon Great Britain. They thought England was already as hostile as it was going to get, and that its policies were the result of passionate hatred rather than natural self-interest. They resented Great Britain's policies more than Hamilton did partly because they expected more of nations. "Let vain speculists, in the sequestered recess of study and retirement, invent frigid maxims of policy, and lay it down as an invariable rule, that States are actuated by self-interest alone . . . , those who are conversant with human nature and public affairs, will despise the fallacious doctrine and illiberal tenet," wrote Madison. Honesty, gratitude, and virtue had a place in foreign policy, he went on, especially in relations with France, "who first espoused our hopeless cause with an enthusiastic fervor, and then with persevering assistance and magnanimous exertion protected our infant fortunes."[36] Because Jefferson and Madison expected magnanimity as well as self-interest and hatred in foreign relations, they reacted more strongly against Britain's conduct than Hamilton did. England seemed intractably hostile, anxious to see the American experiment fail so that she could pick up the shattered pieces of the Union.[37] The British insisted on identifying their interests with the destruction of the United States instead of seeing that their long-range interests were best served by matching America's virtuous regard for the rights and interests of others.[38] Only avarice and passionate dislike of the United States could explain the blindness of the British to their true interests. "Nothing will bring them to reason but physical obstruction, applied to their bodily senses," Jefferson concluded.[39] Failure of America to resist would convince the British that hostility ran no risk of punishment, inviting further aggressions not only from England, but from all nations "lest [Britain] should exclusively enjoy the superior and peculiar advantages, arising from her conduct."[40]

Still other principles reflected in the domestic policy of Jefferson and Madison helped determine them to resist the policy of Great Britain. Their belief that economic independence was vital to human liberty and dignity led them to resent being bound "in commercial manacles" to England. So they tried to free the United States from financial dependence on England despite the material costs of such a policy. Their principle of checking and balancing superior power also dictated resistance to Great Britain, since she was the greatest power in the world of that time and the only nation capable of mounting a major military effort against the United States. Rather than joining Great Britain, as Hamilton was wont to do, they favored Britain's weaker opponents. Thus they continued to support the French alliance.

After the French Revolution, they were further inclined to support France because of their democratic sympathies and their belief that republics were more disposed to peace and friendly relations than monarchies or oligarchies. But the French Revolution did little more than confirm them in their earlier policy. The direction of that policy had been settled years before the French Revolution, when Madison and Jefferson both regarded England's form of government as a sort of half-way house between the absolutism of the French monarchy and the libertarian republicanism of the United States.

Most important to the foreign policy of Jefferson and Madison, however, was not the determination that the United States *should* resist the wrongs of foreign nations but that it *could* do so. Hamilton argued that the United States lacked the most basic elements of national power—an army, a navy, domestic manufactures, an extensive and invulnerable source of revenue, and a powerful central government. Had Jefferson and Madison accepted that argument, they would have been faced with the choice of appeasing Great Britain or building powers destructive of the domestic happiness, liberty, justice, and tranquillity that foreign policy was supposed to protect. They avoided this dilemma by rejecting Hamilton's concept of the nature and extent of power necessary for the United States to resist the wrongs of Great Britain and Spain. They judged that the United States did not need an army, manufactures, extensive national revenue, nor a consolidated government. They even came to reject the need for a navy, of which they themselves had been advocates prior to 1789. They did not do this because they were blind idealists who failed to balance goals with the power available. On the contrary, they balanced them very carefully. They simply thought the United States already had power of a nature and extent capable of securing America's foreign policy goals without endangering its domestic system.

Jefferson and Madison decided that there were only two areas where the United States might be required to defend its interests with force—its borders and its ships at sea. Regarding the borders, they thought the United

States had little to fear. Certainly there was no need for a regular army to defend them. America's distance from the European nations whose colonies bordered its territory meant that "No European nation can ever send against us such a regular army as we need fear, and it is hard if our militia are not equal to those of Canada and Florida."[41] Jefferson and Madison counted on America's tremendous population growth to achieve inevitably and peacefully whatever the United States wanted on its frontiers.

This was especially the case with Spain. As early as 1784, Madison thought the United States so powerful "as not to be despised by Spain," and claimed that "soon [Spain's] possessions in this quarter of the globe will be more dependent on our peaceableness than her own power." Jefferson agreed and thought the Spanish border territories could not be in better hands: "My fear is that [the Spanish] are too feeble to hold them till our population can be sufficiently advanced to gain it from them peice by peice [sic]. The navigation of the Mississippi we must have. This is all we are as yet ready to receive."[42]

Jefferson believed that European embroilments would soon provide the United States with an opportunity to force from Spain the right to navigate the Mississippi. "I should think it proper for the Western country to defer pushing their right to that navigation to extremity as long as they can do without it tolerably; but that the moment it becomes absolutely necessary for them, it will become the duty of the maritime states to push it to every extremity," he wrote in 1788. "A time of peace will not be the surest for obtaining this object. Those therefore who have influence in the new country would act wisely to endeavor to keep things quiet till the western parts of Europe shall be engaged in war."[43]

Thus, four factors would make it unnecessary for the United States to raise a regular army for defense of its interests along the Spanish border—Spain's weakness, America's growing population, America's distance from Europe, and the balance of power in Europe which diverted forces from America during Europe's frequent wars. As a result of these factors, Madison thought the Spanish would give up the Mississippi without a fight;[44] and even if war were required, the militia could handle it without any danger to America's internal liberties.

Madison and Jefferson were somewhat less optimistic regarding the border with England. They were not ready for an outright attack on the British posts, for this would bring on war. But they knew they could bring pressure on the British by destroying their Indian allies who constituted the major defense of the posts. Nor would this require regular troops. Even after the Northwest Indian Confederacy had disastrously defeated two American expeditions, Jefferson opposed raising an army of regular troops to march with Anthony Wayne against them. He was convinced that regular troops "were useless and that 12, or 1500 woods men would soon end the war, and at trifling expense."[45] He also proposed building a post at Presqu' Isle and beginning a navy there for the Great Lakes. Hamilton said this would mean war, and the idea was dropped.[46] But the incident showed Jefferson's confidence that the United States had nothing to fear on its borders, even from England. Though America might not wish to attack the posts directly, the defeat of the Indians and America's growing population would make the British position untenable. And if England became embroiled in another war in Europe, it might relinquish the posts even sooner.[47] Meanwhile, America could use commercial weapons to force a change in Britain's hostile policy.

Jefferson and Madison thought there was far more danger of a major war on the sea than on the frontier. American power would soon be so overwhelming on the frontier that no one would dare resist the nation's just interests there. But the ocean was something else again. The determination of Americans to share in the world's shipping and commerce meant "Frequent wars without a doubt," as far as Jefferson was concerned. "Their property will be violated on the sea, and in foreign ports, their persons will be insulted, emprisoned &c. for pretended debts, contracts, crimes, contraband &c. &c. These insults must be represented, even if we had no feelings."[48]

Jefferson thought it would have been better for the peace and liberty of the United States to "practice neither commerce nor navigation, but stand with respect to Europe precisely on the footing of China."[49] He feared that too great an increase of trade "will probably embark us again into the ocean of speculation, engage us to overtrade ourselves, . . . divert us from Agriculture which is our wisest pursuit, because it will in the end contribute most to real wealth, good morals and happiness. The wealth acquired by speculation and plunder is fugacious in its nature and fills society with the spirit of gambling."[50] He realized, however, that "our people are decided in the opinion that it is necessary for us to share in the occupation of the ocean." Believing it the "duty in those entrusted with the administration of their affairs to conform themselves to the decided choice of their constituents," he determined "to share as large a portion as we can of this modern source of wealth and power."[51] Still, he hoped to keep trade merely a "handmaiden to agriculture," carrying off America's surplus crops and bringing back only the vital supplies that the United States could not produce for itself.[52]

If Jefferson and Madison saw the potential for war and depravity in trade, however, they also saw its potential for peace. Both realized that trade created a community of interest that might deter nations from war with one another for fear of losing valuable commerce. Both thought that an international system of free trade would exploit this community of interest to the maximum.[53] When Jefferson and John Adams obtained a trade treaty with Prussia which approached their ideal of free trade, they wrote that they were leading the way to an "object so valuable to mankind as the total emancipation of commerce and the bringing together all nations for a free intercommunication of happiness."[54]

The restrictions that England and the rest of Europe imposed on American trade after the Revolution soon convinced Jefferson and Madison that free trade was out of reach. In 1785 Madison wrote, "A perfect freedom [of trade] is the System which would be my choice. But before such a System will be eligible perhaps for the U.S. they must be out of debt; before it will be attainable, all other nations must concur in it."[55] Since other nations did not concur, he reluctantly decided that the United States had to "retort the distinction."[56]

Yet even commercial retaliation could be an instrument of peace, Jefferson and Madison believed. In fact, their whole policy toward England was dedicated to that proposition. They were convinced that commercial retaliation could avoid the danger of war brought on by appeasement while at the same time avoiding the war that would come as a result of military resistance. It would forcibly remind the British that their long range interest was in conciliating the United States and protecting the community of interest which their mutual trade afforded. It would enable the United States to challenge Great Britain immediately without building an army, a navy, domestic manufactures, extensive revenue, or a consolidated government.

As we have seen, Madison, with Jefferson's support, introduced legislation favoring the trade of nations who negotiated trade treaties with the United States over those, like Great Britain, who refused. Later, Madison favored measures that would simply reciprocate whatever treatment American trade received in the ports of foreign nations. Both measures were designed to force Britain into a treaty with the United States formalizing Anglo-American trade, opening the West Indies to American ships and more American products, and turning the frontier forts over to the United States as stipulated in the Treaty of Peace. Hamilton and his followers in Congress argued that retaliatory measures would bring on a commercial war rather than improve Anglo-American trade, and that such a war would ruin the United States without materially harming Great Britain.

Jefferson and Madison acknowledged that commercial war was a possible outcome of retaliation against England, though they thought it improbable. Jefferson said, "they will be agitated by their avarice on one hand, and their hatred and their fear of us on the other. The result of this conflict of d[irty passions] is yet [to be] awaited."[57] Madison avowed that, "If we were disposed to hazard the experiment of interdicting the intercourse between us and the Powers not in alliance, we should have overtures of the most advantageous kind tendered by those nations."[58] Still he considered British counterretaliation possible. Like Jefferson, however, he did not fear its effects. He told the first Congress in 1789, "We soon shall be in a condition, we now are in a condition to wage a commercial warfare with that nation. The produce of this country is more necessary to the rest of the world than that of other countries is to America." He was not afraid that America would suffer in the contest, for England's "interests can be wounded almost mortally, while ours are invulnerable."[59]

Hamilton, of course, thought this was nonsense. He believed the United States desperately needed British manufactures and the revenue derived from duties on British trade to support American credit. Jefferson and Madison rejected this notion. In their opinion, the United States was almost totally self-sufficient, producing all the three essentials of life—food, clothing, and shelter. British imports were not necessities, but "gew-gaws." The value of these luxuries exceeded that of American exports to England, and the resulting imbalance of trade drained America of its sorely needed capital. "For my part I think that the trade with Great Britain is a ruinous one to ourselves; and that nothing would be an inducement to tolerate it but a free commerce with their West Indies; and that this being denied to us we should put a stop to the losing branch," Jefferson maintained.[60]

A commercial war then would simply do what the United States ought to do of its own accord—cut down Anglo-American trade. It was British credit and America's thirst for luxuries that made British trade important to the United States, and both were harmful. "Fashion and folly is plunging [Americans] deeper and deeper into distress," said Jefferson. "We should try whether the prodigal might not be restrained from taking on credit the gewgaw held out to him on one hand, by seeing the keys of a prison in the other."[61] Madison agreed. He thought, however, that the difficulty in collecting American debts would probably check the propensity of European merchants "to credit us beyond our resources, and so far the evil of an unfavorable balance will correct itself. But the Merchants of Great Britain if no others will continue to credit us at least as far as our remittances can be strained, and that is far enough to perpetuate our difficulties unless the luxurious propensity of our own people can be otherwise checked."[62]

Thus, the credit extended by the British to American merchants which

Hamilton thought vital to the volume of American trade and to the revenue derived from it, Jefferson and Madison thought a temptation to ruin. "It is much to be wished that every discouragement should be thrown in the way of men who undertake to trade without capital; who therefore do not go to the market where commodities are to be had cheapest, but where they are to be had on the longest credit. The consumers pay for it in the end, and the debts contracted, and bankruptcies occasioned by such commercial adventures, bring burthen and disgrace on our country. . . . Yet these are the actual links which hold us whether we will or no to Great Britain," said Jefferson.[63]

But if Anglo-American trade were stopped, what would be done for the necessary manufactures, which along with the gewgaws were imported from England? First, Jefferson and Madison did not propose to develop domestic manufactures. They hoped instead by raising tariffs against England to shift America's dependence for essential manufactures to France. As Madison said in defense of his tonnage bill of 1789, "From artificial or adventitious causes, the commerce between America and Great Britain exceeds what may be considered its natural boundary." Since France had "relaxed considerably in that rigid policy it before pursued," he hoped that favors given to it and other nations in treaty with the United States would "enable them to gain their proportion of our direct trade from the nation who had acquired more than it is naturally her due."[64] His introduction to that bill stated that its purpose was the regulation of commerce and the raising of a revenue; it made no mention of protective duties for manufacturers.

This was certainly in keeping with Madison's former ideas. In 1787 he had written, "There is a rage at present for high duties, partly for the purpose of revenue, partly of forcing manufacturers, which it is difficult to resist. . . . Manufacturers will come of themselves when we are ripe for them." Jefferson, whose agrarian bias exceeded even Madison's, certainly had no desire to "force" domestic manufactures. He was content to "let our workshops remain in Europe. It is better to carry provisions and material to workman there, than to bring them to the provisions and materials, and with them their manners and principles. . . . The mobs of great cities add just so much to the support of pure government as sores do to the strength of the human body."[65]

Jefferson and Madison were confident that France and other European nations could easily supply the few things that the United States really needed to import. The French and the Dutch had the capital to supply essential credit, and French manufactures were as good as the British while being generally cheaper, they thought. Should British shipping be unavailable to supplement American shipping in carrying off America's products, the Dutch would supply it.[66] Also, distributing America's trade among several nations would eliminate American dependence on any one country and help maintain a balance of power in Europe.

Admittedly, however, diverting American trade from Britain to France and the Netherlands involved a decline in the import trade. This would diminish the source of 90 percent of the federal government's revenue which in turn paid the interest and principle on America's debts and established its credit. Jefferson and Madison were not too worried about this aspect. They thought Hamilton's funding and assumption schemes had drastically inflated the national debt, and that substantially less revenue was necessary to pay off the true debt. Nor did they favor extensive federal activities that might in themselves require large amounts of revenue.

As good agrarians, Jefferson and Madison concluded that the only potential benefit that British trade offered was to supply markets for America's agricultural surpluses. The most important of these markets were in the western hemisphere, particularly in the West Indies. "Access to the West Indies is indispensably necessary to us," said Jefferson.[67] "The produce of the U.S. will soon exceed the European demand. What is to be done with the surplus, when there shall be one? It will be employed, without question, to open by force a market for itself with those placed on the same continent with us, and who wish nothing better."[68]

Thus, changing British policy regarding the West Indies was vital not only to America's agricultural prosperity, but to peace as well. And commercial retaliation promised to do just that. The United States stood to lose only the British import trade, the luxury part of which she would be well rid of, the beneficial part of which could be replaced by Britain's competitors. Meanwhile, restrictions on British trade would starve the West Indies, bankrupt British manufacturers, and undermine British finances. Great Britain would be forced to conclude a trade treaty opening its West Indies and evacuating the posts. Probably this would come about without much of a struggle. But if it did require a commercial war, the United States would certainly win. Besides, a commercial war would avoid the shooting war which could easily occur if appeasement led to British miscalculations, if the war with the Northwest Indians led to a clash with the British-occupied frontier posts, or if American surpluses brought about an attempt to open western hemisphere markets by force.

To a large extent these convictions of Jefferson and Madison derived from principles reflected in their domestic policy—that superior power needed to be checked and balanced, that agriculture was vital whereas trade and manufactures were not, that economic independence and frugality were essential to liberty and dignity, and that the federal government needed a kind of power capable of defending the United States against foreign aggression without threatening liberty at home. Their convictions also must have been influenced by their environment in the South. The workings of the southern plantations and farms seemed to prove that the United States was self-sufficient as long as it had a market for its goods, and that British credit and British imports meant bankruptcy.

Jefferson and Madison thought that their policies would be the most likely of any to avoid war with Great Britain. But what if they were wrong, and war with England did result from commercial retaliation? Would America then not require a powerful central government, revenue, credit, domestic manufactures, an army, and a navy? Jefferson and Madison answered that question in a slightly different way after Hamilton had shown his intentions as secretary of the treasury than they had before. At both times they relied primarily on the financial hardships that the expenses of the war and the loss of American trade would inflict on Great Britain to bring the war to a speedy and victorious conclusion. At both times they expected America's distance from Europe to make it impossible for England to send and supply an army large enough to conquer the United States. And at both times they expected to be forced to "abandon the ocean where we are weak, leaving to neutral nations the carriage of our commodities; and measure with [the British] on land where they alone can lose."[69] America could safely rely on foreign shipping for vital supplies in times of war because "Neutral nations, whose rights are becoming every day more and more extensive, would not now suffer themselves to be shut out from our ports, nor would the hostile Nation presume to attempt it," predicted Madison.[70] Meanwhile, the American merchants could turn their vessels into privateers to harass enemy trade. This reliance on neutral ships to supply vital materiel, a militia army and privateer navy to do the fighting, and distance and financial hardship to sap the spirit of Great Britain allowed Jefferson and Madison to minimize the necessity for a consolidated government, domestic manufactures, a standing army, and heavy expenditures.

All of these assumptions remained constant in the thought of Jefferson and Madison between the end of the Revolution and the Jay Treaty crisis. But after Hamilton took office, the two Virginians abandoned certain other war preparations they had advocated in the Confederation period. The first of these was the domestic manufacture of war implements. Neutral shipping could supply most of the goods America might need to import, but belligerent nations could legally intercept war materiel as contraband. Thus, in

1787, when Madison was rejecting the need for most domestic manufactures, he said that "As far as relates to implements of war which are contraband, the argument for our fabrication of them is certainly good." In 1788 Jefferson too thought that the United States should make provision for "magazines and manufacturers of arms."[71] After these men began their opposition to Hamilton's policies, they promoted this idea no longer.

Far more important, they abandoned their support for a navy. Prior to Hamilton's taking office, Jefferson and Madison had zealously advocated a navy as the best means of defense involving the least danger to internal liberty.[72] "I consider that an acquisition of maritime strength is essential to this country," said Madison; "what but this can defend our towns and cities upon the sea-coast? or what but this can enable us to repel an invading enemy?"[73] Jefferson agreed; without "a protecting force on the sea . . . the smallest powers in Europe, every one which possesses a single ship of the line may dictate to us, and enforce their demands by captures on our commerce."[74] Jefferson thought that a small navy of some eighteen ships of the line and twelve frigates would be about adequate.[75] A small American navy could cope with even the strongest naval powers because

Providence has placed their richest and most defenceless possessions at our door; has obliged their most precious commerce to pass, as it were in review before us. To protect this, or to assail, a small part only of their naval force will ever be risked across the Atlantic. The dangers to which the elements expose them here are too well known, and the greater dangers to which they would be exposed at home were any general calamity to involve their whole fleet. They can attack us by detachment only; and it will suffice to make ourselves equal to what they may detach. Even a smaller force than they may detach will be rendered equal or superior by the quickness with which any check may be repaired with us, while losses with them will be irreparable till too late. A small naval force then is sufficient for us, and a small one is necessary.[76]

Hamilton's policies evidently led Jefferson and Madison to fear federal taxation and power more than the lack of a navy. So they decided that privateers could threaten the West Indies, the fisheries, and the western trade routes as well as a regular navy. Madison signaled the retreat from his former ideas in 1790, when he told Congress that although he favored a maritime force, he did not favor a navy; he sought only to increase those resources that might be converted into such a marine force as would be absolutely necessary in an emergency.[77] By the time of the Jay Treaty crisis, Jefferson had adopted the same policy, and it became an important plank in the platform of the nascent Republican party. Jefferson and Madison remained confident, however, that the United States had the power to challenge British policy even without a navy and domestic sources of war implements. America could still handle a shooting war with Great Britain in the unlikely event that commercial retaliation or other circumstances should lead to it.

This and other basic principles of the foreign policy of Jefferson and Madison were vividly illustrated in Jefferson's response to the Nootka Sound crisis. As war threatened between Spain and England, Jefferson hoped for peace, but was entirely ready to make use of the European embroilment if it occurred. His preferred policy was to maintain American neutrality, making American ships the carriers of belligerent supplies, and pressuring Spain and England to modify their policies concerning the Mississippi and the western posts.[78] It was at this time that Hamilton was relaying from Beckwith the supposed desires of Great Britain for an alliance. But Jefferson did not alter his belief that it was better to pressure Great Britain than to ally with that nation. If the object of the alliance was honorable, it was useless; if it was dishonorable, it was inadmissable.[79] Instead of appeasing Great Britain, he instructed Gouverneur Morris to tell the British that America would remain neutral if Britain would *"execute the treaty fairly* and *attempt* no conquests adjoining us."[80]

But what if the British did attempt to conquer Spanish Louisiana or Florida and requested permission to cross American territory to do so, Washington asked Jefferson? It must be resisted, Jefferson answered. If Britain acquired Spanish Louisiana and Florida, "Instead of two neighbors balancing each other, we shall have one, with more than the strength of both." Great Britain would

possess a territory equal to half ours, beyond the Missisipi [sic]. She will reduce that half of ours which is on this side of the Missisipi. By her language, laws, religion, manners, government, commerce, capital. By the possession of New Orleans, which draws to it yet dependence of all ye waters of Mississippi. By the markets she can offer them in the gulf of Mexico and elsewhere. She will take from the remaining part of our States the markets they now have for their produce by furnishing those markets cheaper with the same articles, tobacco.rice.indigo.bread.lumber.naval stores.furs. She will have then possessions double the size of ours, as good in soil and climate. She will encircle us completely, by these possessions on our land board, and her fleets on our seaboard.[81]

He concluded that "we ought to make ourselves parties in the *general war* expected to take place, should this be the only means of preventing the calamity."[82] War was a last resort, however, and should be undertaken only if France also supported Spain.[83]

Meanwhile, war should be deferred as long as possible. If the British did request permission to cross American territory, Jefferson advised Washington to avoid giving any answer at all. Britain might then decide not to attack Florida or Louisiana, or it might fail if it did attack, or France and Spain might reconquer them. Of course, should all these contingencies fail, the United States would have to fight. But delay would mean that the United States could choose the time and place at which the war would begin. So he told Washington, "if we are obliged to give an answer, I think the occasion not such as should induce us to hazard that answer which might commit us to the war at so early a stage of it; and therefore that the passage should be permitted."[84] If America refused passage and Britain defied the answer, the United States "must enter immediately into the war, or pocket an acknowledged insult in the face of the world; and one insult pocketed soon produces another."[85] Finally, if Britain passed without asking permission, he would "be for expressing our dissatisfaction to the British court, and keeping alive an altercation on the subject till events should decide whether it is most expedient to accept their apologies, or profit of the aggression as a cause of war."[86]

The contrast with Hamilton's policy was striking. Jefferson sought to balance the superior power rather than join it in an assault on the Mississippi. He did not see America's choices limited to acquiescence or suicide. Damaging as a war might be, it would not be fatal. In any case, appeasing Britain by pocketing insults was far more likely to lead to war than would resistance to aggression. This was especially the case since resistance could take many forms, from commercial retaliation to merely waiting until Britain's guard was down before striking her. Jefferson had no use for the *code duello*. He did not look upon war as a road to glory, to be fought according to the set rules of gentlemen. He saw no dishonor involved in winning a war by cleverness, deception, delay, and taking advantage of the enemy's weaknesses. Like many men of peace, Jefferson and Madison found war so noxious as to be outside the scope of their usual rules of honor. Thus during the Revolution, Madison had proposed shooting prisoners in retaliation for the burning of American towns, while Jefferson introduced a bill of attainder for a traitor and made violent threats of reprisal against the British for their treatment of Ethan Allen.[87]

To say that Jefferson and Madison never felt it necessary to balance their goals with the power available is simply ridiculous. They expended a great deal of intellectual energy doing just that. Their policy was at least as much determined by their certainty that the United States was already powerful enough to challenge Great Britain as by their conviction that it ought to challenge her.

It is true, however, that there were certain problems with their attempt to balance goals with power available. First, a great deal of their confidence in the ability of the United States to win a commercial or shooting war rested in the belief that the people of the United States were willing to give up the luxuries attained from the British trade and to endure the hardships imposed by another guerrilla war. They counted on two factors to insure this—the influence of agriculture and hatred of the British. In relying on the influence of agriculture they rested upon a weak reed. Agrarians were as speculative and covetous of riches as any other group in the United States. But dislike of the British almost sufficed to unite the Americans behind the policy of challenging Great Britain. In the South, at least, it worked a fantastic transformation.

During the Confederation period, the South had been a bitter opponent of discriminatory tariffs. South Carolina, Georgia, and Delaware had refused to grant to Congress the control over commerce that was necessary to oppose British pretensions, and the control that North Carolina had been willing to give up was extremely restricted.[88] The South had almost no shipping of its own and opposed any navigation law that would increase the price of exporting its agricultural products. Some southerners even preferred to encourage a British marine over a New England one.[89]

But Madison and Jefferson relied on the fact that most southerners detested Great Britain more than they detested the North. After all, the South had suffered much from British depredations during the War of the Revolution. Even after the war was over, the Negro slaves that had come into the hands of the British army were carried off rather than returned to their masters. Southerners believed this to be contrary to the Treaty of Peace, which stipulated that the British should evacuate the United States without carrying away any slaves or other property. The British commander, Sir Guy Carleton, held that the slaves had become free men the moment they entered the British lines and were therefore not affected by this provision. Whether the British government accepted this argument or not, there was no compensation forthcoming.[90] Finally, southerners, particularly Virginians, were greatly in debt to British subjects. In fact nearly half the unsettled debts owed by citizens of the United States to British subjects were owed by Virginians.[91] Madison had good reason to say that in Virginia, "The prospect of [the tariff] being levelled against Great Britain will be most likely to give it popularity."[92]

If this provided most of the impetus behind the South's increasing willingness to go along with commercial discrimination against Britain, there was a more positive incentive as well. The discrimination had as its most important target the opening of the British West Indies to American vessels, and this was very desirable to the South. Many people, including Madison and Jefferson, had not given up hope of a southern shipping industry.[93] The opening of the West Indies seemed the best prospect to enable the South to compete with its northern neighbors, since the southern states were closer to the islands. In fact, that portion of the West Indies open to American ships seems to have been the only area of shipping in which the southern states participated to any extent after the Revolution.[94]

The opening of the West Indies to American ships was also important to southern agriculture. Though most of the South's produce was permitted into the British West Indies, it had to be carried in British ships.[95] These vessels, sailing from England, found it just as easy to carry European and Canadian as American produce. If American vessels were allowed into the West Indies, the South hoped it would materially increase the demand for its products.*

The needs of the West India planters for cheap American produce, and the inability of British shipping to furnish it in sufficient quantity and at a low enough price, forced the governors of the various islands to open their ports to American ships periodically by proclamation. This did furnish a considerable employment for American ships and produce, but the uncertainty of the trade deprived it of much of its profitability. If vessels were sent to Jamaica, for instance, and the ports were found to be closed, the voyage was ruined. The island was so far to the leeward that the vessels could not return to other islands before the produce was spoiled. Since crops were most often sent on consignment, the planters bore the loss.[96] Thus the South's economic interests and its animosity toward the British combined to change the mind of many southerners regarding commercial discrimination.

But as we have seen, northern opinion was moving in the opposite direction. If retaliation was undertaken, would the people support it, or would they undercut it by smuggling? Even if they did support it, could France and the Netherlands really supply credit and manufactures in sufficient quantity to maintain a reasonable occupation for American merchants and ships? Would there be sufficient imports to furnish a revenue capable of paying off

---

* American ships were smaller and less expensive to build and man, and were not forced to carry ballast on any leg of their journey. Ships coming from England to pick up North American produce and carry it to the West Indies often had to carry ballast on the first leg of their journey.

America's debts and maintaining its credit? And if war should come, would the people be willing to endure the privations of a guerrilla war which destroyed their trade and subjected their coastal cities to naval bombardment?

Jefferson and Madison were confident that if the test came, these questions would all be answered in the affirmative. Perhaps these assumptions were wildly unrealistic. For to think that the people would unite behind a policy that forsook wealth and power in return for austerity and the risk of another guerrilla war, all in pursuit of a simple, republican, economically independent, agrarian nation might seem to verge on insanity to some. One can point to the reaction of the Northeast to Jefferson's embargo and the War of 1812 in support of this view. And certainly Great Britain's interruptions of neutral trade during the Anglo-French wars of the late eighteenth century demonstrate the folly of Jefferson and Madison in hoping that neutral nations could supply America with necessary imports in case of war with England.

Yet in these days we cannot so easily dismiss the dreams of Jefferson and Madison as hopelessly utopian. The examples of Cuba and Vietnam have shown that large groups of people will sometimes sacrifice the promise of greater wealth for national independence and an appealing political vision. Cuba and Vietnam also demonstrate that a people struggling on their home ground can resist the economic or military opposition of great powers for indefinite periods. Had the Americans been willing to make equivalent sacrifices, there is no doubt that they could have realized the dreams of Jefferson and Madison. The question the people of the United States had to decide was whether these goals were worth the sacrifice.

Undoubtedly most did not think so. They may have sympathized with the democratic tendencies and agrarian biases of Jefferson and Madison. But the American people's dreams were of a republicanism based on economic opportunity rather than austerity. In all probability, a commercial or shooting war with England in the 1790s would have resulted in the same kind of disaffection and consequent ineffectuality that characterized the foreign policy efforts of Jefferson and Madison during their administrations.

But of course, Jefferson and Madison were confident in the 1790s that England would surrender to commercial pressure without great resistance. Since we now have access to the British records, we are in a position to judge this prediction more accurately than they were.

6. GREAT BRITAIN HOLDS THE LINE

The British apparently did not fear that the Constitution would unify the United States and give it the power to overturn Britain's harsh policy toward her former colonies. The British actually favored America's attempts to strengthen its government.[1] Many newspapers did point out, however, "the infinite absurdity of gravely framing laws of conventions for what never was, nor most probably ever can be, a nation any more than those quarters of the globe Europe, Africa, or Asia."[2] The United States was no more of a threat under the Constitution than under the Articles of Confederation, they were convinced, for it was "a wretched nation, defeated or abandoned by her own subjects, betrayed by Ministers, ill served by the executive power, and worse yet, . . . by the deliberative and legislative! A state without a single ally, and, more terrible yet, without deserving to have one, unless perhaps the Right Honorable Dey of Algiers."[3]

With so low an estimate of American power, it is not surprising that the British government saw little reason to modify its policy of confrontation. By keeping a monopoly of the navigation to the West Indies, it maintained naval supremacy in the western hemisphere. By holding the posts and supporting the Indians, it throttled American territorial expansion to the north and west, protecting Canada and giving Great Britain the advantage in the race for occupation and exploitation of the territory beyond the Mississippi. The British government was not contemplating the reconquest of America nor the subversion of the republican form of government in favor of a monarchy. It was seeking to maintain what it regarded as the proper status quo between itself and America. The British government did not regard its policy as one of aggression, but of what today we might call containment—the attempt to curb the potential threat to Britain's North American colonies and to their expansion on that continent. If the United States would only leave the Northwest Indians in rightful possession of their lands and accept the undoubted right of Britain to regulate its colonies as it saw fit, the British government proclaimed it saw no reason why England and the United States could not be on the friendliest of terms.

William Pitt and some members of his cabinet may have had doubts about this policy from time to time. He and Lord Grenville, his cousin who was secretary of state for home affairs and then secretary of state for foreign affairs, tended somewhat toward a policy of free trade and evidently doubted the wisdom of monopolizing the navigation of the West Indies. They also must have realized that even Hamilton would not accept the

British version of the status quo forever. Although England might force it upon the United States for a time, this would earn America's enmity for which Britain would pay when America developed to its full potential. Still, the voices of the fur trade interests, of the shipping interests, and of Canadian government officials were strong, and Pitt himself had encouraged the sentiments for a reassertion of British power and prestige which lent popularity to the American policy being followed. Thus, he tended to ignore American problems, and British policy toward the United States was left in the hands of subordinate officials to whom curbing American trade and territorial ambitions was gospel.

Policy toward American trade was the province of David Jenkinson, Lord Hawkesbury, who, in 1786, had become the chairman of the Privy Council's Committee on Trade and Plantations. Often, meetings of the committee were held with only himself and his secretary present, and until 1794 his advice on American matters seems to have been accepted without qualification. John Brown Cutting, a Virginian in Britain, wrote Jefferson that Lord Hawkesbury was "the *commercial minister* and dictates all measures relevant to the United States."[4]

Hawkesbury had been a member of the committee when it had issued its report on the state of the American trade in 1784. The results of the policy set forth in this report seemed to him to bear out the wisdom of continuing the policy of confrontation with regard to American trade. In 1786 the committee reported that, "In consequence of the Restrictions laid on the American Navigation by Your Majesty's Order in Council, for regulating the Commercial Intercourse between Your Majesty's American Dominions and those of the United States, we have almost entirely secured the Markets of our West Indian Islands to our Fisherman which was theretofore wholly enjoyed by the Americans."[5] Hawkesbury saw that the lumbering industries of Canada, Nova Scotia, and Newfoundland were similarly stimulated by the exclusion of American ships from the West Indies, and though exports from the West Indies to the United States also dropped, the dependence of those islands on the United States was considerably lessened.[6]

In 1791 Hawkesbury and his committee observed that barring American ships from the West Indies had contributed to Britain's naval might. The number of British ships trading with the islands had risen from 491 to 559 since the beginning of the Revolution, they reported, and these ships were now made in Great Britain and manned by British sailors, thereby greatly increasing British naval strength.[7] The voyages to the West Indies also helped to make voyages to the remaining British North American colonies profitable. These colonies and the West Indies could be visited in the same voyage, and the number of British ships engaged in that trade increased from 261 to 367.[8] Just as important, the ratio of British to American ships engaged in trade to the West Indies had doubled, and Hawkesbury and his committee asserted that this had resulted more from what had been taken away from American navigation than what was added to the British.[9] Though they would rather have seen that ratio the result of additional British ships rather than fewer American ones, they were not at all unhappy that the number of American ships engaged in all overseas trade had decreased by 850 ships on account of British trade policy, and that about 650 of these had been engaged in the West Indies trade.[10]

Not only had American shipping decreased as a result of British trade policy, asserted Hawkesbury and his committee, but American shipbuilding as well. In 1772, 182 ships were being built in the United States, they said; in 1789 there were only 31 under construction. British vessels were almost wholly engrossing the carrying trade of the United States, the British consul in Philadelphia reported; in fact, all foreign tonnage combined was no more than a quarter of the British tonnage engaged in the American trade.[11] British ships even had the advantage over American ships in carrying American goods to Europe, Hawkesbury and his committee found; for the insurance premiums on an American ship bound from the United States to Europe were double those on a British ship. This was because of the better quality of the British ships and navigation, and because of the war being carried on against the United States by the Barbary States with whom Britain was at peace.[12]

Hawkesbury also had reason to believe that the market for British manufactures was steadily increasing in America. The London *Times* printed a report from New York that "The British have driven every other nation out of the trade of this country; their goods are both superior in quality, and so very cheap, that scarcely any article of manufactured goods has been imported, during these last twelve months, from any other place than Great Britain and Ireland."[13] The British consul in Philadelphia had deprecated American attempts to increase domestic manufactures, saying he did not believe that any measures pursued with whatever energy could have much effect on British manufactures nor essentially diminish their consumption in America.[14]

The balance of trade between the United States and Britain under Hawkesbury's commercial system had also steadily grown in favor of Britain. British exports to the United States had diminished, reported Hawkesbury and his committee, but this had been more than compensated for by the increase in the value of exports to the remaining North American colonies and the West Indies. The committee attributed the decline in exports to the United States entirely to a decrease in re-exports of European goods and pointed out that exports of British manufactures to America had actually increased.[15]

Given these estimates, it is not surprising that Hawkesbury and his committee should feel that their commercial system regarding the United States had been a resounding success, and that the maintenance of that status quo would be much to Britain's interest. They do not seem to have been motivated so much by hostility to the United States as by the desire to pursue British interests.[16] Still their conception of British interests clashed frequently with that of the United States, a fact which did not seem to disturb them. Lord Hawkesbury once favored a plan to encourage the production of tobacco in the Spanish and French West Indies and the selling of it at a free port in the British West Indies. This new product would then be transported home in British ships. "If it diminished the Import from any country," he observed, "it will be from the United States, which is a Consideration not worth regarding."[17] Hawkesbury and his committee also took the initiative in seeing that American trade with the British colony on the Bay of Honduras was stopped.[18]

Knowing that the United States would refuse to settle for a trade treaty which did not open the West Indies to American ships, Hawkesbury and his committee were perfectly happy to leave the regulation of Anglo-American commerce in the hands of the King in Council and to avoid concluding a trade treaty. They were quite heedless of the dispatches from British agents in the United States which argued that such a treaty would be valuable to Great Britain. They ignored Beckwith, who wrote that illiberal treatment of American commerce might drive that nation to lessen its dependence on customs and encourage domestic manufactures. Beckwith fruitlessly recommended more liberal treatment of American commerce and a trade treaty to rivet American dependence on British manufactures. Consul Miller in Charleston recommended the same; and Lord Grenville, the British foreign minister, perhaps somewhat doubtful of the wisdom of Hawkesbury's policy, sent Miller's dispatch to the Committee on Trade.[19]

Yet if the members of the British government did have doubts at any time concerning the policy of confrontation practiced by Hawkesbury, they did little to change it. Trade policy toward the United States remained almost entirely in his hands. In one letter to Hawkesbury, Lord Grenville referred to "the system of commercial intercourse with America which *you* have established."[20] It was the Committee on Trade under Hawkesbury which had supervised the drafting of the Parliamentary Act of 1788, putting into permanent form the orders in council regulating Anglo-American trade.[21] It was Hawkesbury and his committee who drafted the Report on American Commerce of 1791 as guidance for the instructions to be given to the recently appointed British minister to the United States. In fact, it was Hawkesbury who drafted the actual instructions to that minister, instructions only slightly altered by Grenville, the foreign minister.[22]

Hawkesbury's draft of the instructions to George Hammond, the new minister to the United States, shows on what terms he was willing to formalize trade relations with America. Hammond was to propose that the United States relinquish for the duration of the treaty the right to raise duties on British manufactures. If this were unobtainable, he was to fall back in progressive stages to allowing duties no higher than those charged the most favored nation. In turn, America was to receive "most favored nation" treatment. However, those duties known in England as "alien duties," from which the United States alone of all foreign nations was then exempt, might be raised to correspond with those Britain charged other nations. For a limited number of years the United States was to be allowed to continue to send certain merchandise to the West Indies in British ships, but the subject of admission of American ships to those islands Hawkesbury said could not be admitted even as a subject of negotiation. Finally, as to America's discriminatory tonnage duties between American and foreign vessels, the British government would consent that British vessels should be subject in American ports to the same distinctions that existed between British and American ships in British ports.[23]

Grenville's instructions, written from this draft, eliminated all of the particular instructions concerning a trade treaty with the United States, instructing Hammond instead to refer all such propositions to the home government. Hammond was only to say that Britain would treat on the basis of the most favored nation. That Grenville did not contemplate any drastic change from Hawkesbury's conception of a proper trade treaty is evident from the fact that he sent along with Hammond a copy of the Report of the Privy Council of 1791 drafted by Hawkesbury and his committee, which embodied the proposals and reasoning of Hawkesbury's instructions. Grenville told Hammond to be guided by the details and arguments therein.[24] Thus the most that Alexander Hamilton could have hoped for in the way of a trade treaty with Great Britain obtained without coercive commercial measures was a formalization of the status quo.[25] In fact, Hamilton realized this and seemed willing to accept these terms. In 1792 he proposed that, in return for British aid against the Spanish in New Orleans, the United States accept the commercial status quo for ten years, as well as break off her connection with France and rectify the northwest border so as to give Canada access to a navigable portion of the Mississippi.[26]

The British government continued to apply the policy of confrontation on the frontier as well as in the area of trade. The British had kept the posts primarily to give the fur merchants time to remove their capital and cut their losses, and to prevent the Indians from feeling betrayed and turning in their fury upon the Canadian frontier settlements. But the British were not disregarding the possibility of an overall attempt to limit American territorial expansion and even to dismember from that country territory within its acknowledged borders. They certainly saw the benefits to be derived from a strong stand by the Indians on the American side of the Canadian border. The Indians might thus settle a border between Indian lands and the United States far enough removed from the posts and the Great Lakes to secure a British monopoly of the navigation of the Great Lakes, of the fur trade, and of the allegiance of the Indians. The British also seem to have toyed with the idea of courting dissident outlying provinces of the United States, such as Vermont and Kentucky, and forming some sort of connection with them that would help to hold back the flood tide of American population growth and immigration.[27]

The decision to keep the posts had been followed by progressive steps to render the holding of them more tenable. The best way to accomplish this was to keep the Americans as far removed from them as possible, and the best way to accomplish that was to aid the Indians in keeping the Americans at bay. Thus, orders were issued to the British officials implying that secret aid which could be disavowed by the home government should be given to the Indians, and later Governor Dorchester was instructed specifically to supply the Indians with ammunition to defend themselves.[28]

Correspondence with the leaders of Vermont also resulted in concrete steps on the part of the British government. Until Vermont joined the union in 1791, its leaders considered it a sovereign state, independent of the jurisdiction of the United States. Through special trade privileges, the British government sought to bring Vermont close to the British orbit.[29] Although the British government maintained contact with dissident citizens of Kentucky and Tennessee, it seems to have attempted few concrete actions to assist those states in removing themselves from the jurisdiction of the United States.

Though the British government did hold the posts, aid the Indians, and court Vermont, Tennessee, and Kentucky, its whole frontier policy

91

was highly tentative. Despite the best efforts of Governor Dorchester, the home government refused to come to a firm decision on whether the posts were to be held indefinitely or given up. The cabinet told him that he would be correct to resist if America tried to take the posts by force, and that he should recapture them if they were taken. It also authorized funds to place those posts in a "temporary" state of defense.[30] In other words, Britain would continue to hold the posts and to intrigue with America's outlying provinces until events allowed a solidification of this policy or compelled a withdrawal.

Britain's frontier policy continued in its tentative hostility until 1790, when the Nootka crisis and the possibility of war with Spain forced an entire reevaluation of it. The ministers realized that the United States might make use of the crisis to ally with Spain in an attack on Canada or might simply take the posts on its own. Were the posts worth holding in the face of such a contingency? Or should they be given up to assure the neutrality of the United States? Both alternatives were fully surveyed by the British cabinet.

The case for holding the posts was made in a report from Hawkes-bury's committee of the Privy Council, to which Grenville had referred a memorial from Levi Allen proposing a trade treaty between Vermont and Great Britain.[31] The committee's report was dated April 17, 1790, just two weeks before the cabinet decided to make the Nootka incident the basis of an ultimatum to Spain. Not only did the committee recommend the continuance of free trade with Vermont, it recommended the encouragement of trade with other areas bordering Canada so that produce from America's borderlands would be brought into Canada and transported down the St. Lawrence and across the sea in British ships. The committee also asserted that the British should have a monopoly on the navigation of the Great Lakes and the navigable rivers entering and leaving those lakes. It recommended that

the posts which command the Entrance of these Lakes, and which are best situated for securing the navigation of these Rivers should be retained by His Majesty, (if other important Considerations will so permit) and be Garrisoned by a Force sufficient to defend them: For there can be no doubt that the various Settlements which are now forming in the interior parts of America, afford the prospect of a most extensive and valuable Commerce to those Nations, who can secure to themselves the best means of availing themselves of it.

The committee said it would refrain from advising a treaty with Vermont, not feeling itself competent to judge how improper such a treaty

92

would be in view of the peace treaty placing Vermont on the American side of the border, nor could it decide if it was politically prudent to risk the offense such a move might give to the United States. But it did assert that "in a commercial view it will be for the Benefit of this Country to prevent Vermont and Kentucky, and all other Settlements now forming in the Interior parts of the Great Continent of North America, from becoming dependent on the Government of the United States, or on that of any other Foreign Country, and to preserve them on the contrary in the State of Independence and to induce them to form Treaties of Commerce and Friendship with Great Britain."

The committee contended that only the Mississippi River and the Great Lakes–St. Lawrence system provided avenues of commerce for the settlers of the back country, and that circumstances indicated that the St. Lawrence would prove most convenient: "It will be fortunate for Great Britain, if this Channel continues exclusively under her Command; for the Commerce, so carried on, will be attended with this singular Advantage, that the Ships, employed in it, must belong wholly to the Subjects of the British Empire." As for the route down the Mississippi, the committee predicted many contests between Spain and the United States for control of it, and observed that "there will be less danger in encouraging the Navigation of Spain in those Seas than that of the United States, and that the Ships of these States are more to be apprehended, as Commercial Rivals, than those belonging to the Subjects of the Spanish Monarchy." Finally, it urged attention to the interior of the American continent because, with the great and increasing production of manufactures in Britain, "it is necessary to seek for new Markets in every part of the World, in order to afford sufficient scope and further Encouragement to the Industry of His Majesty's Subjects."[32]

The committee's analysis of the commercial and political benefits to be derived from maintaining independent provinces within the borders of the United States and from holding the posts to defend the British monopoly on navigation of the Great Lakes system were certainly not lost on Grenville. At that point, however, he could do little to implement this report beyond instructing Dorchester to allow Vermont to export flour to Quebec "if this concession could be the means of attaching the people of Vermont sincerely to the British interest," since, considering the implications of the Nootka crisis, "The Friendship of the inhabitants of Vermont would under the circumstances of any alarm from the side of the United States, be of the greatest importance." Grenville also told Dorchester to remain on guard for an American attack on the posts, and to point out to the United States the wisdom of attacking south to wrest the Mississippi from Spain rather than north toward the British posts.[34]

The grandiose schemes of the committee for establishing a western commercial empire based on exclusive control of the Great Lakes–St. Lawrence system and protected by the forts seem to have been pushed into the background by the exigencies of the possible war with Spain. Shortly after Grenville received the committee's report, he called in Sir Frederick Haldimand, Canada's former governor, among others to ascertain the consequences of giving up the posts. Grenville concluded that, even if the posts were surrendered, by building comparable posts on the Canadian side of the border Britain would be likely to retain the fur trade and the allegiance of the Indians as well. Thus, Britain seems to have contemplated giving up the posts.[35]

But Spain's surrender to the British ultimatum removed any need to give up the forts. The disastrous defeat of the American General Harmar's expedition against the Northwest Indians in that same year, 1790, made the British feel that the time was ripe to attempt to implement the committee's idea and create a trade empire based on the exclusive navigation of the Great Lakes–St. Lawrence system. Thus, when Grenville was approached by the adventurer William Augustus Bowles, who proposed to lead an Indian Confederacy favorable to Great Britain on the southern borders of the United States, Grenville saw opportunity beckon.

Bowles was an American Loyalist who had ingratiated himself with the Creek and Cherokee nations, and who aspired to displace Alexander McGillivray from the leadership of those Indians.[36] Having persuaded a reluctant Governor Dorchester to advance him £100 for the trip, Bowles had traveled to England from Canada to seek British aid in a war against the Spanish. Bowles also indicated a willingness to fight the United States on behalf of Britain, but his main objective was to secure from Spain two ports in Florida for the use of the Indians. Should these ports not be given, he claimed he could lead a force of Indians and dissident Americans against the Spanish which would drive them from both Florida and New Orleans within two months, after which he would cross the Mississippi and attack toward Mexico.[37] He requested from the British admission to their free ports in the West Indies and, in case of war, provision of arms and military stores.[38] Should this aid not be forthcoming, he warned that the Indians would have to seek an alliance with the Americans, the first object of which would be the British posts.[39]

Upon receipt of this extraordinary request, Grenville wrote to Hawkesbury concerning the admission of these Indians to Britain's free ports. He told Hawkesbury that Bowles exaggerated the ability of the Indians and back settlers of America to harass the Spanish colonies, and that in this matter no encouragement was to be given him. Bowles's proposal concerning resistance to the Americans, however, Grenville felt more worthy of regard. He wrote Hawkesbury:

It is unquestionably true that the Americans have for these last two or three years been meditating attempts against our Posts, and that nothing could be so effectual for opposing them in case of an attack as a general confederacy of those Indians and back settlers. This makes me desirous of complying with the request of admission into our free ports if it could be done with safety, as nothing would tend so much to establish intercourse and connection with them: But I doubt whether any direction could with safety be given for such connivance as was formerly practiced when this whole subject was less the object of attention and jealousy.

Grenville suggested that the parliamentary act concerning free ports be modified on some pretense that would not point to the real object, and it could then be explained to Bowles how to avail himself of the modified act. "Perhaps on consideration this may not be practicable, but at least I think it worth attending to and trying, as I am really much impressed with the importance of the ultimate object of attaching these People," he wrote. It was unfortunate that Bowles was of questionable character, he mused, "but you will know that the utility of things of this sort very often stands on very different grounds from that of the honesty of the persons employed in them." He concluded by pointing out to Hawkesbury that the project was "closely connected with the system of commercial intercourse with America which you have established."[40]

Evidently Hawkesbury agreed, for Grenville wrote to Dorchester on March 7 that such of Bowles's requests "as related to views of hostility against the United States have met with no kind of encouragement, but they will in some degree be gratified in their wish of intercourse with the British Dominions by an admission to the free ports in his Majesty's West Indian Islands, supposing that they should find themselves in a situation to avail themselves of this indulgence."[41]

Despite this action, Grenville indignantly denied having anything to do with Bowles when Jefferson voiced his suspicions that Britain was secretly behind him. Grenville wrote Hammond that Bowles was not an instrument of British policy to reestablish the Creek border in Georgia, and that Britain had never promised him reenforcements. That was true, of course, but it was somewhat hypocritical of him to write that Jefferson's assertions to the contrary "can have no other Effect than to raise groundless Jealousies between the two Countries, in the Room of that Harmony and good Understanding which it is so sincerely our Object to establish," and to assert that Jefferson's idea of British policy was "extremely different from that which has been uniformly pursued."[42] It is obvious, however, that Grenville felt himself perfectly justified in denying any aggressive intent regarding Britain's connection with Bowles. He viewed the encouragement of an Indian confederacy in the southwest as a defensive measure designed to maintain the territorial status quo, to check the territorial ambitions of the United States, and to pave the way for a British trade empire along the Mississippi, Great Lakes, and St. Lawrence waterways.

Grenville and the British cabinet had the same purposes in concocting a scheme far more grandiose than that connected with Bowles—a neutral Indian barrier state. The surrender of Spain in the Nootka crisis and the defeat of General Harmar had led Grenville and the rest of the cabinet to abandon any thought of giving up the posts unless compensated by large concessions from the United States which would further Britain's projected trade empire. In return for giving up the posts, the British decided to demand that the Indians be guaranteed in perpetuity almost all of the land on the American side of the Canadian border and north of the Ohio River, as well as certain other lands. This would effectively bar American expansion to the northwest even to the borders already granted by the Peace Treaty of 1783 and would secure the British monopoly of the fur trade and navigation of the Great Lakes.

To pave the way for such a project, Grenville instructed Hammond at the beginning of his mission as the first minister to the United States that, even if America now complied with the articles of the peace treaty concerning debts and Loyalists, the British would not be bound to evacuate the posts, since it was evident that "no measures that can now be taken can replace the Loyalists and British Creditors in that situation to which they were entitled by the Articles of the treaty of peace."[43] Obviously Grenville intended that further concessions on the part of America would be necessary to secure British abandonment of the posts.

The conditions necessary to an evacuation of the posts were not long in coming to Hammond. The British government proposed to mediate between the United States and the Indians and, through this mediation, to establish boundaries between them mutually guaranteed by Britain and the United States. These boundaries would place a barrier of Indian lands between Canada and its southern rival. Grenville told Hammond that the general ground on which he was to negotiate a settlement between the Americans and the Indians was

the securing to the different Indian Nations along the British and American Frontiers, their Lands and hunting Grounds as an independent Country, with respect to which both His Majesty and the United States shall withdraw all Claims of possessions whatever, shall agree never to establish any Forts within the Boundaries to be expressed in such Agreement, and shall bind themselves to each other not to acquire, or to suffer their Subjects to acquire, by Purchase or otherwise, from the Indians, any Lands or settlements within the said Boundaries.[44]

But for the Indian state to be an effective barrier, it would have to extend the entire length of the Canadian-American border; and although the Indians had valid claims in the American Northwest, they did not have many further east. Thus, Grenville told Hammond that "it may be a point of material Convenience, that some new Arrangement should be made respecting the Frontier on Lake Champlain to which the Indian claims are understood not to extend."[45] The new boundary on Lake Champlain, Grenville told Hammond in a later letter, "is purely and evidently defensive, and the Sacrifice on the part of the Americans must be allowed to be extremely small, when compared with the private Losses and public Expences, which as I have already mentioned, have been incurred by this Country in Consequence of the Infractions of the Treaty by the States."[46]

Thinking that the Canadian provinces were threatened by the United States, realizing that time would increase the power of the United States relative to Canada, and fearing that the Americans would do their best to turn the Indians against Canada if they ever secured ascendency over them, the British government thus sought to take advantage of America's momentary weakness to cripple permanently her possibilities of expansion, and to do this by erecting within American borders a barrier of Indian lands backed by a British guarantee. The gratitude of the Indians toward the British for securing their lands would maintain British ascendency over those people and forestall any attempts by the Americans to turn them against Canada. Grenville also realized from the survey of the posts made during the Nootka crisis that forts could be erected on the Canadian side of the border to control the navigation of the Great Lakes system. Since the Americans would be prevented by the barrier state from erecting forts on their side of the border, the British control of the navigation of the Great Lakes system would be complete.

The British, however, found the American government adamantly opposed to British mediation between itself and the Indians within its borders. As a matter of fact, the whole idea of an Indian barrier state obtained by British mediation had arisen through a misinterpretation of one of Hamilton's remarks to Beckwith. During the Nootka crisis, Beckwith, as directed, had mentioned that, far from aiding and inspiring the Indians to war upon the United States, the British desired peace, especially since the war was ruining the fur trade. Hamilton had responded that Governor Dorchester might use his influence to bring that peace. Dorchester interpreted this as a request for his intervention and wrote Beckwith that he could take no step in this direction without specific authorization from one or the other of the contending parties together with the terms they would be willing to accept.[47]

When Beckwith presented Hamilton with this idea, the secretary of the treasury completely repudiated any idea of British mediation, saying that he could not even submit such a paper for the president's consideration. He had suggested only that, since it was in the British interest that peace be established, "if Lord Dorchester would suggest that a friendly accommodation and settlement would be a pleasing circumstance to your Government it might have a tendency to promote it."[48]

Despite this discouragement, Grenville and the home government had seized on the idea of British mediation as the foundation for their Indian barrier-state project. Hammond's first instructions had included a direction to sound the Americans on the possibility of a British mediation even before the entire barrier-state project had been worked out. In an interview with Hamilton, Hammond intimated that a request for British intercession to bring peace with the Indians would not go unheeded. Hamilton answered that the United States was determined to bring the Indians to terms, by war if necessary, and that official British mediation would not be asked. However, Hamilton continued, "if the voluntary interposition of the King's government in Canada could tend to accomplish it, such a measure would be received with the greatest gratitude."[49]

Despite receipt of this discouraging news from Hammond, Grenville sent on further instructions outlining the final form of the barrier-state project.[50] A few days later he responded to the doubts expressed by Hammond of American acquiescence in the idea of British mediation. He asserted that the recent statement of American violations of the treaty of peace which had been handed to Jefferson by Hammond must have made a great impression on the minds of the Americans. Grenville was confident that the United States would now realize the enormity of its sins and be disposed to give compensation to Britain for the losses she had incurred thereby. Since another American expedition against the Northwest Indians, this one led by General St. Clair, had only recently been defeated disastrously, Grenville said the Americans should be even more inclined to accept British mediation and the proposed barrier state.[51] The timing of the presentation of such a proposal to the Americans, however, was left to Hammond.

Dutifully Hammond continued to sound opinion in the American government on British mediation, but soon he wrote back to Grenville that the project was hopeless, that the Americans would never accept it, and that he was suspending his activities on its behalf to await further instructions.[52] Grenville, evidently convinced by Hammond's arguments that such a project involved the cession of too much settled territory for America to accede to it, finally wrote that he approved entirely of Hammond's "prudent conduct."[53]

Thus, the Indian barrier-state project seemed dead. But the project came up again in 1792 when Hammond received news that there was to be a meeting between the Indian Confederacy and the United States in a last desperate attempt to secure peace before a new American expedition under General Anthony Wayne took up the fight against the Northwest Indians. Hammond suggested to Lieutenant Governor John Graves Simcoe of Upper Canada that a "voluntary" request from the Indians for Simcoe to mediate at the coming meeting might bring the United States to accept such a plan.[54] Simcoe repeated the suggestion to Alexander McKee, a British Indian agent, and the "voluntary solicitation" was quickly forthcoming.[55] The United States, however, refused to accept British mediation, though it did consent to permit British agents to come to the meeting as observers and to explain to the Indians the implications of any offers America might make.[56]

Despite the best efforts of the British Indian agent, McKee, the Indians and the Americans could not come to terms at the treaty meetings of 1792–1793. The only way in which the British could secure their Indian barrier state, as Simcoe and Hammond agreed, was another crushing defeat of the Americans by the Indians such as that which had occurred during St. Clair's campaign.[57] To this end the British gave their best efforts, attempting to unite the Indian Confederacy and dispensing supplies in order to enable the Confederacy to resist Wayne's imminent march.

As long as Britain had hopes of throttling America's westward expansion and preventing American navigation of the Great Lakes, a truly conciliatory policy toward England was doomed. Hamilton might accept the status quo in Anglo-American trade, but even he could not tolerate the status quo on the frontier. He was willing to cede sufficient territory in the Northwest to give Britain access to a navigable portion of the Mississippi in return for the aid of British ships in an attempt to eliminate Spanish control of the Mississippi.[58] But as long as the power of the Indian Confederacy and the weakness of the United States gave England hopes of erecting a trade empire in the West based on a monopoly of the Mississippi–Great Lakes–St. Lawrence system, the United States could offer nothing that would deter British confrontation.

Despite British activities on the frontier, Hamilton still clung to his policy of conciliation. He opposed challenging Britain by restricting her trade or by attacking the posts. Instead he advocated acceptance of the status quo in Anglo-American trade and an undermining of Britain's position on the frontier by eliminating the resistance of the Northwest Indian Confederacy. He realized that Britain's plans for the frontier rested on the ability of the Indians to hold the Americans in check, and that once the resistance of the Indians was eliminated through negotiation or war Britain's position in the posts would be untenable. By concentrating on the Indians rather than on attacking the posts directly, the United States could force Britain to a reasonable frontier settlement without risking open war or the disruption of Anglo-American trade.[59] Hamilton would thus have the United States follow a friendly and conciliatory policy toward Britain and await the outcome of Wayne's campaign against the Indians.

Jefferson did not differ greatly from Hamilton on frontier policy. He saw the wisdom of avoiding an attack on the British posts and concentrating on the elimination of the resistance of the Indian Confederacy.[60] Thus he generally opposed a direct challenge to British confrontation on the frontier.[61] Yet, while he did avoid a direct challenge to the British on the frontier, he advocated far more vigorous measures than Hamilton in the realm of commerce. He did not think, as Hamilton did, that the United States had to make do with the status quo in Anglo-American trade, believing that commercial retaliation against Britain would not only force her to open the West Indies, but probably to give up the posts and abandon the Indians as well. Was Jefferson correct?

Britain certainly was concerned by the movement in the United States to retaliate commercially against her navigation. In response to the tariff of 1789 discriminating between American and all foreign ships, the Privy Council began to collect information for a report on American trade. The threat of retaliatory commercial legislation in 1791 accelerated this effort, and the report was completed that same year as a guide to the British minister to be appointed to the United States.[62]

Immediately after the decision was made to send a minister to America, Grenville so informed Colonel William S. Smith, an American then returning from London to the United States. Grenville hoped that news of the appointment would counteract the discriminatory movement that Beckwith's correspondence and that of the other British consuls in America had informed him was afoot.[63] He even had the packet held at Falmouth until Smith arrived to board it, so that the news would lose no time in reaching the proper ears.[64]

Though these events do show concern on the part of the British government that the discriminatory movement in the United States might succeed, it does not show that such measures would have forced Britain to change her trade policy. In spite of Hawkesbury's advice to the contrary, Grenville's instructions to Hammond did not authorize him to conclude a commercial treaty. He was authorized only to "express His Majesty's readiness to enter into such a negotiation, and to consent to stipulations for the benefit of commerce and navigation, on terms of reciprocal advantage."[65] Hammond was given no power except to refer American offers home, a fact that Jefferson was quick to ferret out of him.[66] Since the ministers were still ready to delay negotiation of a trade treaty, they could not have been too frightened of American commercial retaliation.

It seems likely, in fact, that American retaliation not only would have failed to change Britain's policy, but that it would have brought about counterretaliation. Grenville told Hammond that, unless the United States was ready to agree that British and American ships should be treated precisely the same way in the ports of each country, retaliation would take place. "You will state your persuasion that measures for that purpose will be adopted by the Parliament of Great Britain, and You will let it be understood that a plan of this nature has already been formed, tho' it will be with the greatest reluctance that His Majesty's Servants will feel themselves obliged to bring it forward," Grenville wrote.[67]

Grenville's threat that Britain's retaliation would not wait upon new discriminatory measures, but would eventually take place if those already extant were not repealed, may not have been totally empty. The report of 1791 drawn up by Hawkesbury's committee made the same point. The report pointed out that American discrimination had not depressed British shipping, and that British ships enjoyed other advantages to compensate for it. British ships paid lower insurance premiums than American ships, and British port charges such as lighthouse dues and pilotage fees were higher for American ships than for British.

Still, the committee asserted, the government ought to seek to counteract the American distinctions: Great Britain "has never yet submitted to the imposition of any tonnage duties by foreign nations on British ships trading to their ports, without proceeding immediately to retaliation."[68] If the American distinctions were acquiesced in without remonstrance, the United States might be encouraged "to increase these distinctions, so as to make them, in the end, effectual for the purpose for which they are intended," it warned, and pointed to the attempts in the House of Representatives to do just that.[69] It asserted that the Liverpool merchants were disposed to immediate retaliation, but that the merchants and shipowners of London, Bristol, and Glasgow were not. "They think that it will be advisable to endeavor first, by negotiation, to remove the present unfavorable distinctions; but if justice cannot in this way be obtained, that it will be necessary, in the end, to proceed to retaliation."[70]

The committee agreed that negotiation should be tried before retaliation,

but it will be right, in an early stage of this negociation, explicitly to declare that Great Britain can *never submit*, even to treat on what appears to be the *favourite object* of the people of these States, that is, *the admission of the ships of the United States into the ports of your Majesty's Colonies and islands*: it may be proper also to make them understand, that Great Britain has measures in view sufficient for the protection and support of its own commerce and navigation, in case congress should proceed to make further distinctions to the detriment of these important objects, and should refuse to consent to a fair and equitable plan of accommodation.[71]

Such retaliation was to take the form of higher duties on American tobacco, rice, and other articles imported in American ships than were charged on the same articles imported in British ships.

Hawkesbury himself was strongly in favor of such a course of action. When Henry Wilckens, representing a meeting of Liverpool merchants and shipowners, wrote him concerning the American Tariff and Tonnage Acts of 1789, Hawkesbury answered that the merchants should make some representation concerning them, keeping Hawkesbury's name out of it since such a representation should come from themselves rather than by his suggestion.[72] Wilckens' response was a letter to Hawkesbury asking quick action to counter "American arrogance."[73]

The sentiments expressed by Grenville, Hawkesbury, and the Committee on Trade of the Privy Council leave little doubt that Britain would have retaliated against any further discrimination against their trade, and particularly so if such discrimination favored French as well as American shipping over that of the British.[74] As John Adams had commented in 1785, "The words 'Ship and Sailor,' still turn the Heads of this People. They grudge to every other people, a single ship and single seaman. . . . They seem at present to dread American Ships and Seamen more than any other. Their Jealousy of our Navigation is so strong, that it is odds if it does not stimulate them to hazard their own Revenue."[75]

Thus, American attempts to coerce Britain into a liberal trade treaty through discriminatory tariff and tonnage measures would quite likely have led to British retaliation and a commercial war. Could the United States have won such a war?

Britain was certainly confident that America could not. Hawkesbury and his committee were determined not to open the West Indies at any price. By continuing its monopolistic navigation system, the British government had already shown itself willing to sacrifice the interests of the West India planters to the necessity of protecting British shipping. The government also thought that the exclusion of British manufactures and shipping from American markets, while it might hurt England, would destroy the United States. Although the British may have exaggerated the effects of a commercial war on the United States, it does seem that the new nation would have suffered more from such an event than Britain; and it seems doubtful that the United States could have made up for its economic disadvantages with determination and willing self-sacrifice, especially in view of the rather pro-British sentiments of the Northeast.

Clearly, the policy of Madison and Jefferson was a risky one. There was little chance that commercial retaliation by itself would force the British to open the West Indies to American navigation, let alone make them cease their support of the Northwest Indians and give up the posts. The attempt would probably have engendered a commercial war that would have threatened the entire financial structure of the infant American nation. On the other hand, Jefferson and Madison were prepared for the contingency of British resistence and were convinced that the United States would win the resulting war. If Americans really were willing to accept the austere and simple life of the agrarian that Jefferson and Madison visualized for the United States, then probably the country could have withstood this commercial war. But judging from the nation's reaction to Jefferson's embargo policy of 1807, it is unlikely that the American people would have accepted such sacrifices. Even if they had, Britain might have been just as stubborn.

All in all, it seems that Washington, Adams, and Jay followed the proper policy. Growing prosperity and the magnitude of the other problems facing the new government rendered an immediate settlement with Great Britain less urgent than it had been during the Confederation. To avoid challenging Britain and bringing on a crisis while building the strength of the new nation was undoubtedly the wisest course, especially in the light of our present knowledge that Great Britain would have retaliated rather than surrender to commercial discrimination. On the other hand, it was wise to avoid making all the concessions that Hamilton advocated in order to achieve a settlement and perhaps an alliance with England. Britain was as yet unready to give up its dreams of throttling America's chances to expand westward, and any settlement brought about by conciliation would have cost the United States dearly on the frontier. To hold matters with England in abeyance while building America's strength seems from a twentieth-century vantage point to have been the best possible course between 1789 and 1793.

But in 1793, the situation changed drastically. France declared war on Great Britain, and Europe was engulfed in a holocaust that would last for more than fifteen years. Almost immediately, the problems between England and the United States came to a head in what was to be known as the Jay Treaty crisis. No longer could the United States put off a settlement with Great Britain. It must either settle or fight. No one of importance wanted to fight. The only question was how to achieve a settlement that would avoid both war and the sacrifice of America's vital interests on the frontier and the high seas. Now the alternative foreign policies of Jefferson, Madison, and Hamilton locked in mortal combat, seeking to win the adherence of Washington, Jay, Adams, the Congress, and ultimately the people of the United States. The debate emerged from the privacy of cabinet discussions, executive position papers, personal correspondence, and congressional committee maneuverings into pamphlets, newspaper articles, soapbox orations, and massive popular petitions. It stirred great passions and helped to make organized political parties out of congressional factions. The ideas on foreign policy formulated by Hamilton, Jefferson, and Madison between 1789 and 1793 became the rallying points of these parties, and the choice between them involved the nature and perhaps the very existence of the United States.

Part III

CRISIS AND RESOLUTION: ANGLO-AMERICAN RELATIONS AND THE JAY TREATY, 1793-1796

7. THE STRUCTURE OF AMERICAN NEUTRALITY

In the spring of 1793, Washington managed to escape from the capital for a brief rest at his beloved Mt. Vernon, only to have those rare days of contentment shattered by a letter from Jefferson reporting the rumor (hopefully unfounded) that France had declared war against almost every power in Europe.[1] A few days later, the catastrophe was confirmed by a letter from Hamilton.[2] Washington knew that war between France and England would arouse the passions of Americans. Hoping that the general desire for peace would override sympathies for one or the other of the belligerents, he decided on a policy of strict neutrality.[3] He issued what came to be known as his Proclamation of Neutrality, enjoining the American people against participation in the war on behalf of any of the belligerents.

Such a policy was easier to proclaim that to define. America had treaties with France promising special benefits to her above all other nations should she be involved in a war. These benefits included the right to bring prizes into American ports (a privilege denied France's enemies), a denial to France's enemies of the right to fit out ships in American ports, and a guarantee of French possessions in America.[4] Was it not unneutral to give these privileges to France while denying them to her enemies? On the other hand, was it not unneutral to break treaty commitments to France in favor of the claims of her enemies?

Even impartial actions enforced against all belligerents were likely to favor one belligerent more than another. For instance, if all belligerents were permitted to raise troops on American soil, France would be more benefited than Britain. France could mount an attack from American soil against the British in Canada or Britain's Spanish allies in Florida and Louisiana, while there was no adjacent French territory for Britain to attack.[5]

It was difficult enough to satisfy both belligerents and the factions at home, but Washington's problems were even further complicated by having as his two principal advisers men who had opposing concepts of what constituted neutrality. The idea that neutrality was supposed to be "friendly and impartial" to all belligerents was a new departure in international relations. Custom and international law at that time permitted a nation to do almost anything short of actual fighting and yet to retain their designation as a neutral nation. Both Hamilton and Jefferson, while genuinely desiring that America remain neutral, favored making use of the latitude given to nations by custom and international law to stack America's neutrality in favor of either England or France, as their predilections dictated. Hamilton feared the triumph of revolutionary France and its principles, acknowledging that "I am glad to believe, there is no real resemblance between what was the cause of America and what is the cause of France—that the difference is no less great than that between Liberty and Licentiousness."[6] Jefferson, on the other hand, saw the success of the French Revolution and French arms against Britain as vital to the freedom of America. If France's enemies were successful, "it is far from being certain they might not choose to finish their job completely, by obliging us to a change in the form of our government at least," he wrote.[7]

While ideology played an important part in determining the stance of neutrality desired by Hamilton and Jefferson, their conceptions of power also played an important part. Hamilton was now even more cautious not to offend Britain; whereas Jefferson's policies before might have resulted in commercial war, he reasoned, they now risked a shooting war. In a series of articles entitled "Pacificus," he told the American people that it was impossible to imagine a more unequal contest than a war between Britain and the United States: "With the possessions of Great Britain and Spain on both flanks [Spain being allied with Britain at this time], the numerous Indian tribes under the influence and direction of those Powers, along our whole interior frontier, with a long extended seacoast, with no maritime force of our own, and with the maritime force of all Europe against us, with no fortifications whatever, and with a population not exceeding four millions . . . ," war with England would bring the destruction of American trade "and the most calamitous inconveniences in other respects."[8]

Hamilton regarded the aid that France could render America in such a case as negligible. He claimed that the assistance given by France during the American Revolution "was afforded by a great and powerful nation, possessing numerous armies, a respectable fleet, and the means of rendering it a match for the force to be encountered. The position of Europe was favorable to the enterprise; a general disposition prevailing to see the power of Britain abridged. The co-operation of Spain was very much a matter of course, and the probability of other Powers becoming engaged on the same side not remote. Great Britain was alone and likely to continue so." Now, however, "France is . . . singly engaged with the greatest part of Europe, including all the first-rate Powers except one; and in danger of being engaged with the rest. . . . Her internal affairs are . . . in serious disorder; her navy comparatively inconsiderable."[9]

Hamilton believed that Great Britain, involved in a life-and-death struggle with France, would be little inclined to brook American interference on behalf of France. He feared that even the slightest gestures toward France might bring on a war. Consequently, he set out to establish a neutrality as little offensive to Britain as possible.

To accomplish this, Hamilton advocated provisional suspension of the alliance with France. He particularly sought to avoid America's pledge to defend the French West Indies.[10] This was justified on several grounds, he maintained. First, the French had changed governments, and though a nation had such a right, it had no right to involve other nations in the consequences of those changes. If those changes "render treaties that before subsisted between it and another nation useless, or dangerous, or hurtful to that other nation, it is a plain dictate of reason, that the *latter* will have a right to renounce those treaties."[11] Also, he said, the government should be an *"undisputed* organ of the national will," and there were indications that the present French government was not.[12] If neither of these reasons were sufficient, the guarantee of the islands was contained in a *defensive* alliance, and France had been the one to declare war on England. The fact that France was not involved in a defensive war thereby freed the United States from its obligation.[13] Finally, Hamilton asserted, the United States could avoid the guarantee by declaring itself too weak to carry it out, which he deemed the worst course of the four.

Hamilton further argued that since the United States could justly consider the treaties not binding, deciding to be bound by them would be equivalent to making a new treaty and would be unneutral. England thus might justly treat the United States as an enemy. He passed off the objection that suspension of the treaties might involve the United States in a quarrel with France by saying that such a degree of intemperance on France's part would finally force a fight with her anyway.[14]

Washington decided, however, that the French treaties should not be suspended. Thereafter, Hamilton expounded the view that observance of the treaties was not incompatible with a friendly and impartial neutrality so long as observance of them did not make the United States an associate in the war. He agreed to the provisions giving France the right to bring prizes into American ports and denying the right of her enemies to fit out ships in American ports, but he continued to press for a renunciation of the guarantee of French possessions in America.[15] He adapted his positions to the immovable fact that most Americans favored the French cause, making an outright pro-British policy impossible.

Despite Jefferson's approval of the French Revolution and his belief that in some measure American liberty depended on French successes, he too was a strong advocate of neutrality. When writing to President Washington to tell him that war had actually come, Jefferson commented that it was "necessary in my opinion that we take every justifiable measure for preserving our neutrality."[16] Nevertheless his conception of neutrality was quite different from that espoused by Hamilton, which Jefferson characterized as offering "our breech to every kick which Great Britain may chuse to give it." Hamilton, he said, was for "Proclaiming at once the most abject principles, such as would invite and merit habitual insults."[17]

Jefferson believed that the United States should withhold any announcement of its neutrality until the belligerents had a chance to bid for it. As its price, the United States should ask "the broadest privileges of neutral nations," he thought.[18] Thus, he opposed the issuance of Washington's Neutrality Proclamation.[19] But the best that Jefferson could secure was the elimination of the word "neutrality" from the proclamation, in the forlorn hope that Britain might concede something to have a neutral policy spelled out by the United States in even more specific terms.

While Hamilton saw danger in the war between Britain and France, Jefferson saw opportunity. Jefferson thought that England, already in a life-and-death struggle with France, would not be anxious to gain additional enemies and would be willing therefore to make concessions to the United States. He believed that Britain had an Achilles heel—its finances. A month after news of the war had reached America, he wrote that the British, issuing financial paper based not on land but on pawns of thread and ribbons, would "soon learn the science of depreciation, and their whole paper system vanish into the nothing on which it is bottomed."[20] The United States could play on Britain's economic weakness to extort concessions from her by "pinching her commerce."[21]

This was not Jefferson's way of drawing the United States into the war. He sincerely desired peace. He simply felt that a strong stand was the best way to preserve that peace. "The part we have to act is delicate and difficult . . . with respect to that nation which from her overbearing pride, constant course of injustice and propensity to eternal war, seems justly to have obtained for herself the title of *hostis humani generis*," he wrote. "No moderation, no justice on our part can secure us against the violence of her character, and that we love liberty is enough for her to hate us. That any line of conduct either just or honourable will secure us from war on her part, is more to be wished than counted on."[22] He did not believe, as Hamilton did, that commercial retaliation against Britain would bring on war. "This would work well in many ways, safely in all, and introduce between nations another umpire than arms," he wrote Madison. "It would relieve us too from the risks and the honors of cutting throats."[23]

Feeling as he did, it is not surprising that Jefferson spoke often in cabinet meetings for giving all aid possible to France within the scope of neutrality. Once he even went beyond this. He wrote a letter of introduction to the governor of Kentucky for a Frenchman he knew was going to raise forces there for an attack on New Orleans.[24]

Still, he was careful to draw back short of war. Despite all his lectures as to the inviolability of the French alliance and the need for the United States to adhere strictly to the terms of the treaties, he hoped to avoid the guarantee of the French possessions in America. He agreed with Hamilton that, if performance of the guarantee were impossible, nonperformance was not immoral. But he opposed the immediate renunciation of the guarantee which Hamilton favored, and he thought the United States should make some diplomatic effort to save the islands for France.[25]

Jefferson's relief was apparent when Edmund Genet, the new French minister to the United States, arrived and told him that France did not mean to invoke the guarantee.[26] This left Jefferson and Madison much freer to indulge their antagonism to the sort of neutrality advocated by Hamilton and in part agreed to by Washington. With Jefferson's encouragement, Madison wrote a bitter public attack on the Proclamation of Neutrality and on the idea that the United States should reject in advance an adherence to the guarantee.[27]

Although Jefferson opposed what he considered the supine approach toward England advocated by Hamilton, he did oppose concessions to France when he thought they might endanger America's neutrality.[28] He wrote to his son-in-law that "the predilection of our citizens for France renders it very difficult to suppress their attempts to cruise against the English on the ocean, and to do justice to the latter in cases where they are entitled to it."[29] He also revoked the *exequatur* for the French vice-counsul in Boston. He told Washington that he could stop the action, but that if he thought, "as I confess I do, that an example of authority and punishment is wanting to reduce the Consuls within the limits of their duties," he should forward it.[30] It is clear that for Jefferson, neutrality and peace came first, the French cause second.[31]

Though Jefferson had much support for his policy among the people and the lower house of the legislature, he found himself alone in the executive councils. Henry Knox, the secretary of war, acknowledged himself to be ignorant of most affairs save the military and could usually be counted on to favor the opinions of Hamilton. On one occasion Jefferson wrote scathingly that Knox submitted an opinion "acknowledging at the same time, like a fool as he is, that he knew nothing about it."[32] When rumors of the coming resignations of Knox and Hamilton reached Madison, he commented that "Knox as the shadow follows the substance."[33] Though Knox was generally a faithful second of Hamilton, Madison's description was somewhat inappropriate, since, weighing over 300 pounds, Knox must have been the most substantial shadow in America.

Jefferson also found opposition in executive councils from Vice-President John Adams. The pride of John Adams had made him refuse the opportunity to join the discussions of the heads of departments, whom he considered inferior in position to the vice-president. But in April 1793 Washington asked him for an opinion concerning the proper structure of neutrality. Adams' opinion closely paralleled Hamilton's, seeking to render the Franco-American treaties null and void. Still, he had not lost his suspicion of England. He was a passionate defender of impartial neutrality, and regretted that there was "but little that I can do, either by the functions which the constitution has intrusted to me, or by my personal influence [to maintain American neutrality]; but that little shall be industriously employed, until it is put beyond a doubt that it will be fruitless, and then, I shall be as ready to meet unavoidable calamities as any other citizen."[34]

Doubtless Jefferson had anticipated such a policy from Adams. As early as 1783 he had written that Adams "hates the French, he hates the English. . . . His dislike of all parties, and all men, by balancing his prejudices, may give some fair play to his reason as would a general benevolence of temper."[35]

Attorney-General Edmund Randolph was more sympathetic to the French and to the feelings of his fellow Virginians, Jefferson and Madison, than were Knox, Adams, or Hamilton. But he was an exponent of a stricter neutrality than Jefferson or Madison. He believed that it was "always advisable for a neutral nation, to avoid even a suspicion of its neutrality."[36] Randolph opposed revocation of the French treaties, but told Washington explicitly that, if France demanded execution of the guarantee, it should be declined.[37] He attempted in many cases to tread the line between Jefferson and Hamilton and often succeeded only in alienating both. Hamilton and his cohorts believed him to be among the "frenchified slaves," while Jefferson heaped scorn and derision on his head as "the most indecisive [man] I ever had to do business with. He always contrives to agree in principle with one, but in conclusion with the other."[38] Although Randolph probably was weak in conviction and decision, Washington had confidence in him, and

Randolph's opinions were closer to those of Washington than those of any of Washington's other advisers.

Whereas John Adams balanced between his antipathies and Randolph between his fears, only Washington owed his balance to self-control and studied impartiality in the interest of peace for America and justice to all belligerents. Jefferson, Madison, and Hamilton were impartial only when they had to be, Adams and Randolph when their antipathies or fears balanced; but Washington presided over his emotions. His was a balance much less fragile than that of his advisers.

The principles of Washington's neutrality were "to adhere strictly to treaties, according to the plain construction and obvious meaning of them, and, regarding these, to act impartially towards all the Nations at war."[39] To this line Washington firmly adhered. Despite a sympathy for the French,[40] he refused to allow his personal feelings to become known and kept the government impartial in language as well as in action. "Having determined, as far as lay within the power of the Executive, to keep this country in a state of neutrality, I have made my public conduct accord with the system," he wrote in 1794; "and whilst so acting as a public character, consistency, and propriety as a private man, forbid those intemperate expressions in favor of one Nation, or to the prejudice of another, which many have indulged themselves in, and I will venture to add, to the embarrassment of government, without producing any good to the Country."[41] Although he issued the Neutrality Proclamation, Washington generally favored Jefferson's policy of refusing to concede neutral privileges in advance of necessity, rather than Hamilton's policy which Jefferson characterized as promising beforehand so much that the belligerents had no time to ask anything. Washington was not satisfied "that we should too promptly adopt measures, in the first instance, that is [sic] not indispensably necessary. To take fair and supportable ground I conceive to be our best policy, and is all that can be required of us by the Powers of War."[42]

When Washington announced his policy in the Neutrality Proclamation, he temporarily dampened the pro-French fervor of the nation. But many observers noted that within a month after the Proclamation, pro-French sentiment was on the rise again. One prominent New Yorker reported that the arrival of a French ship in the harbor

seems to have at once awakened the dormant spirit of Seventy-Six—Some imprudent *Anglified* Americans were unguarded enough to utter the wishes of their hearts as to the frigate and the nation to which she belonged and to send them without discrimination to the devil—this has produced for four or five

Nights past a meeting of some hundreds of the Republicans at the Coffee house to repress this English Spirit—and Yesterday a Cap of Liberty was put up over the Bar and several Enormous Bowls of Punch drank to its Support—Tho' it must have been "*bitter beer*" to the taste of many to whom it was offered, yet no one dared refuse the Draught.[43]

The arrival of Edmond Genet as minister to the United States from revolutionary France, and his triumphal tour from his port of entry in Charleston to Philadelphia raised emotions even further, until the frenzy threatened to sweep the United States into war with England. The followers of Hamilton, now becoming known as Federalists,* sought desperately to stem the tide. They begged Americans to remember that the Spirit of Seventy-Six regarded the British as "enemies in *war*; in peace *friends*." They scoffed at democratic factions that were often led by "a nabob in a gilt coach drawn by four of six horses and a train of servants, [who] talks with great distinctions in society—while he hears of titles with terror, his slaves tremble at his nod."[44] Hamilton, Rufus King, Noah Webster, and John Quincy Adams took to the newspapers with eloquent essays on the benefits of impartial neutrality. But it was Genet himself who did most to dampen the French fervor. Even Jefferson found him impossible, saying he was "Hotheaded, all imagination, no judgement, passionate, disrespectful and even indecent towards the President in his written as well as verbal communications, talking of appeals from him to Congress, from them to the people, urging the most unreasonable and groundless propositions, and in the most dictatorial style etc. etc. etc. If it should be necessary to lay his communications before Congress or the public, they will excite universal indignation."[45]

Universal indignation was just what Genet's conduct did inspire. The Federalists saw to it that his transgressions were well publicized, and Robert R. Livingston wrote from New York that Genet was making "a very strong and disadvantageous impression upon the public mind thro'out the whole state."[46] In South Carolina the reaction was strong enough to carry Robert

* From here on in this book, the followers of Hamilton will be designated as Federalists, and those of Jefferson and Madison as Republicans. I realize that in 1793 Federalists and Republicans were no more than loosely organized coteries composed of a few congressional leaders along with their allies in the cabinet. They certainly were not political parties in the modern sense, and most members of Congress operated independent of these factions. But despite their small membership and lack of official status, these two groups were quite well coordinated by 1793 and clearly provided the leadership in Congress. Examples of this fact are sprinkled throughout the following chapters. In addition, as the Jay Treaty crisis wore on, these factions acquired more members, more power, and more formal organization, taking on more and more of the characteristics of modern political parties. This development too will be traced in the following pages.

Goodloe Harper and others from the Jeffersonian or Republican to the Federalist camp.[47]

Frantically, Jefferson and Madison sought to extricate the French and Republican cause from the cause of Genet. Jefferson told Madison that "it will be true wisdom in the Republican party to approve unequivocally of a state of neutrality, to avoid little cavils about who should declare it, to abandon Genet entirely with expressions of strong friendship and adherence to his nation and confidence that he has acted against their sense. In this way we shall keep the people on our side by Keeping ourselves in the right." Madison agreed.[48]

Genet had forced the Republican leaders to abandon their attack on the Proclamation of Neutrality. Desperately they set about organizing a campaign to win back public enthusiasm. Madison sent a sketch of ideas concerning neutrality to many leaders around the nation which they might modify and have approved at county meetings. Thus he began a process of party organization.[49]

While the Republicans squirmed, the Federalists rejoiced. "What a pleasant thing it is to see Jefferson, Randolph and Genet by the ears!" wrote one Federalist. John Adams' son-in-law, William S. Smith, wrote Hamilton, "You will be delighted with the Anti-Gallican Spirit which has lately burst forth in this State."[50]

The Federalists saw that there were still too few who thought "right" about France but were happy that at least the people were less "frenchified" than formerly. "I like the horizon better than I did," wrote Fisher Ames; "there are less clouds."[51] He could not see just over the horizon where lurked a cloud of gigantic proportions—the Anglo-American war cloud of 1794.

8. THE WEAPONS OF AMERICAN NEUTRALITY

The rise of opinion against the French which so encouraged the Federalists was rudely interrupted in December 1793, when news reached the United States that England had negotiated a truce between Portugal and the Algerian pirates. Portugal had patrolled the Straits of Gibraltar, keeping the Algerian corsairs bottled up in the Mediterranean Sea. England wanted the Portuguese ships to fight the French, and so negotiated the truce to free its ally from this diversion.[1] The truce, however, allowed the pirates to ply their trade in the Atlantic. American ships bore the brunt of this, for the United States was the only nation with a large Atlantic trade that did not have a treaty with the Algerian pirates.[2] Naturally, the Americans thought the truce had been negotiated by the British with the specific intention of interrupting American trade with France.[3] Even good Federalists believed that the British had "let the Algerines loose upon us."[4]

The Portuguese-Algerian truce was the first event in a series of British diplomatic moves that brought England and the United States to the brink of war. Concern in the United States now turned from the structure to the weapons of neutrality. Addressing Congress in December 1793 following the Algerian truce, Washington admonished, "I cannot recommend to your notice measures for the fulfillment of *our* duties to the rest of the world, without again pressing upon you the necessity of placing ourselves in a condition of compleat defence, and of exacting from *them* the fulfillment of their duties toward us. If we desire to avoid insult, we must be able to repel it; if we desire to secure peace, one of the most powerful instruments of our rising prosperity, it must be known, that we are at all times ready for War." So saying, Washington requested of Congress further arms and military stores for the country's arsenals, a reorganization of the militia, and the establishment of a military academy.[5]

While Washington spoke of military preparedness as the means of defending America's neutrality, his secretary of state spoke of other means. He revived the movement for commercial retaliation. He presented to Congress the report on the state of American trade which had been requested of him by that body in 1791, but which Hamilton had worked so successfully to delay. Needless to say, Britain's trade policy showed up in a very poor light. Jefferson pointed out that before the war between France and England, France had allowed American vessels into her West Indies along with American salted provisions, whereas Britain had not. Though the United States exported to Great Britain twice as much as it did to France and imported from Great Britain over seven times as much, the tonnage of American ships involved in the French trade was double that which was able to participate in the Anglo-American trade, he reported. Making good use of the intercepted report of 1791 of the British Committee for Trade and Plantations, he pointed out that Britain itself claimed that its policy had cost the United States between eight and nine hundred vessels. Though there were other differences between French and British trade policy, some of which reflected favorably on Britain, all of these paled before Britain's hostile policy toward American shipping.

After reporting on the state of American trade, Jefferson went on to propose a remedy for the ills affecting it. With nations willing to treat on a reciprocal basis (and Jefferson pointed out in his report that France was at that time proposing to enter a new treaty of commerce on liberal principles, having already relaxed some of the prohibitions mentioned in the report), friendly negotiations tending toward free trade should be attempted. "But should any nation, contrary to our wishes, suppose it may better find its advantage by continuing its system of prohibitions, duties, and regulations, it behooves us to protect our citizens, their commerce and navigation, by counter prohibitions, duties, and regulations also. Free commerce and navigation are not to be given in exchange for restrictions and vexations; nor are they likely to produce a relaxation of them." Retaliation was necessary, because American navigation needed to be protected and encouraged. "As a branch of industry, it is valuable, but as a resource of defence, essential. . . . The position and circumstances of the United States leave them nothing to fear on their land-board, and nothing to desire beyond their present rights. But on their seaboard, they are open to injury, and they have there, too, a commerce which must be protected." He made sure, however, that his support for a navy did not include a naval building program, stating that the protection of commerce "can only be done by possessing a respectable body of citizen-seamen, and of artists and establishments in readiness for ship-building."[6]

Jefferson's recommendations were quickly embodied in a series of resolutions introduced in the House of Representatives by James Madison. These resolutions proposed discriminatory duties against nations that did not have a trade treaty with the United States. The revenue so derived was to defray the expenses resulting from violations of America's neutral rights.[7]

Desperately, Hamilton and his friends sought to counter the logic and facts behind the resolutions. Hamilton, making use of information he had been collecting since 1791 to counter Jefferson's report, gave Representa-

117

tive William Loughton Smith of South Carolina a speech with which to oppose Madison's resolutions. Sliding over the fact that Britain's policy toward the imports of American goods compared unfavorably with that of France, Smith and Hamilton made maximum use of the fact that the British treated American trade more favorably than that of any other foreign country. American ships, Smith pointed out, paid less duty than did other foreign ships in British ports. The British discriminated in favor of the United States on tobacco; they gave America a monopoly on rice and wood shipped to the British West Indies (in British ships only, of course); and their discriminatory duties allowed American naval stores to compete in England with those of the Baltic countries. Smith admitted that France treated American shipping more favorably than Britain, but he pointed out that Jefferson had exaggerated the differential in the American tonnage employed in the French and the British trade. By counting the number of inward entries of each vessel rather than the number of vessels engaged in the trade, a vessel making four entries in a year from the French West Indies was credited with twice the tonnage of a vessel of the same capacity making two entries from British or European ports.[8] In any case, the French were making concessions to American shipping for their own interest, Smith stated. Britain provided better products, a better market in which to sell and purchase, and better credit to American merchants.[9]

The questions raised by Madison's resolutions went far deeper than a mere rearrangement of American trade. They affected American neutrality and, in Federalist eyes, threatened war itself. Fisher Ames, member of Congress from Massachusetts, wrote home to Christopher Gore,

The debate on the war regulations (for so they ought to be named) is yet open. ... The ground is avowedly changed. Madison & Co. now avow that the political wrongs are *the* wrongs to be cured by commercial restrictions, which, in plain English is, we set out with a tale of restrictions and injuries on our commerce, that has been refuted solidly; pressed for a pretext, we avow that we will make war, not for our commerce, but with it; not to make our commerce better, but to make it nothing, in order to reach the tender sides of our enemy, which are not to be wounded in any other way. You and I have long believed this to be the real motive; I own I did not expect to hear it confessed.[10]

He reported to another friend, "It is all French that is spoken in support of the measure. I like the Yankee dialect better."[11]

In attacking Madison's resolutions, the Federalists warned time and again of the danger of war. William Loughton Smith told Congress that commercial restrictions would never be successful in forcing the British to open their West Indies to the ships of the United States. The "Navigation Act of

Great Britain, the principles of which exclude us from the advantages we wish to enjoy, is deemed by English politicians as the palladium of her riches, greatness and security," he avowed. England would not yield to American extortion without a serious trial of strength, for it would encourage all countries to try the same. A trade war would disturb only one-sixth of Britain's trade, but one-half of America's, leaving little doubt about who would suffer most. "If we should seize the present moment to attack her in a point where she is peculiarly susceptible, she would be apt to regard it as a mark of determined hostility," he said, and went on to warn that "War is as often the result of resentment as of calculation." The United States was growing in power; it should be patient, and put off trials of strength.[12]

Smith quickly garnered support for his position within the House. One member advised negotiation until patience was exhausted, and then an attack on the western posts: "Away with your milk-and-water regulations; they are too trifling to effect objects of such importance. Are the Algerines to be frightened with paper resolves, or the Indians to be subdued, or the Western posts taken, by commercial regulations? When we consider the subject merely as a commercial one, it goes too far, and attempts too much; but when considered as a war establishment, it falls infinitely short of the mark, and does too little."[13] Another member pointed out that discrimination against countries with no trade treaties would involve Spain, Portugal, Denmark, Russia, Hamburg, Bremen, and other Hanse Towns, as well as Great Britain.[14]

"Madison and Co." did not receive these attacks in silence. The lack of reciprocity in Anglo-American trade was obvious and the remedy apparent, Madison asserted; the idea that England would declare war in retaliation for American commercial restrictions was ridiculous, for these resolutions did not even reciprocate for what England was already doing to the United States. Abraham Clark of New Jersey recalled the success of nonimportation before the Revolution and said that the British would surely accede to American demands should Madison's resolution pass. Many British manufacturers were already starving for want of employment, so American commercial restrictions would add further to their distress and bring the government to its senses.[15]

Hamilton rushed into print the Federalist contention that Madison's resolutions meant war, and the cry was carried throughout the country.[16] Pressures mounted against the resolutions from outside the House of Representatives, and tempers frayed within. Members labeled opponents "British agent" and "garrulous old man." When the Federalists noticed that Madison and some of his followers were absent from one of the sessions, they tried to bring the resolutions to a vote and were barely beaten down.[17] Finally, Madison's ranks broke. John Sherburne of Massachusetts, one of two New Englanders who had previously voted for the resolutions, now moved their postponement on the grounds that four-fifths of the American people were against them.[18] The Federalists sensed victory and sought to forestall postponement. They hoped that the more timid members would vote against Madison's resolutions if they were forced to a decision before they could learn the sense of their constituents.[19] Madison and his supporters now thought it best to support the postponement and barely succeeded in passing it.[20]

While waiting for the resolutions to come up again, both Republicans and Federalists sought to organize meetings of citizens to support their respective positions, with the Federalists evidently more successful than their opponents. In Boston a meeting called by the Republicans to support Madison's resolutions ended with the defeat of those resolutions by a majority of more than two-thirds.[21] Theodore Sedgwick, representative from Massachusetts, now gloated that the resolutions were doomed, "there being certainly a majority against them in the Senate."[22]

But Sedgwick was wrong. Madison's resolutions were not yet done. In supporting postponement, Madison had shrewdly calculated that subsequent news from England could be expected to strengthen arguments for retaliation.[23] His expectations were not disappointed.

By late February 1794, a rumor had already reached the United States that American ships carrying French West Indian produce were being seized by British cruisers.[24] Soon it was apparent that these seizures were a calculated effort on the part of Great Britain to interrupt the carrying trade between the French West Indies and the French mainland, a trade that France had abandoned into the hands of neutral American ships. News reached America in early March that an order-in-council dated November 6, 1793, had instructed British commanders to intercept and bring in for adjudication all ships bound to or from the French colonies. As Madison suspected, the orders had been given the commanders secretly, and the American minister in London had not been informed until it was too late to warn ships plying the French West Indies trade of the new British policy.[25] As a result, close to 250 American vessels were captured and most of them condemned.[26]

These English outrages gave new life to Republican efforts to retaliate commercially against Great Britain. Yet Madison found it advisable to further postpone his resolutions. Sedgwick, concluded, perhaps wistfully, that this was because Madison "was manifestly fearful to take them into consideration."[27] Madison, however, had quite different reasons. He and his supporters were talking of substituting sterner measures, such as an embargo.[28]

In the wake of anti-British passions inspired by the West Indian captures, the embargo was brought to a vote in the House of Representatives. Surprisingly, it was defeated by two votes.[29] Four days later, however, the embargo was given new life when Washington submitted evidence to Congress of the great hardships endured by the captains and crews of American ships being illegally detained by the British in the West Indies.[30] About the same time, news reached Philadelphia of a speech by Lord Dorchester to the seven Indian nations of Canada. Dorchester told the Indians that because of American aggressions the border between the Americans and the British drawn in 1783 no longer existed, and that, "from the manner in which the People of the States push on, and act, and talk on this side, and from what I learn of their conduct towards the Sea, I shall not be surprised if we are at war with them in the course of the present year; and if so, a Line must then be drawn by the Warriors." The Americans, he told the Indians, had destroyed their right of preemption of Indian lands on the American side of the border. Thus, all American purchases from the Indians since 1783 he considered "an infringement on the king's rights: and when a Line is drawn between us, be it in Peace or War, they must lose all their Improvements and Houses on our side of it; those People must all be gone who do not obtain leave to become the King's Subjects. What belongs to the Indians will of course be confirmed and secured to them."[31]

News of these outrages so angered the House of Representatives that on March 25, 1794, four days after defeating the general embargo, the House reversed itself and enacted an embargo of one month's duration by a large majority.[32] The Senate quickly concurred. Though many Federalists had reservations about the embargo, they felt compelled to go along.[33] If the measure had little chance of starving the West Indies, as the Republicans hoped at least it would keep American ships out of the hands of the British, the Federalists reasoned.[34] They were careful to see that the embargo applied to ships destined for any foreign port whatsoever, and thus they avoided a direct challenge to Britain.

Unsatisfied with the general embargo, Republicans pushed for more stringent commercial measures to be directed specifically at Great Britain. The first such measure was a motion to sequester debts owed to the British by American citizens and to use the money to compensate Americans for losses occasioned by British actions. Such was the indignation toward Great Britain that a Federalist, Jonathan Dayton of New Jersey, introduced the motion, and Sedgwick mourned that even William Loughton Smith had "Sailed down the tide." Sedgwick predicted that the proposition would be carried in the House by a two-to-one margin.[35]

The ardor of Congress was cooled, however, by news that the British had issued a new order-in-council mitigating effects of the order of November 6. The day following receipt of this news, Sedgwick predicted that though sequestration might pass the House, it could not pass the Senate; two days later, John Adams was confident it would not even pass the House.[36] Eventually, the Federalists were able to prevent sequestration from ever coming to a vote, though Madison asserted that a majority in the House favored the measure.[37]

News of the milder British order-in-council did not defeat the whole movement for commercial retaliation, however. On April 15, 1794, the House Committee of the Whole passed a bill to prohibit commercial intercourse with Britain by a vote of 54 to 44.[38] But the following day President Washington sent to the Senate his nomination of John Jay as envoy extraordinary to Great Britain, empowered to negotiate the differences between England and the United States. Hamilton and his followers in Congress had engineered the appointment to defeat the Republican campaign for commercial retaliation against Britain. In this they were to be completely successful.

The Federalist plan for dealing with the British war crisis consisted of two parts—to arm in preparation for war while attempting to negotiate a peace. They were ready to fight if Britain forced them to,[39] but they did not think, as many Republicans did, that this was Britain's intention. Negotiations might lead to a settlement; and even if negotiations failed, they would furnish time for the United States to build its defenses while allowing "foreign nations to waste their strength and their fury."[40] In the meantime, they thought it best to avoid any measures that might further stir England's hostility. While they did not think England wanted to force war upon the United States, it seemed plain to men like Rufus King that if the Americans sought it England would "feel no reluctance again to measure swords with us."[41] Under these circumstances, commercial retaliation would bring war, not forestall it. Some Federalists thought the Republican program was designed to do just that, to bring the United States into war on the side of France and enable southerners to repudiate their debts to the British.[42]

To save the peace, the Federalists sought to turn congressional thoughts from commercial retaliation to military preparedness and from reprisals to negotiations. Alexander Hamilton was the unquestioned leader of this effort, and he assumed the vital task of bringing President Washington to its support. Taking up one of Washington's favorite themes, Hamilton asserted in a letter to the president that "to be in a condition to defend ourselves, and annoy any who may attack us, will be the best method of securing our peace." He recommended fortifying the principal ports, raising 20,000 troops, and giving the president the power to lay an embargo. In the light of future events, it is also interesting that he recommended consideration of measures to organize all the neutral powers for common defense.[43]

While Hamilton sought the chief executive's support for the Federalist program, Theodore Sedgwick attempted to put the program through the House of Representatives. "The whole of my system is the fortification of our harbours, the ports, and naval armament . . . , Vesting the president with the power to lay an Embargo & to prevent the exportation of produce for a limited time, and the raising imediately [sic] an army of 20,000 men," he wrote pretentiously. His program was almost exactly that outlined by Hamilton, and even his detailed description of the way the men were to be called up, paid, and employed matched that in Hamilton's letter to Washington. "The President most compleatly and explicitly approves of this project, but I am not certain his extreme caution will permit him to bring it forward," Sedgwick concluded.[44]

Congress debated the Federalist proposals concurrently with the Republican measures of commercial retaliation. In fact, by the time Sedgwick wrote, two of the measures comprehended in "his system" had already passed the House of Representatives, including a provision for building six frigates and one for fortifying the major American ports. Few of Madison's supporters opposed fortifying the ports, but building frigates they thought a very different matter.

The frigate scheme was a direct outgrowth of the truce between Portugal and Algiers. The House had debated it before news of the British captures in the West Indies reached the United States. Avowedly, the frigates were for the purpose of fighting Algerians, but no one lost sight of the fact that they might also be used against the British. The measure seemed to command great popularity. Even Benjamin Bache's *General Advertiser*, a rabidly Republican newspaper, at first supported the measure.[45]

Nonetheless, the Republican leaders in the House of Representatives fought the measure vehemently. "History does not afford an instance of a nation which continued to increase their navy and decreased their debt at the same time," William B. Giles of Virginia told the House. "A navy is the most expensive of all means of defence, and the tyranny of Governments consists in the expensiveness of their machinery," he continued, asserting that the expenses of the British navy would probably destroy Great Britain.[46]

Although the navy threatened civil liberty, it could not threaten the Algerians, Republican leaders asserted. Madison maintained that if the navy were adequate to its task, it would be opposed by the country that had set the Algerians loose upon the United States in the first place.[47] A Republican senator wrote that the United States "was creating ships for the sport of every superior naval power."[48] Shortly before the vote, Bache's *General Advertiser* abandoned its support of the frigate scheme and fell into line with the Republican leadership by printing a slashing attack on it.[49] But sentiment for a navy—sentiment that Jefferson and Madison themselves had done much to foster in earlier days—was too strong. The authorization to build six frigates passed the House, 50 to 39.[50] The measure was doubtless helped by news of the British captures in the West Indies, which reached Congress shortly before the House voted on the measure. Three New Englanders who had voted against the frigates in the Committee of the Whole before the news,[51] reversed themselves on the final vote. Madison reacted quite differently, however. "As the danger of a war has appeared to increase, every consideration rendering the frigates at first unwise, now renders them absurd," he wrote.[52]

The greatly increased danger of war gave impetus to the Federalist attempt to build an army as well as a navy. In 1794 the army consisted of a total of 3,861 men, most of whom were with Wayne in the Northwest.[53] Sedgwick brought forward a plan that would authorize the raising of 80,000 militia and fifteen additional regiments of regular troops totaling 15,000 men plus officers, to be dissolved in two and a half years if no war should break out with any European foreign powers. His purpose, he told the House, was to preserve peace by being prepared for war. A militia, he believed, was perfectly capable of defending America from invasion, for it was "not in the power of any nation to conquer America, or to dismember it, and possess themselves of any section of it." But, he went on, "As long as we depend on a militia alone for repelling foreign injury short of a direct attack on our territory, European nations will not consider us able to retaliate, and assert our rights." He made clear that he thought an atttack on "adjacent rich Dominions" proper retaliation.[54]

Even though these troops were to be used against Great Britain, the Republicans wanted no part of them. Most of them agreed to the raising of the militia, and that bill passed the Committee of the Whole.[55] But to the raising of regular troops they objected strenuously. Nonetheless, under the impetus of the war cloud, the House of Representatives passed a resolution to raise the regular troops, and actually increased the number to be raised to a total of 25,000.[56]

While the Federalists fashioned the stick, they also prepared to extend the carrot. They urged Washington to send an envoy extraordinary to Britain to make one last try for a settlement between the countries. Preparedness and negotiation were part and parcel of the same program. As Sedgwick wrote, "Today I reported three bills 1. for a detachment from the militia— 2. for raising a corps of 800 artilery [sic] 3. for a regular force of 25,000 men. . . . The President now ought not to delay for a moment to send an Envoy Extra to London."[57]

The idea of an envoy extraordinary seems to have occurred simultaneously to many people. Rufus King received a letter from Christopher Gore in Boston stating that the merchants of that city favored a special mission to England.[58] Edmund Randolph claimed that he was among the first to suggest the idea to Washington.[59] Aaron Burr, a leader of the Republicans in the Senate, passed around a paper that suggested several measures to deal with the crisis, including an envoy extraordinary.[60] But a caucus of influential Federalist senators adopted the project as its own and succeeded in shaping that mission to fit the overall Federalist program.

On March 10, shortly after the order-in-council of November 6 became known, Caleb Strong, George Cabot, and Oliver Ellsworth met with Rufus King in his room to seek a way to avoid war and yet save the national honor by procuring indemnification from Great Britain. They decided that it would be advisable to build America's military forces, to find a means of internal taxation to replace the revenue that would be lost if war interrupted America's foreign commerce, and to send a special envoy to England. They delegated Oliver Ellsworth to take their plan to the president and suggested that Hamilton or Jay be selected as the envoy, with Hamilton being the particular favorite. By these means they hoped to stop all further inflammatory congressional proceedings and to gain time for the nation to prepare for war if the envoy could not reach an agreement with the British government.[61]

Ellsworth related to the president the thinking of the men he represented.[62] Washington promised to take the matter into consideration but apparently did nothing until March 27, when news arrived that the order of November 6 had been revoked and replaced by somewhat modified instructions.[63] The next day, Washington called in Robert Morris to confer with him on appointing an envoy extraordinary.

Until March 27, Washington evidently had felt that Britain was bent on war and that negotiations could do little good. He had believed that Dorchester's speech to the Indians implying inevitable war between Britain and the United States had "spoken the Sentiments of the British Cabinet at the period he was instructed." He held some hope that British troubles on the Continent might have changed the minds of the British cabinet, but believed such a change to be problematical. He went so far as to request from Governor George Clinton of New York the extent of British fighting strength in Canada.[64]

After he received the news that the order of November 6 had been revoked, Washington apparently thought that chances of peace were much better. On April 6 he wrote to the manager of his estate at Mount Vernon that the capture of American vessels by British cruisers and the American embargo naturally had occasioned a temporary fall in the prices of provisions. He was confident that "as soon as the present impediments are removed the prices of flour will rise to what it had been (at least) for which reason hold mine up the prices mentioned in my last."[65] Washington must have been confident that America's embargo would be lifted in the near future and that no war would intervene to interrupt American commerce. He may have been even more encouraged the following day. That day Hammond told Rufus King that he did not believe Dorchester's speech had been authorized by the British home government.[66]

As evidence mounted that Britain was not totally determined on war and that negotiation might be of some benefit in deterring hostilities, Washington seems to have considered the proposal to send a special envoy to England more seriously. This news must have leaked, for the president was the recipient of several strong letters from influential Republicans objecting to the mission in general and to Hamilton in particular.[67] But Washington did not remove Hamilton's name from consideration until Hamilton himself, seeing that by remaining in contention he was jeopardizing the whole mission, withdrew and recommended Jay.[68]

The same day he received Hamilton's letter recommending Jay, Washington called the chief justice in and offered him the envoyship. Pressed by Hamilton, Strong, Cabot, Ellsworth, and King, Jay finally accepted. In doing so, he told the president that he wished the House to avoid legislation aimed at menacing Great Britain. He thought such legislation would and should cause Britain to refuse to treat with the United States.[69] Washington accepted his advice, writing to Secretary of State Randolph, "My objects, are, to prevent a war, if justice can be obtained by fair and strong representations (to be made by a special Envoy) of the injuries which this Country has sustained from Great Britain in various ways; to put it into a complete state of military defence, and to provide *eventually*, such measures, as seem to be now pending in Congress, for execution, if negotiation in a reasonable time proves unsuccessful."[70] He thus accepted in its entirety the

Federalist conception of how the Anglo-American crisis should be handled and placed the negotiations in the hands of one of their number.

Led by Aaron Burr, the Republicans in the Senate fought Jay's nomination bitterly. They argued that the business could be handled by the minister already in residence there and decried Jay's appointment to a second federal post without his first having resigned as chief justice. Nonetheless, the Senate approved his nomination by a vote of 18 to 8.[71]

Despite the requests of Jay and Washington to avoid legislation menacing to Great Britain, Jay's appointment did not completely halt the course of the Republican-backed legislation aimed at Britain's commerce. The House of Representatives proceeded to pass the nonintercourse resolution that had been pending since late March. It did soften the measure, however. The original bill had stated that the boycott of British trade would not be terminated until the forts and Negroes had been restored and compensation made for the spoliations of American ships and merchandise. This ultimatum was eliminated, and the nonintercourse resolution then passed the House of Representatives 58 to 38.[72] "Such madness, my friend, such madness!" mourned Sedgwick.[73] But Madison was also mourning that, though the measure had a majority in the House, it would probably be defeated in the Senate.[74]

He was right, but barely so. Only three days after the nonintercourse bill had passed the House of Representatives, the Senate voted on it and found itself in a tie, 13 to 13, with the deciding vote in the hands of Vice-President Adams.[75] Though the Republicans had come close to passing their measure, there was little or no doubt how it would fare at the hands of Adams. He was no lover of Great Britain at the time, writing to his wife that though the English faction exulted at the prospect of the French West Indies being captured by the British, "I am no more delighted with the idea of the West Indies in the hands of the English, than I was with Brabant and Flanders in the power of Dumourier."[76] Nevertheless, he wanted peace with England and considered it the job of the Senate to block legislation that menaced peace. "We the old Sachems have enough to do to restrain the Ardour of our young Warriors.—We shall Succeed however, I still hope, in preventing any very rash Steps from being taken," he wrote during the crisis.[77] The nonintercourse measure in particular he considered a mischievous measure which would probably lead to war, and he had foreseen that the success or failure of the measure might come to lie in his hands. "The House yesterday passed a resolution in committee of the whole, whose depth is to me unfathomable," he had written his wife. "The Senate will now be called upon to show their independence, and perhaps your friend to show his weakness or his strength."[78] He cast his vote against the bill, and the Republicans were defeated.[79]

The Republicans had foreseen that the "executive maneuver" of nominating John Jay as envoy extraordinary to Britain probably meant the defeat of the retaliatory legislation. In fact, they believed, the whole purpose of nominating an envoy had been to remove the issue from the House of Representatives, where the Republicans predominated, and to settle the crisis by treaty, over which the Federalist executive and Senate had control. As Jefferson later wrote, "A bolder party-stroke was never struck. For it certainly is an attempt of a party, which finds they have lost their majority in one branch of the legislature, to make a law by the aid of the other branch and of the executive, under color of a treaty, which shall bind up the hands of the adverse branch from ever restraining the commerce of their patron nation."[80] Thus, they opposed the special mission to England. The whole Federalist approach to the Anglo-American war crisis they considered humiliating and dangerous.

The Republicans were not opposed to negotiations with Britain as such, so long as they were in the hands of men who could be trusted. (Before it was known that Jay would be the envoy, Burr himself had proposed a special mission to England.) But they did think it humiliating to send an envoy to beg for peace in the face of Britain's many insults. They thought some sort of retaliatory legislation should precede the negotiations. Such measures would be so effective, they believed, that Great Britain would gladly settle the points in dispute with the United States and accord the broadest privileges of neutrality in order to have them revoked. Commercial retaliation would have put the United States "on the right ground for negotiations," wrote Madison.[81] On the other hand, the appointment of a Federalist envoy extraordinary to negotiate in the face of British insults without retaliatory legislation behind him was the most degrading measure which could be proposed, Jefferson believed; "we have borne so much as to invite eternal insults in future should not a very spirited conduct be now assumed."[82]

The Republicans did not believe that their "spirited conduct" would bring war with England. Certainly they did not intend it to do so, as the Federalists suspected. The Republicans realized that war with England meant destruction of America's commerce, and though they did not have ships on the sea to be captured by British vessels as did the Northeast, such an event would prevent the exporting of their crops. As one Republican wrote James Monroe, "If there is any reason to apprehend a rupture between Great Britain & America it will . . . very much effect [sic] prices in general and our wheat on hand I fear [will] not readily find a market such will be the fear of capture. War certainly should be avoided if with any degree of propriety it can be done."[83]

Republicans in fact believed their program far more likely to avoid war "with propriety" than the Federalist plan. Madison said that Britain would "push her aggressions just so far and no farther, than she imagines we will tolerate. I conclude also that the readiest expedient for stopping her career of depredation on those parts of our trade which thwart her plans, will be to make her feel for those which she cannot do without," he wrote.[84] Weak conduct would draw on a war which firmness might have prevented.

But despite much public scoffing at the Federalist contention that commercial retaliation might bring war, the Republican leadership privately did not deny that this was a possibility. Though certain that American commerce made it Britain's interest to avoid war with the United States, the Republican leadership was well aware that Britain's passion might overrule its intellect. Jefferson, commenting on the nonintercourse bill, admitted that war might result from it. "If it does," he said, "we will meet it like men: but it may not bring on war, and then the experiment will have been a happy one."[85]

If the Republicans admitted that war was a possibility, how could they bring themselves to oppose measures of preparedness? First they claimed that they did not oppose "sensible" measures of preparedness. "A Calm Observer" pointed out in one newspaper that the Republicans did vote to raise enough regular troops to fill the already established quota of 5,000 men, to fortify ports and harbors, to raise a corps of 800 artillerists to garrison those fortification, to fill the arsenals with arms, to pay up to one million dollars for peace with the Algerians, and to call on the states to raise and train 80,000 militia.[86] The other preparedness measures, they maintained, were not sensible. The "foolish frigate scheme" was inadequate to its task, expensive, and would place the ships in the water too late to do any good in the present crisis.[87] A large regular army was unconstitutional and dangerous in the hands of a Federalist government. The Federalist plan to raise such troops was "a Jesuitical . . . contrivance to cripple Madison's plan of commercial restrictions," wrote one Republican.[88]

Yet the Republican leaders must have been torn by the preparedness issue. They must have been stung deeply by the Federalist cries that they were proposing measures which could well bring war, but opposing measures to place America in a state of defense. They must have been particularly torn on the issue of building the frigates, a favorite scheme with Jefferson and Madison in the period preceding the Constitution. Many of their followers, particularly in the north, favored it also.

Still the Republicans were confident that even without an army or navy, American strength was adequate to secure concessions from the British. If Britain responded irrationally to American pressure and declared war, the United States would have to give up the sea, but American privateers would wreak havoc with British commerce, and America's militia was competent to defend the country from invasion, to capture the posts, and even to conquer Canada, they thought. Besides, depriving Britain of America's market and supplies in the midst of her titanic struggle with France would bring her soon to the point of collapse.[89] They scoffed at the Federalists cry that war with England would mean extinction for the United States, "As if the experience of the last war, an established government, and the duplication of our numbers had enfeebled us, and rendered us less capable than we were in 1776 of resisting a nation evidently fallen from her former greatness."[90] Thus the Republicans did not advocate standing firmly against Britain merely because America's cause was just, but because they thought America would win.

Of course, the Federalists had believed that the whole Republican program was foolish even before the European war had broken out; now it seemed sheer madness. The sincere friends of peace, said Hamilton, were for negotiating while "leaving things in a state which will enable Great Britain, without abandoning self-respect, to do us the justice we seek. The others are for placing things upon a footing which would involve the disgrace or disrepute of having receded through intimidation. This last scheme indubitably ends in war."[91]

The Federalists thought that war with Great Britain threatened the very existence of the United States. British naval power in the western hemisphere was overpowering. The *Gazette of the United States* reported that in Martinique alone, the British had twenty-one ships of war and six gunboats.[92] The United States had none of either. If war came, the only American ships left on the seas would be merchant ships converted to privateers, and though these would hinder Britain's trade with the West Indies, the Federalists thought the United States would lose more than it would gain.[93] War would deprive America of a supply for which "no substitute can be found elsewhere—a supply necessary to us in peace, and more necessary to us if we are to go to war," wrote Hamilton. The revenue lost by such an event could not be repaired from other sources, he continued, and the loss of such revenue would bring the Treasury to an absolute stoppage of payment, "an event which would cut up credit by the roots."[94] Stopping Britain's trade with the United States and subjecting its other commerce to the depredations of American privateers "could not fail to be seriously distressing to her," Hamilton remarked; "Yet it would be weak to calculate upon a very decisive influence of these circumstances." They would not arrest Britain's actions, nor "overrule those paramount considerations which brought her into her present situation."[95]

The Federalists hoped that fortification of America's harbors would protect coastal cities against all attacks from the sea except formal, serious operations. But if Britain chose to undertake such operations, they had no doubt that the cities would be lain in ashes. They also feared operations by Indians and British troops on the frontier. Yet the Federalists thought that under the circumstances the United States was secure from the total conquest by Britain.[96] They even believed the United States capable of mounting an attack on Canada and Florida, though they thought this would require a regular army and considerable exertion.[97]

But Federalist confidence in America's ability to resist British conquest was premised on the unity of the nation, a concern for which lay at the base of the political philosophies of Washington, Jay, Adams, and most of Hamilton's followers. The United States was secure from conquest, Hamilton had asserted in 1783, only "if internal dissensions do not open the way."[98] The Federalists thought that war sparked by commercial retaliation would lead to such internal dissensions. The northern states would oppose a war unless it was forced on the United States, asserted Hamilton, and many would not consider a war that resulted from Republican commercial measures as one forced on America.[99] Timothy Dwight wrote to Oliver Wolcott confirming Hamilton's opinion: "A war with Great Britain, we at least, in New England, will not enter into. Sooner would ninety-nine out of a hundred of our inhabitants separate from the Union, than plunge themselves into such an abyss of misery."[100] John Quincy Adams and his father also feared internal dissensions would result from a war with Britain,[101] and Fisher Ames wrote that in case of war, "I dread anarchy more than great guns."[102]

The Republicans, of course, did not think that there would be internal dissension if war came as a result of commercial retaliation. They considered the Federalist party to be composed of a few active leaders and no followers. Jefferson wrote that a war with England "would be vastly more unanimously approved, than any one we ever were engaged in; because the aggressions have been so wanton and barefaced, and so unquestionably against our desire."[103] The Republicans thus scoffed at Federalist fears of conquest.

But scoff as the Republicans might, the Federalists made good use of the war issue in opposing the Republican program. One Federalist reported from New England that an early opinion in favor of commercial retaliation had been dispelled by pointing out the anomaly of Republicans favoring commercial retaliation while opposing naval preparedness.[104] The Federalists were evidently making good progress on their program, which Fisher Ames characterized as "Peace, peace, to the last day it can be maintained; and war, when it must come, to be thrown upon [the Republican] faction, as their act and deed."[105]

Ames's desire to allow any blame for a war with Britain to fall exclusively on the Republicans is an indication that the Federalist program was not determined exclusively by considerations of power, but by partisan and sectional motives as well. The Federalists were undoubtedly more concerned than agrarian Republicans about the effect of war on American commerce, and they were also undoubtedly fearful of the effect that a war would have on their party's domestic financial program. Thus they sought to keep Anglo-American affairs in the hands of their party and section by removing such matters from a hostile House of Representatives and placing them in the hands of a Senate and executive that sympathized with their aims.[106]

But it is going too far to say, as Alexander DeConde has, that the Jay Treaty was a result primarily of partisan motives, that Jay's mission was "conceived by Federalists to be executed by Federalists for the benefit of Federalists."[107] The Federalists sincerely believed that the protection of American commerce and of Hamilton's financial system was in the interest of the nation, and that the Republicans, out of a desire for sectional and partisan advantage, would bring war and the destruction of America's commerce, credit, and perhaps national existence itself. Jay's mission was conceived by Federalists to be executed by Federalists for the benefit of the United States.

Undoubtedly, the Federalists' dislike of France also influenced their approach to the Anglo-American war crisis. This must not be overemphasized, however. The conduct of Britain toward the United States during this period angered most Federalists almost as much as it did the Republicans. "If John Bull is a blockhead, and puts himself on his pride to maintain what he has done, and should refuse reparation, it will, I think, be war," wrote Fisher Ames.[108] "We are ill-treated by Britain, and . . . it is owing to a national insolence against us," John Adams wrote his wife.[109]

Federalist ideology, however, had more influence. The Federalists' love of balanced, orderly, and somewhat authoritarian government on the British model made many of them unwilling, despite their anger at Britain, to take the side of France against her. "Such indeed are the injuries which we have received from Great Britain that I believe I should not much hesitate on going to war, but that we must in that case be allied to France, which would be an alliance with principles which would prostrate liberty and destroy every species of security," wrote Theodore Sedgwick.[110] Fisher Ames agreed saying that "The English are absolutely madmen," and that their stupid policy would Frenchify the United States.[111] Most Federalists seemed to wish a plague on both their houses. George Cabot, senator from Massachusetts, believed it would be "for the interest and peace of *our* country that they should on all sides suffer deeply, and no one triumph. On the one hand, the haughtiness of England, in case of success, would become intolerable to our maritime commerce; and, on the other hand, French principles would destroy us as a society."[112]

Thus the Federalist and Republican approaches to the Anglo-American war crisis were direct continuations of the policies formulated by Jefferson, Madison, and Hamilton in the period immediately following ratification of the Constitution. Now, however, the consequences of miscalculation were far greater. As before, the approaches of both sides were affected by considerations of ideology and partisan advantage. But, also as before, their major considerations were to balance their goals with the power available to the United States.

The instructions and advice that Jay received from his fellow Federalists before he left for England reflected their consciousness of American weakness before the might of Britain. Hamilton wrote that it would be "our error to overrate ourselves and underrate Great Britain; we forget how little we can annoy, how much we may be annoyed. 'Tis enough for us, situated as we are, to be resolved to vindicate our honor and rights in the last extremity. To precipitate a great conflict of any sort is utterly unsuited to our condition, to our strength, or to our resources."[113] Thus they felt that negotiations should not be accompanied by reprisals or threats that would make concessions by Britain seem a humiliating surrender.[114] It was folly to believe that

Great Britain, fortified by the alliances of the greatest part of Europe, will submit to our demands, urged with the face of coercion, and proceded by acts of reprisal. She cannot do it without losing her consequence and weight in the scale of nations; and, consequently, it is morally certain she will not do it. A proper estimate of the operation of human passions, must satisfy us that she would be less disposed to receive the law from us than from any other nation.[115]

To make sure that Jay got the point, Hamilton, Strong, Cabot, Ellsworth, and King went to him to press him to accept Washington's offer of the envoyship and, at the same time, to urge him to reinforce the opinion he had already given Washington that the measures before the House of Representatives for commercial reprisals would embarrass the negotiation. They even told him to threaten to decline the appointment unless these were eliminated.[116] Military preparations, however, contained nothing offensive and gave rise to no point that could be a bar to amicable negotiation, they believed. These rather than commercial resolutions were to supply the threat behind the amicability of the envoy.

With this approach to the negotiations, the Federalists sought to secure a great deal. Hamilton wrote Washington and Jay that America should attempt to get indemnification for the captures under the November 6 orders, which he believed should be a sine qua non. He wanted a settlement of the unexecuted portions of the Peace Treaty of 1783, especially British evacuation of the posts and compensation for the Negroes carried off by the British. He wanted more liberal treatment of neutral American commerce by British ships, and a treaty that would permit American ships to trade with the West Indies.[117]

The Federalists, however, believing that they were negotiating from a position of weakness, were willing to give a great deal to get these concessions. Except for compensation for spoliations, they were obviously willing to accept less than they asked in order to secure peace. Jay's official instructions, though drawn up by Edmund Randolph, were modeled closely on the advice of Hamilton, and nothing was made a sine qua non except compensation for spoliations. There was no great confidence among the Federalists that Jay would be able to secure much from Britain. "The President has sent Mr. Jay to try if he can find any way to reconcile our honour with Peace. I have no great Faith in very brilliant Success: but hope he may have enough to keep us out of war," John Adams wrote Jefferson.[118] Evidently Washington did not expect much more.[119]

Although Jay's appointment succeeded in defeating the nonintercourse bill, it did not end the Republican attempt to pass commercial reprisals against Britain designed to force Jay to negotiate from a position of strength. But the Republicans found the attempt hopeless. Representative Clark, who had proposed the original nonintercourse measure, attempted to insert an additional duty on British manufactures into the ways and means bill, but desertions among Republican ranks forced him to withdraw it.[120] Against Madison's wishes, another representative forced the yeas and nays on a discriminating duty against British tonnage. Again the Republicans were left "in a very feeble minority."[121] Two Virginia senators, in pursuance of instructions from their state's legislature, rather sheepishly introduced a motion to suspend payment of British debts until the British had fulfilled their part of the Peace Treaty. "When the question was put, forteen [sic] voted against it, two only, the Virginia delegates, for it, and all the rest, but one, ran out of the room to avoid voting at all, and that one excused himself," gloated John Adams.[122] With sentiment clearly against risking war with commercial reprisals, the embargo was lifted by general agreement,[123] although the president was given the power to renew the embargo if he found such an action necessary.

In the middle of May, news reached the capitol that Lieutenant Governor Simcoe of Canada had built a new fort on the rapids of Miamis River, well into acknowledged American territory. Had this news arrived before Jay's appointment, Congress probably would have passed the Republican program. As it was, the news did little good for the Republican cause. A new nonintercourse measure failed in the House by a resounding vote of 46 to 24.[124]

The Federalists also sought to make use of the news of Simcoe's aggression. They tried to inject new life into the proposal to raise additional regular troops, a measure that had passed the House Committee of the Whole during the war crisis. Yet despite Federalist attempts to save the bill by striking out the call for 25,000 troops and leaving the number to be raised blank, it failed in the House by a vote of 50 to 30.[125] The Senate revived the plan over the broken Republican party in that house and voted to authorize the raising of 10,000 troops, but the measure was strangled in the House.[126] The Federalists did succeed in splitting the Republicans with a proposal to build a few gunboats to protect America's coasts, Madison telling the House he was uncertain on the question. With Madison abstaining, Congress ordered ten of them to be built.[127] The Federalists also passed some new taxation bills, including a hotly contested carriage tax, to support defense measures. Except for these measures, however, Jay's nomination had sidetracked all-important legislation concerning Anglo-American relations. These relations lay completely in the hands of John Jay in London.

All in all, the Federalists were quite satisfied with the way things had gone. "The session of Congress is about to close better than I expected," Hamilton wrote Jay. "All mischievous measures have been prevented, and several good ones have been established. . . . Men's minds have gotten over the irritation by which they were some time since possessed, and if Great Britain is disposed to justice, peace, and conciliation, the two countries may still arrive at a better understanding than has for some time subsisted between them."[128]

The Republicans, of course, were not so elated. Fisher Ames told of Senator John Taylor of Virginia shaking his head over the fact that the Federalists, though a minority, had carried and were carrying all their measures

—frigates, taxes, and negotiations.[129] Madison wrote to Jefferson, "The influence of the Executive on events, the use made of them, and the public confidence in the President are an overmatch for all the efforts Republicanism can make. The party of that sentiment in the Senate is completely wrecked; and in the House of Representatives in a much worse condition that at an earlier period of the Session."[130] Events in London, however, were conspiring to revive Republican fortunes.

9. NEGOTIATIONS

From the very beginning of the war between France and Great Britain, the British sought to keep the United States neutral. Lord Grenville instructed George Hammond to make clear to the American government that France had declared war on Britain and that, since the treaty between France and the United States was a defensive one, the United States was not bound to intervene.[1]

At first, the American response was totally unsatisfactory to Britain. In May 1793, when London received word that privateers were being fitted out in American ports for use against the British, the newspapers began weighing the possibility and consequences of a war against the United States.[2] But the Proclamation of Neutrality and the Genet affair soon had the papers announcing satisfaction with American conduct.[3] They hailed Washington as the epitome of prudence and virtue, and John Jay found the President's popularity among the English to be second only to that of the king.[4] Even Grenville, with memories of several bitter clashes over America's neutral policy, was forced to admit that the American government sought a fair neutrality.[5]

Yet the British were not totally convinced that the American government would be able to enforce a true neutrality. They realized that the people were strongly Francophile and thought the federal government too weak to hold them in check.[6] The British government distrusted Secretary of State Jefferson and his successor, Edmund Randolph. Hammond reported that "Mr. Jefferson is so blinded by his attachment to France and his hatred of Great Britain, as to leave no doubt upon my mind, that he would without hesitation commit the immediate interests of his country in a measure which might equally gratify his predilections and his resentments."[7] When Randolph succeeded Jefferson and carried on his policies, Grenville told Hammond to talk with some of his friends in America about forcing Randolph to adopt a different tone, "or at least, to place him in a Situation where his personal Sentiments may not endanger the Peace."[8]

The chance that the emotions of the people or of the secretary of state might drive the American government from its policy of strict neutrality must have been a source of some anxiety for the British government. Its military operations against the French West Indies could be materially affected by the operations of American privateers or an American embargo. In addition, Britain's position in Canada was quite weak; and should war break out, Canada was in danger of being overrun by American troops.

Nevertheless, England doggedly proceeded to fight its war without much regard for American interests or American power. The British attacked the West Indies despite America's guarantee of the French islands there. British Home Secretary Henry Dundas even ordered three regiments stationed in Nova Scotia and New Brunswick to go to the West Indies, leaving those provinces with only one regiment.[9] The whole of Britain's North American colonies now contained a total of thirty-five hundred regular troops, including those in Nova Scotia and New Brunswick.[10] The frontier posts were greatly undermanned. Detroit and Niagara had a few more than three hundred men apiece guarding the walls, but Michilimachinack had only sixty-one, Erie thirty-nine, and Ontario fifty-four.[11] The fortifications themselves were in a ruinous state.[12] Lieutenant Governor Simcoe commented that "any Post on the Continent if attacked, must be considered as necessarily sacrificed."[13]

On the Great Lakes, Britain had only nine gunboats,[14] and Simcoe wrote home that the navy there was more semblance than reality.[15] Governor Dorchester reported that the Canadas were outnumbered in population by the United States fourteen to one, and could not stand a contest with that nation without reinforcements of four or five thousand infantry and several ships.[16] Despite valiant attempts to organize a militia, he and Simcoe found they could expect little or no help from the French, who formed the predominant proportion of Canadian settlers.[17] In the light of this information, the British cabinet must have been quite disturbed to hear reports that General Anthony Wayne was marching against the Northwest Indians with more than five thousand men, and that the Indian Confederacy, which had been the major source of protection for the forts, had broken apart.[18]

The British home government, however, merely continued counseling the Canadian officials to train the militia and to do everything in their power to avoid offending the Americans. The governors were ordered to offer conciliatory language, but to do or say nothing that would endanger the continued possession of the posts. Nor were the governors to cease supporting the Indians, as long as it could be done without directly involving the British government. The home government hoped that the Indians might be reunited and made plans to gradually increase the naval force on the Great Lakes. But the British counted most on the threat of a naval attack on American commerce and coastal cities to deter the Americans from taking the posts. The British deterrent would be even further strengthened, they reasoned, when the conquest of the West Indies was completed.[19]

If the British had little regard for American interests or power on the frontier, they regarded them even less in matters of neutral rights. The

United States wished the belligerents to be guided by the rule of "free ships, free goods" in their treatment of neutral shipping. This principle stated that any merchandise aboard a neutral ship was protected from capture by the belligerents, even if that merchandise was owned by citizens of one of the belligerent nations. Such a principle would allow American ships to carry either French or British merchandise without fear of molestation and would give them a competitive advantage over belligerent shipping which was subject to capture. The French also favored such a procedure, for British naval supremacy prevented the French merchant fleet from adequately supplying its war effort in the colonies or at home. American ships, protected by the principle of "free ships, free goods," could carry on this trade.

The British, however, made known early in the war their determination to ignore this principle. Grenville wrote Hammond, "It is indeed necessary to state on this occasion, that the Principle of Free Ships making Free Goods is one which has never been recognized by this Country, and that undoubtedly will not be allowed in the present case." He pointed out that observance of this rule would afford "to the French those means of Subsistance, and of carrying on the war, which, from the nature of their present situation, and of the Force employed against them, they must otherwise be unable to procure."[20]

The British instead followed the older principle of the *consolato del mare*, which allowed the capture of enemy property aboard neutral ships but protected neutral property aboard enemy ships. Thus, French property would be subject to capture anywhere it might be found, and the French war effort could not be supplied by shipping French property aboard neutral American vessels.

It soon became obvious that the Americans were not willing to do much more than protest the failure of Britain to abide by the principle of "free ships, free goods." Hammond discussed the problem with Hamilton and discovered that the secretary of the treasury thought the British government justified in refusing to adhere to the principle.[21] In addition, Hammond deduced from Jefferson's "moderate and lukewarm" reaction to the news of British intentions that any contrary propositions offered by the Americans "are not meant to be seriously enforced."[22]

The definition and treatment of contraband threatened relations between England and the United States far more seriously than the dispute over "free ships, free goods." Great Britain, determined to make full use of its naval supremacy, regarded as contraband all things "of such a Nature as to enable the Enemies of this Country to carry on the War against Us."[23] Under this definition, British cruisers would be able to stop American ships and seize not only all French property and all American owned war material bound for France, but American-owned foodstuffs and other items as well. Although at first Britain did not specify just what was to be regarded as contraband, British privateers adopted a most liberal interpretation. The government encouraged this by issuing letters of marque that were much more expansive than those of the past. Formerly, privateers had received all profits from the prizes they took, but had been forced to pay the damages for any ship they captured which the admiralty courts judged illegal prize. In the war against the French revolutionaries, however, privateers received only half the value of the prize while the Admiralty paid the damages if the prize was judged illegal. Any inhibitions that might have tempered the conduct of the privateers toward neutral commerce were thus removed.[24]

On June 8, 1793, the British made official their policy of treating foodstuffs as contraband. The government issued an order-in-council instructing British armed vessels to send into British ports all ships carrying grain, flour, or meal to the ports of France or to ports occupied by the French army. These provisions were to be purchased on behalf of the British government.[25] Even Hamilton reacted violently to this announcement of British policy. He told Hammond that it was harsh and unprecedented, and that since neutral Denmark and Sweden were exempt from its operation by virtue of previous treaties with England, it seemed to be directed particularly against the United States.[26]

Yet even before news of America's reaction to the order had reached Britain, the British government had gone far beyond the principles enunciated on June 8. On November 6, the British government issued the order-in-council which directed British vessels to bring in for adjudication all neutral ships bound to or from the French colonies. It was this order, issued secretly, that resulted in the capture of over two hundred and fifty American ships and brought the United States and England to the brink of war.[27]

The British government had taken this drastic step for several reasons. When the war began, the French had thrown open their West Indies islands to American ships. The British cabinet was informed by its officials in the West Indies that the purpose of this policy was to make neutral Americans the carriers for the islands, because the French had neither ships nor men to perform this task. Since Americans would purchase goods in the West Indies and then sell them in France, the goods were American property while on the sea, and neutral goods were immune to capture according to the *consolato del mare*.[28] The British, however, suspected that much of this produce actually belonged to the French, and that supposed American purchases were frauds designed to protect French goods with the neutral

American flag. They had warned early in the war that they would not tolerate such a practice. One ministerial paper accused the Americans of indulging in "barefaced equivocation," expressing the hope that such conduct would not be tamely suffered by Great Britain and commenting that "the insidious character of the Americans is not now to be learnt; it has long been known."[29]

Much of this trade was already being interrupted by the British under the Rule of the War of 1756. The British claimed that by this rule, international law forbade neutrals to engage in any sort of trade with a belligerent which had not been open to them in time of peace. The British did not explain how this recently devised rule had become international law when the principle of "free ships, free goods," which had every bit as much claim to being international law as the Rule of 1756, had not.

In late 1793, the British cabinet heard that American trade with the French West Indies was about to increase greatly in both scope and importance. The revolt of the Negro slaves on the French island of Santo Domingo had forced many landowners to export great quantities of their produce in hopes of saving it from destruction. The Americans were beginning to buy up these vast stores in order to ship them to France. The British evidently felt that the emergency justified the harshest of steps. Their order of November 6 directed the capture even of those American ships engaged in that portion of the West Indies trade which had been open to them before the war, thus transcending the Rule of 1756.[30]

The mere detention of the ships did not mean that the British courts of Admiralty to which the captured ships were brought for adjudication would necessarily condemn them. The British later claimed that the order of November 6 did not authorize the condemnation of ships and cargoes that were trading within the Rule of 1756. Technically, they were correct. But their Admiralty courts in the West Indies were notorious for their loose interpretation of the rules governing condemnation; and under the order of November 6, they outstripped even their previous reputation.

In late December, when Thomas Pinckney, American minister to Great Britain, was finally told of the new order, he emotionally informed the British Foreign Office that the measure would be bitterly resented by America.[31] The cabinet did not need Pinckney to tell them this, for it certainly had known the probable reaction of America to the order and had issued it anyway. Perhaps the order had been intended to be only a temporary measure, designed to surprise and capture the produce suddenly exported as a result of the slave revolt, and then to be revoked quickly in hopes that American indignation could be checked short of hostilities.

Grenville told Hammond later that the order had been intended as a temporary measure from the first,[32] and the manner of the order's revocation tends
to bear this out.

On January 6, 1794, Hawkesbury's Committee on Trade, with only
Hawkesbury and one other member present, read an address by a committee of British merchants trading with America. This address informed
the government that the order of November 6 might lead to a rupture between the United States and England. The Committee also heard from a
Frenchman representing the islands of Martinique and Guadaloupe that
by law Americans had been permitted before the war to export from the
French West Indies syrup and rum and to import certain enumerated items,
mostly provisions, in ships of more than sixty tons. They also heard that
the governors of the French islands had opened the islands by proclamation
to a great deal more American trade than that provided for by law, and that
the Americans had been in possession of most of the trade of those islands.

Upon hearing this, the Committee on Trade recommended that the
order of November 6 be revoked and that another be issued. This new order
would detain ships with produce from the West Indies only when they were
bound for France. Of course, all produce belonging to the French, wherever
bound, would still be subject to confiscation. The committee further recommended that neutral ships and goods bound for the West Indies should only
be detained if they attempted to enter a blockaded port or if they carried
naval or military stores.[33] Their recommendations were accepted, the order
of November 6 was revoked, and a new order embodying the proposals of
the committee was issued on January 8. Thus Britain returned essentially to
the policies that had been followed prior to November 6. The whole procedure smacked of preplanning, for the cabinet could not have been ignorant of the facts presented to Hawkesbury's committee when it issued
the November order, and news of the American reaction had not reached
Great Britain to induce a retraction from fear that America's indignation
had exceeded its expectation.

As soon as the order of January 8 had been issued, Grenville hastened
to head off the anticipated American reaction to Britain's former policy.
He sent Hammond a copy of the order of November 6, evidently the first
one the minister to the United States received, along with a copy of the
order of January 8. "It is possible that, with respect to the former of these
orders, a considerable degree of dissatisfaction may have arisen in America," he commented with magnificent understatement. "If anything is stated
to you on the subject, you will confine yourself to observing, that this order
no longer subsists," he directed. Grenville also told Hammond to justify the

measure by pointing to the unusual quantity of French goods bound for France which had accrued on account of the slave revolt, and to say that in this situation, none of the principles by which ordinary intercourse was regulated could apply. He pointed out that the ships were brought in for adjudication and were not necessarily thereby condemned. He also emphasized that by the order of January 8, trade in flour and sugar between America and the French West Indies was exempted from capture even though such trade had not been open before the war. Finally, Grenville explained that the truce negotiated by Britain between Portugal and Algiers had not been for the purpose of harming American commerce.[34]

The British government then sat back to await developments in the United States. Perhaps they counted on Hamilton and Washington to keep American passions in check, as one prominent American traveling in England suspected.[35] They also hoped for a victory of the Indian Confederacy over General Wayne which would dampen American belligerence.[36] Above all they counted on Britain's naval supremacy to keep the United States from acting rashly.

Vagaries of transportation deprived the British government of official dispatches describing the growing war cloud in the United States until June 10, 1794. Only then did February dispatches from Canada and the United States begin to arrive. In fact, the government did not receive official notice of Jay's mission until two days after the emissary had landed in England. But the British had had ample warning of the contents of those dispatches much earlier from private sources, for news of the war cloud began to be reported in the London newspapers in late April. It was soon obvious that Anglo-American relations were in a state of crisis. These reports of the war cloud might have stirred such alarm among the people that the British government would have been inclined to make more concessions to the American negotiator than they ultimately did; but the sequence in which the news from America arrived and the manner in which it was presented seem to have minimized the threat of war and its impact on Great Britain.

The first news of the war cloud seems to have reached London around April 26, 1794. The opposition newspaper, the *Morning Chronicle*, reported America to be extremely angry over the capture of between two and three hundred American ships taken *"upon principles now abandoned by our Ministers."*[37] Three days later the same paper claimed that the outbreak of hostilities was considered certain and was seconded in its report by another opposition paper, the *World*. Both papers were forced to add however, that the American Congress had defeated a proposed embargo by two votes.[38] Ministerial papers immediately countered by reminding their readers that Congress had been acting under the false supposition that the November 6 order was still in effect, and that even then the embargo had failed. They added that news of the revocation of that order had reached America, "and a perfect reconciliation has ensued."[39] The ministerial papers repeated these assertions periodically through the first two weeks of May, while reporting without alarm the passage of the American naval armament bill. One paper even asserted that Hammond had offered reasonable compensation for the capture of American ships, and that four respectable American merchant congressmen were on their way to England to settle accounts.[40]

On May 20, alarm must have been stirred again when the *World* printed a long report on Sedgwick's proposition for an army and commented that the House of Representatives had postponed Madison's resolutions because they were too weak.[41] This alarm was doubtless heightened the following day when it printed the news that Congress had established an embargo.[42] But the ministerial papers moved once again to squelch any apprehensions. The editors of these papers evidently believed that news of the passage of the embargo was a correction of the earlier report that an embargo had been defeated, rather than a report of a later and entirely separate action. Therefore, they assumed that the measure had been passed at an earlier time than was actually the case, and they expressed confidence that it would be repealed when Congress learned that the order of November 6 was no longer in effect.[43]

Although the ministerial papers may have been successful once more in squelching alarm, the opposition papers doubtless revived it on May 24. The *World* reported that the embargo had been produced not only by the order of November 6, but also by the Algerian truce, and above all by Lord Dorchester's speech, an account of which had just reached London.[44] On May 26, Lord Shelburne read an account of Dorchester's speech to the House of Lords, and accompanied it by a stinging attack on the government's policy.[45] All of this might have stirred new fears of war between the United States and Britain. But the same day that Shelburne delivered his speech, and the day before it was reported in the papers, the *Morning Chronicle* wrote that the American government was sending Thomas Jefferson to negotiate its differences with England.[46] This news must have allayed any fears of an immediate outbreak of hostilities. The *Oracle and Public Advertiser* grew so enthused that it claimed Jefferson was already in England and had been present at the House of Lords during Shelburne's speech on American affairs.[47]

While the report of Jefferson's presence in England was quickly discredited, the British continued to believe that Jefferson was on his way until June 10, when, at long last, the official dispatches from Britain's officials in the United States and Canada arrived.[48] Now the people read that the House of Representatives had passed a nonintercourse bill and was considering bills to raise an army of 18,000 men and to suspend British debts.[49] They also read that John Jay rather than Jefferson was to be the American negotiator.[50] The following day they heard that Jay had actually landed; and the day after that, June 13, they were told in an amazing mixture of fact and falsehood that the nonintercourse bill had been defeated by the tie-breaking vote of Washington himself and that all had been left to Jay's negotiations.[51] Thus through misinformation, rumor, design, and the fortuitous sequence of the arrival of various bits of news from America, the impact on the British people of the war threat seems to have been blunted. John Jay's negotiating position was not to be enhanced by the alarm such news might have stirred among many elements of the British nation had it arrived differently.

Even so, the British ministers must have been disturbed about the extent of the war cloud blowing up across the Atlantic. If they had counted on Hamilton to keep the passions of the American people in check, they must have been chagrined to read in a dispatch from Hammond that Hamilton was almost as indignant about British policy as the people whose passions he was supposed to dampen. He was demanding compensation for the damages of the British captures under the order of November 6 as a condition for continued peace, and talking of raising a strong party in Britain to favor the American cause.[52] In addition the British ministers received news that Simcoe had built his fort on the Miamis in acknowledged American territory.[53] This must have convinced them that war between Britain and America was indeed near, and that certain concessions would have to be made if Britain wished to keep the peace between herself and her former colonies. Now the ministers had to decide how much they were willing to give up to insure that peace.

Peace was worth a great deal to Britain at that moment. The war on the continent was going badly, and Spain seemed on the verge of leaving England's coalition. America's embargo emphasized the importance of American trade to the well-being of the British colonies in the West Indies. Canadian dispatches forced the cabinet to conclude that "The broken condition of the Indian Confederacy . . . will certainly relieve General Wayne from any material apprehensions on their account."[54] Finally, the British cabinet was hearing disturbing reports of the rise of an Armed Neutrality, promoted by France, and to be composed of Sweden, Denmark, and perhaps the United States.[55] These circumstances have led the most authoritative student of the Jay Treaty to conclude that "the diplomatic situation, as it would have been viewed by a shrewd diplomatist who knew all the cards, all the players, all the stakes in the great international game, would have been pronounced favorable for the United States."[56]

Yet the situation was not all that favorable. The disintegration of the coalition, which threatened to disrupt land operations on the Continent, might only increase British determination to maintain supremacy on the sea against all American claims of broad neutral rights. As much as the British might desire peace with the United States, they would feel they could not give in to America's demands unless they wished to give up the war entirely.

The embargo did give some cause for the British home government to worry. Hammond admitted that it was an event which "may . . . essentially affect the islands."[57] On April 22, the British government heard from Lieutenant Governor Bruce of Dominica that his colony was short of flour, and his letter was dated even before the embargo had taken effect.[58] Phineas Bond, the British consul in Philadelphia, apprehended some shortages on St. Christopher's, St. Kitt's, and Antigua and perhaps in the British garrisons conducting operations on Santo Domingo, remarking, however, that it was hoped "the operation of this embargo may not be generally inconvenient."[59]

As it happened, reports of actual shortages on the islands caused by the embargo were few and caused little consternation in the government. The official correspondence from all the islands except Jamaica either failed to mention the embargo or spoke lightly of its effects.[60] Fears for the troops on Santo Domingo must have been allayed when Sir Charles Grey, the commander of the British Forces in the West Indies, raised no complaints about the embargo or a shortage of provisions.[61] In late August a letter from Stephen Fuller was laid before Dundas in which Dundas was informed that as of the middle of June there was such a shortage of flour on Jamaica that bread was being baked in loaves as small as five ounces, two of which had been sent to England as a curiosity.[62] But evidently this letter made little impression on Dundas or the rest of the government. John King, who had given the letter to Dundas, wrote Fuller that the embargo had been lifted since these reports of mid-June, and that in any case, the correspondence of the lieutenant governor of Jamaica had not mentioned any scarcity there, even though his last letter had been dated June 28.[63]

Two weeks later the British ministers did indeed receive confirmation from the lieutenant governor of Jamaica of a severe shortage of flour in his colony, and they also heard of some shortages in Grenada.[64] But these seem to have been the only authoritative reports of real distress caused by the embargo received by the British government during the Jay negotiations, and they came long after the embargo had been lifted, thereby dulling their impact considerably. Contributing even further to the dulling of this impact was a dispatch from Governor Hamilton of Bermuda received just before the official complaint of scarcity on Jamaica, which reported as of June 21 that American ships loaded with provisions were already swarming in the ports of Bermuda and were headed south.[65]

Thus, it is doubtful that the embargo did a great deal to advance Jay's cause. Grenville wrote Hammond during the negotiations that though the intention of the Americans in laying the embargo had been to injure Britain, "a short trial was sufficient to prove that its immediate effect was to injure themselves, and that a continuance would have been productive of very fatal consequences to their own Interests. It was therefore withdrawn before the unfriendly purposes for which it had been calculated were effected, and it was withdrawn by the very party by whom it had originally been brought forward."[66] Grenville realized that the West Indies needed American provisions, and he was therefore willing to make some concessions to the United States in that area. But he was confident that the United States would suffer more than Britain by attempting to deprive the West Indies of provisions, and so his concessions were minimal.

The situation on the Canadian frontier was doubtless more distressing to the British. With the Indian Confederacy broken, the British realized Canada's situation would be quite desperate should the United States attempt an invasion in force. Here was the place the British would be willing to concede the most to preserve peace between the Americans and themselves. But even here the British government did not feel it necessary to abandon its claims entirely. A stinging rebuke was sent Dorchester for his speech to the Indians, and his order to occupy the Miamis post was disapproved.[67] But no specific order was given to abandon the Miamis fort, and it was not returned to America until 1796, when the rest of the posts were surrendered.

In fact, the British were somewhat encouraged during the negotiations by reports that the Indians were reuniting. Portland, who replaced Dundas as home secretary in 1794, wrote Dorchester of his satisfaction "at the general Reunion of the Indians, particularly as it may lead in its consequences, to their obtaining and perhaps thro' our mediation, such a Boundary as may render them of greatest utility to the Canadas."[68] The British realized that Canada would be difficult to conquer in its entirety if the Northwest

Indians contributed energetically to its defense. They knew that Quebec was a formidable fortress; they were confident that they could exact more from America on the sea than America could gain in an invasion of Canada.[69] Thus, even in the area of its greatest strength, the United States was not in a position to coerce all it wanted from Great Britain.

The revival of the Armed Neutrality was another source of worry for Grenville and the rest of the British cabinet. Its avowed purposes were to keep warships of distant belligerent nations out of the Baltic and to protect neutral shipping in all parts of the world. Grenville told Hammond that the matter was too important to admit of delay and instructed him to "exert yourself to the utmost, to prevent the American Government from acceding to the Measure now proposed to Them."[70] The vehemence with which Grenville addressed Hammond shows that Grenville attached some importance to the project, and at least two London newspapers noted that on the day that news of the intention of Denmark and Sweden to conclude an Armed Neutrality reached London, stocks fell 1 percent.[71]

Still, Grenville realized that Sweden and Denmark were not capable of carrying on a naval war against Great Britain, Holland, Spain, and Russia, and that they could exert little influence on the Baltic without the aid of Prussia and Russia, who were fighting on the British side. Grenville pointed out to Hammond that Sweden and Denmark were hardly capable of raising the agreed on number of eight ships apiece to enforce the armed neutrality, let alone aiding distant America.[72]

Most important of all, Grenville and the British cabinet were well aware of the importance of British trade to the structure of American finance and the stability of America's government. British representatives in the United States had written often of this fact. Grenville thought that war between the United States and Britain would be inconvenient for England, but fatal to America. Throughout the negotiations Grenville's tone was that of one negotiating from strength. He was not under such pressure from the people or Parliament as might have induced him to soften his position materially, perhaps because the impact of news of the war cloud had been dulled by the manner of the arrival of that news. Although it is true that Britain wanted to maintain peace with the United States and was willing to make some concessions toward that end, it is hard to see how the diplomatic situation could have been pronounced favorable for the United States, if by that it is meant that John Jay was in a position to demand from Britain most or all of what his government sought with regard to the frontier, trade, and neutral rights.

Certainly Jay did not believe that the United States was in a position to demand all it wanted from Great Britain. It is quite evident that Jay was on the defensive throughout the negotiations. Anxious for a quick settlement, he was determined to avoid aggressive tactics that might result in a breakdown of the negotiations. He wrote Hamilton toward the end of September, "If I should be able to conclude the business on admissible terms, I shall do it and risk consequences, rather than by the delay of waiting for and governing myself by opinions and instructions, hazard a change in the disposition of this court."[73]

Jay was convinced that diplomacy was dependent on grasping opportunities as soon as they appeared and taking advantage of temporary circumstances. He believed the British government to be favorable toward a settlement with the United States. But he was fearful that untoward actions by American citizens or members of their government would disturb this favorable atmosphere before a treaty could be signed. He railed against the effusively pro-French speeches of James Monroe, the minister to France; he protested Randolph's highly sympathetic letters to the French government; he remonstrated against the anti-British resolutions passed by the legislatures of Kentucky and North Carolina.[74] He thought that threats from him or from the United States would prick Britain's pride and make it more difficult to secure an agreement.

Meanwhile, Jay sought to cultivate the good will of the British cabinet, especially that of Lord Grenville. He attended many dinner parties given by members of the government, telling Hamilton, "I think it best that they should remain unmentioned for the present, and they make no part of my communications to Mr. Randolph or others. This is not the season for such communications; they may be misinterpreted, though not by you."[75] His communications with Grenville were marked throughout by restraint, friendliness, and deference. The most critical portions of the treaty, without which there could have been no agreement, he furthered with the utmost delicacy. He does not seem to have uttered a harsh word or wielded a threat throughout the entire negotiation. He wrote Hamilton, "I will endeavor to accommodate rather than dispute; and if this plan should fail, decent and firm representations must conclude the business of my mission."[76] He obviously thought that unless the agreement were concluded in an aura of good will, with both sides intent on carrying out their pledges, then the most liberal of treaty terms coerced from Britain would be worthless.

This did not mean that Jay was unaware of the need for power to reinforce his negotiation. He favored the acceleration of the war preparations that took place during his mission.[77] He also noted that Britain's position in the negotiation was weakened by the fact that a war with the United

States would have been unpopular in England unless the United States provoked it.[78] But he thought that the British government did not need reminding from him of these factors or of the general disadvantages to Britain of adding another to the list of her enemies in those difficult moments of her war with France. He was a decided advocate of Theodore Roosevelt's later dictum concerning soft words and big sticks, commenting often to the effect that "No strong declarations should be made unless there be ability and disposition to follow them with strong measures."[79] He was not ready to make these strong declarations until it was certain that conciliatory measures had failed. He believed with the other Federalists that the United States would have to be unified to stand against Great Britain, and that this unity would not be forthcoming unless it was demonstrated conclusively that war had been forced on the United States.[80]

It is difficult to tell to what degree the shortcomings of the Jay Treaty were attributable to Jay's pro-British bias or to the flattery and good treatment of him by Grenville and the rest of the British government. There is no doubt that Jay favored the British over the French revolutionaries. Beckwith as early as 1790 had commented that in a conversation with Jay the American chief justice had "marked clearly to me, a preference in favour of an English interest, and that he wished to show it."[81] Yet during the negotiations, he encouraged preparations for war, inveighed in letters to Washington against political connections with any country, and told Hamilton that the United States should not consent to a delusive settlement with Britain in order to avoid war.[82] Despite some pro-British bias, Jay probably expressed most accurately his attitudes toward the belligerents when he commented, a year after the negotiations: "As to the issue of the war, I am far from desiring that either France, Britain, or Germany, or any other power should acquire a decided preponderance in Europe. In my opinion, it would conduce more to the welfare and peace of those nations, and also of the United States, that they should remain in capacity to limit and repress the ambition of each other."[83]

The British knew of Jay's generally friendly attitude toward them and did their best to cultivate that feeling and turn it to their benefit. Jay's secret report to Congress in 1786, the contents of which he had revealed to a British consul, had justified Britain's holding the posts until the United States observed its part of the Peace Treaty. It also had been less vehement in defending the American position regarding the abduction of Negro slaves after the Revolution than might have been expected.[84] In addition, Grenville had received by way of Lord Auckland a letter from the former British lieutenant governor of New York who professed to know Jay well and who commented that despite great talents, a cool head, and good judgment, Jay could be attached by deference and good treatment.[85] Thus Jay's conciliatory and deferential approach was reciprocated. Jay and Grenville, both rather stiff, humorless, and very conscious of their own integrity, found much to admire in each other's character. As a consequence, the whole negotiation was marked by the most cordial of atmospheres.

Yet Jay was well aware that a satisfactory settlement was not necessarily the outcome of cordiality between negotiators. "So far as personal attentions to the envoy may be regarded as symptoms of good-will to his country, the prospect is favorable," he wrote Washington. "These symptoms, however, are never decisive; they justify expectation, but not reliance."[86] Thus, he was quite able to separate friendly attitudes on the part of Grenville from the concrete points to be settled. One who reads Jay's correspondence cannot avoid the feeling that he was a man of great integrity and, though slightly vain, the last one to allow personal feelings to come between himself and his duty. It is difficult to believe that he would accept terms less desirable that he thought possible to obtain. Whatever Jay failed to secure in his treaty that was not due to America's relative weakness was more likely the result of his desire for peace and his determination to avoid risking a settlement by asperity or threats.

Was there, in fact, any more that Jay could have secured from Grenville by pressing his case more vigorously? This is an extremely difficult question to answer. The written records of the negotiations give only a few hints of what actually went on between the negotiators. Most of the contacts between Jay and Grenville were in private; and by mutual agreement, no records of the conversations were kept. Even their personal secretaries were denied access to these conversations, Jay's secretary commenting, "Sir James Bland Burgess and myself, had a real holiday for a month."[87] Yet from the instructions to Jay, the various projects exchanged by the negotiators, and some of their correspondence, it is possible to obtain at least a few hints as to the relative success of each side in the negotiations.

Jay did succeed in several of the most important of his assigned tasks. He did secure the surrender of the frontier posts; he succeeded in having the matter of spoliations under the order of November 6 assigned to a mixed commission for arbitration; he achieved the right for American vessels of less than seventy tons burden to trade with the British West Indies for a period of two years, and the right for American ships of all sizes to trade with her East Indies. The surrender of the posts and compensation for spoliations under the order of November 6 satisfied at least the minimum demands of America and, if nothing else, postponed war between the two countries until 1812. But these concessions were dearly bought, and the Jay Treaty was to be roundly castigated despite its success in keeping the peace.

When the treaty terms became known, many Americans objected that the posts were not to be evacuated until June 1796. They also objected to the lack of reciprocity in an agreement to allow inland trade across the Canadian border. This permitted the British to trade throughout the United States, but forbade Americans to trade in that part of Canada within the limits of the Hudson's Bay Company. A provision referring the British debts to a mixed commission came in for several criticisms. It did not deny the commission the right to award interest accumulated on the debts during the period of the Revolutionary War, and it did not require that British creditors first exhaust the judicial resources open to them in the United States before referring them to the commission. The latter criticism seemed especially just, since Americans having claims against British spoliations had to exhaust judicial resources in England before going to the spoliations commission. Many criticized Article IX, which permitted British subjects owning land in America to hold it or pass it on to their heirs under the same laws as American citizens, with reciprocal rights for Americans in England's dominions. This particularly stirred fears in North Carolina, where the Grenville family had claims to vast tracts of land.

Many were extremely angry at a provision which prohibited the sequestration of debts, and one which forbade America to raise her tonnage duties on British vessels for twelve years, yet permitted Britain to raise her alien duties on American vessels to equal charges on British ships in American ports. By this provision the Republicans were divested of their treasured commercial weapons. Even good Federalists like Hamilton believed that at least the 10 percent differential on British and American tonnage should have been left intact, for it was notorious that the lighthouse and Trinity fees charged American ships in British ports exceeded the tonnage duties charged British ships in American ports.[88]

In addition, even those who favored the treaty opposed Article XII, which permitted American ships of 70 tons or less to trade with the West Indies. The concession was vitiated by a provision that the United States was to prohibit the exportation from her territory of molasses, sugar, coffee, cocoa, and cotton, whether the produce of the British West Indies or not. This provision meant the end of the profitable trade that brought these products from the French West Indies to America and then reexported them to France and the rest of Europe. It also meant that the export trade in cotton, which was just beginning to be significant in the economies of Georgia and

South Carolina, would be nipped in the bud. The South also complained that the treaty failed to provide compensation for the Negroes carried off by the British following the Revolutionary War.

Most heavily criticized were the concessions the treaty made to Britain's view of neutral rights. The treaty did not explicitly adandon the principle of "free ships, free goods"; in fact it provided for future discussions of it. But tacitly it accepted Britain's right to confiscate enemy property aboard American ships by providing for the way in which ships detained on this account should be treated. In the same manner, the treaty did not explicitly acknowledge provisions as contraband of war, but provided that in cases where they were seized as contraband, they should be purchased rather than confiscated. This seemed to the French and their friends in the United States an outright betrayal of the Franco-American alliance, which specifically recognized the principle, "free ships, free goods," and exempted foodstuffs from the contraband list. It seemed to make a mockery of the provision in Jay's treaty that nothing in the treaty should operate contrary to treaties already binding on the signatory nations. Finally, the treaty failed to prohibit the impressment of American seamen.

To what degree was Jay responsible for these flaws in his treaty? Jay claimed that he had pressed for an earlier date of evacuation of the posts, but could not obtain it.[89] The provisions for treatment of the British debt seem as liberal as Jay could have obtained. The British were going as far as they could in agreeing to leave the issue of the interest accrued during the period of the war to the commission. In fact, Grenville was going against the wishes of a powerful group of British merchants in referring the question to an arbitral commission at all. These merchants pressed him for a large lump sum payment, the amount of which Grenville told them was in excess of "what could on any reasonable supposition have been recovered from Individuals under the Treaty of 1783 even if that Treaty had been exactly fulfilled by the United States in all its parts and without the smallest delay."[90]

Jay pressed Grenville to require the exhaustion of America's judicial remedies before permitting appeals to the commission, and Grenville had evidently been willing to acquiesce in this arrangement. But he seems to have been forced to compromise with the British merchants and, in return for their support of the arbitral commission, to allow immediate appeals to it.[91] Jay tried to secure the same rights for Americans claiming damages under the order of November 6, but wrote that this plan, along with many others devised to speed adjudication of these spoliations, was "perplexed with difficulties, which frustrated it."[92]

The provision that allowed Britons owning lands in America to deal with them in the same way as native Americans cannot be blamed on Jay or on his Federalist cohorts. He was instructed to accede to the abolition of alienism regarding land by Secretary of State Randolph.[93]

Rather than protesting the prohibition of the sequestration of debts, Jay seems to have welcomed it. He wrote Randolph that it would be "useful," since it would encourage British investment in American funds.[94] As for the elimination of America's discriminatory tonnage duties and the prohibition on raising those duties for twelve years, Jay claimed that this was part of the quid pro quo for the opening of the British West Indies to American navigation.[95] He seems to have overestimated the magnitude of Britain's concessions, regarding it as possibly the beginning of the end of Britain's monopolistic navigation policy.[96] Thus, he was willing to prohibit the exportation of tropical products from the United States and to level tonnage duties between the countries to secure it. Doubtless he was not overly disturbed by the fact that this agreement eliminated the commercial weapons of Republican foreign policy and forced a resort to the Federalist approach.

Although few Americans ultimately believed that the British concession to American navigation in the West Indies was important enough to have sacrificed all that Jay did for it, so far as the British government was concerned it was a concession of major importance. Lord Hawkesbury fought it bitterly. As soon as he heard that Grenville proposed to consider opening Britain's islands to American ships of limited tonnage, his office exploded into activity. He rushed copies of William Loughton Smith's speeches on Anglo-American commerce into print, to prove "out of their own mouth" how favorable Great Britain's regulations had been to American commerce.[97] He sent Smith's speeches along with some of Lord Sheffield's writings to the cabinet ministers, and he and his assistants began writing for support from other experts on Britain's commerce.[98] He personally drafted a memorandum for the ministers which asserted that opening the West Indies even to ships of limited tonnage would make the islands dependent on the United States, infect them with republican principles, double the amount of American shipping on those seas, and allow the United States to challenge British naval supremacy there. This would in turn encourage the United States to press for complete freedom of trade to those islands.[99] When Hawkesbury saw that the cabinet was determined to open the West Indies, he asked to be excused from any further meetings on the treaty.[100] With opposition such as this, the opening of the West Indies was a major success for Jay, even though he paid much too high a price for it.

Jay's secret report of 1786 had acknowledged the justice of Britain's refusal to return the slaves captured during the Revolution. But it also claimed that compensation should have been made for them. During the negotiations, however, Jay reported himself convinced by Grenville that even compensation was not justly due America, and so he dropped the subject.[101] He was active in the antislavery movement, and this may well have brought him to give up his attempts to secure compensation prematurely. As we have seen, both Gouverneur Morris and John Adams had judged from their conversations with the British government that there would be little difficulty in securing such compensation. Of course, Grenville had deduced from Hammond's accounts of his conversations with Hamilton that the Americans would make little difficulty over the issue, and thus may have been inclined to maintain a strong resistance to Jay's arguments on this subject.[102] Whether Jay could have secured compensation for the Negroes it is impossible to say, but it is quite certain that, as in the cases of debt sequestration and discriminatory tonnage duties, he did not press America's case with much vigor.

Jay's failure to secure an article prohibiting impressment is probably not to be blamed on his lack of vigor, however. His instructions did not even mention impressment, for the British had not yet begun the practice of impressing sailors from American ships on the high seas. They were taking them in British ports, where the consequences were not so disastrous. Therefore, the problem did not loom so large as it later did. Jay nevertheless pressed for an article forbidding impressment of American seamen and, at one stage of the negotiations, secured agreement to such a provision.[103] But the article prohibiting impressment was dropped for some reason, and Jay had to make do with a promise from Grenville that orders against the impressment of American citizens would be renewed.[104]

The article was not all that important anyway. It would probably have done very little to stop either the purposeful or mistaken abduction of American citizens by overambitious British officers and press gangs. Since there was little distinction in language and appearance between Briton and American, cases of mistaken identity were bound to occur. To add to the difficulties, England did not recognize the right of her subjects to renounce their British citizenship and become American citizens, whereas the United States readily granted citizenship to British subjects. Thus, there could be no agreement between England and America on certificates of citizenship to distinguish between British and American seamen and to prevent impressment of the latter. Some Americans did receive certificates, but they proved of little value. One American seaman told a London newspaper that his certificate of citizenship, signed by the secretary of state, "did not protect him in any other place than the vessel he was aboard, and that he was obliged to send for his taylor to measure him for cloaths aboard, because he was in danger of being impressed if he came on tower-Hill."[105] The only thing that would stop impressment of American sailors was prohibition of all impressment from American crews. This the British were unwilling even to consider. Already the American merchant marine was a haven for British deserters and for the ordinary British seamen that England needed so desperately to man her fleet. Henry Knox reported that in one of America's major ports, only one-fifth of the sailors aboard American ships were actually American citizens.[106] Under these circumstances, the omission of the article prohibiting impressment of American citizens was of little moment.

The omission of one other article was actually to Jay's credit. Grenville sought the cession of sufficient American territory in the Northwest to given Great Britain access to a navigable portion of the Mississippi through Canada. The Peace Treaty of 1783 had provided that the Canadian-American border would run on a line due west from the Lake of the Woods to where that line intersected the Mississippi. When Grenville found that the Mississippi did not extend so far north, he maintained that the purpose of that line had been to give Great Britain access to a navigable portion of the river. Thus Britain might make use of her right to free navigation of the Mississippi, as stipulated in the Peace Treaty, without having to pass through American territory to reach it. Jay resisted this claim, which Hamilton at an earlier time had been willing to grant. Jay pointed out that it was well known at the time the Peace Treaty was signed that the Mississippi was not navigable above the Falls of St. Anthony, and that the line drawn by that treaty would have struck the river far above those falls. He succeeded in deferring the whole matter until a joint survey of the Mississippi was made to ascertain definitely whether or not a line could be drawn from the Lake of the Woods due west to intersect with the river.[107]

On September 30, 1794, Jay submitted to Grenville a draft of a suggested treaty. Included in this draft were provisions to prevent the use of Indian allies in case of war between England and America, to prohibit treaties or political connections between either country and the Indians on the other side of their border, and to prevent the supplying of Indians engaged in war against either nation. It also provided for the demilitarization of the Great Lakes and the Canadian border and for extensive neutral rights, including "free ships, free goods." It exempted raw materials, provisions, and naval stores from the contraband list, although provisions might become contraband where there existed a "well-founded expectation of reducing the enemy by the want thereof." In such a case they were to be preempted and paid for, rather than confiscated. With the exception of the article on preemption of foodstuffs, none of these articles appeared in the final treaty.[108] Samuel Flagg Bemis has suggested that a major cause of Jay's inability to secure the concessions in his draft was Grenville's receipt of a dispatch from Hammond. In this dispatch, Hammond reported that according to Alexander Hamilton, the United States had no intention of joining the Armed Neutrality being instigated by Sweden and Denmark.[109]

From a survey of the negotiations, it is highly unlikely that Hamilton's injudicious revelation had much effect. Jay probably did not expect to get all the concessions he applied for in the draft of September 30. Certainly nothing had been said that would lead him to expect that Britain would accept the principle of "free ships, free goods" or the other rights Jay sought to secure for America's neutral shipping.[110] Hamilton's indiscretion could have had no effect here.

It is also highly unlikely that Grenville would ever have accepted the demilitarization of the Canadian border. British officials in Canada had maintained that regular troops, forts, and naval supremacy on the Great Lakes were the only means by which to provide a successful defense of Canada. Nor is it likely that Hamilton's revelation affected Britain's attitude toward the agreements concerning the Indians, judging by Britain's response to the news of General Wayne's complete victory over the Indians which arrived in London in mid-October.[111] Although the negotiations were all but completed at this time, the news must have applied some pressure to Grenville. Evidently, however, Grenville still feared the consequences of abandoning the Indians. After conclusion of the treaty, he instructed Hammond to make use of the time before evacuation of the posts to attempt to mediate a settlement between the Americans and the Indians which would involve a British guarantee of the agreement.[112] If Grenville stood firm on the frontier settlement even after the news of Wayne's victory, there was little that Jay could have done to better his terms in that quarter. Grenville knew that a failure to come to an agreement with Jay meant war whether the United States ahered to the Armed Neutrality or not, and news of Wayne's victory must certainly have added to the strength of Jay's position far more than might have been lost by Hamilton's revelation. Jay's failures were not the result of the sudden undermining of America's bargaining power.

If there were failures because of Jay's lack of vigor in pressing his objectives, they probably came in the areas of compensation for the Negroes and sequestration of debts. He also may have agreed to lower America's tonnage duties because he overestimated the value of Britain's concessions in the West Indies. But, as far as one can tell from the limited material available, Jay seems to have attained most or all of what Grenville and the British cabinet were willing to concede to America's power.

John Jay was under no illusions concerning the liberality of the treaty. John Quincy Adams, who went over the projected treaty with Jay and William Vaughan shortly before Jay signed it, commented that it was far from satisfactory to those gentlemen, but that it seemed to them preferable to a war.[113] Although it was not so liberal as Jay had hoped, he did believe it to be an honorable treaty, one that was generally "equal and fair." As he wrote Secretary of State Randolph, "I have no reason to believe that one more favorable to us is attainable."[114]

10. RATIFICATION

While the country waited impatiently for news of the outcome of Jay's negotiations, Republicans exchanged bitter words about the wrongheadedness of the Federalists. Monroe wrote Madison of his fears that Jay would combine with the British to foist a dishonorable treaty on the American people; if only the president could be appraised of "the principles and crooked policy of the man, disguised under the appearance of great sanctity and decorum."[1] Madison, too, distrusted Jay. He tried to organize the Republicans in the House in order to force Washington to report to Congress the contents of Jay's instructions, the progress of the negotiations, and the terms of the treaty if known. But his colleagues refused to go along with him.[2]

Despite this distrust of Jay, however, the Republicans began to conclude during the period of the negotiations that his treaty would be a good one. This would not be a result of Federalist sagacity, but of England's troubles. "Opinions respecting Mr. Jay's negociable qualities are varient," wrote Republican Josiah Parker. "But it is agreed by all that he may have an easy task. The unparrelelled [sic] successes of our magnanimous allies against the coalesced despots has reduced Great Britain to the Verge of Bankruptcy, Humility and disgrace. . . . Mr. Jay has nothing to do but to exhibit the *Sine qua non* of the House of Representatives the last Session to the British Minister to acquire all he has a right to ask."[3] Madison thought the same. "It is expected here that he will accomplish much if not all he aims at," he reported to Jefferson.[4] England's difficulties convinced even many Federalists that the treaty would be favorable.[5]

From this, Josiah Parker concluded that "if we do not get all we ask it must be the fault of our Negociator at the Court of London."[6] Others were inclined to agree.[7] Thus, success would be attributed to England's defeats in Europe; shortcomings would be blamed on the passivity or treachery of the Federalists. Fisher Ames decided the whole situation was a Republican plot. Before the terms of the treaty became known, the Republicans would raise the expectations of the public by maintaining first "that we have every thing granted, and nothing given in return; and secondly, that the treaty, when published, has surrendered everything."[8]

In early 1795, rumors of treaty terms began to circulate in the United States, many of them quite informed and quite unfavorable.[9] Writing to Jefferson, Madison detailed the rumors that "the bargain is much less in our favor than might be expected from the circumstances which co-operated with the justice of our demands."[10] Commenting that it was wrong to prejudge, Madison still could not restrain a suspicion that "Jay has been betrayed by his anxiety to couple us with England, and to avoid returning with his finger in his mouth. It is apparent that those most likely to be in the secret of the affair do not assume an air of triumph."[11] His comment might have referred to John Adams, who wrote to his wife, "I am very much afraid of this Treaty! but this is in confidence."[12]

While rumors flew, Congress remained in session, hoping to receive the treaty and act upon it. But the ship that carried two copies of the treaty was attacked by a French privateer and both copies were thrown overboard to avoid capture. A messenger carrying another copy of the treaty attempted to reach America before Congress adjourned. But his ship had to fight strong west winds from the moment it left England. Though the messenger plied the sailors with a small cask of rum he had brought along to improve their performance, it took the ship over three months to make the passage to America. En route, the ship was stopped and boarded by the crew of a French cruiser in search of the treaty. Then, when the ship attempted to land at the head of the Elk River, it found the river blocked and had to put in at Norfolk. The messenger hired a horse, but it foundered after a day and night trip to Richmond, and he found it impossible, despite applications to the governor himself, to secure another. So he took a stage until he could finally find another horse. With frostbitten hands and feet, he delivered his charge on the morning of March 7, 1795, nearly four months after the document had started its journey, and three days after Congress had given up and adjourned in disgust.[13] Upon receipt of the treaty Washington and Randolph decided to keep the terms a secret between themselves, and they issued a call for a special session of the Senate to begin deliberations on July 8, 1795.

The silence of Washington and Randolph was compensated for by the noise of Republican denunciations of the unknown though suspected terms of the treaty. One correspondent of the *Argus* even announced the development of a treaty machine with which, "to the wonder of mankind, a treaty for captures by sea, a treaty of commercial intercourse, a treaty for giving up the Western posts, a treaty of friendship with our dear mother country, and a treaty with every power but France can be struck off in fifteen minutes." If called on by the government, he claimed that it would give a performance "never equalled but by one."[14] Edmond Randolph wrote Adams, "If you are not a subscriber to Bache's scandalous chronicle [the *Aurora*], it may be a subject of momentary amusement to be now informed, that it is filled with discussion on the treaty; not one word of which, I believe, is known thro' a regular channel to any person here, but the President and myself."[15]

When the treaty was finally submitted to the Senate, the Federalists secured a Senate resolution to continue holding the terms secret during the deliberations.[16] This stirred the Republicans to a fury, and their attacks on the unknown terms seemed even more justified. "No doubt that the treaty will be unacceptable to the public; for if it would prove agreeable to them, it would not be concealed," stated one newspaper editor.[17] It was not only the secrecy that indicated the tenor of the treaty. "Lord Grenville boasts of it as a child of his own nurturing; as eminently favourable to the British Commerce: Mr. Pitt speaks of it as far from implying submissions," trumpeted the *Argus*.[18] If the British approved of it, it must be inimical to American interests. Attacks on the unknown terms were justified in any case, Republicans thought, for the treaty could not possibly be as beneficial to the United States as it might have been. Had debt sequestration only been passed, "it is capable of mathematical demonstration, that there would long since have been a general peace throughout Europe," wrote the *Aurora*.[19]

In the teeth of this storm, the Senate set about considering the treaty. The Federalists were themselves greatly disturbed by Article XII. This article permitted American ships of limited tonnage to trade in the British West Indies, but prohibited the exportation from America of tropical products including produce grown within the United States. Since Republican attacks were aimed particularly at this provision, the Federalists, on the advice of Hamilton and Rufus King, moved to accept the treaty but to suspend the operation of the offensive article.[20]

Five days later, the Republicans attacked in earnest. Aaron Burr moved to postpone consideration of the treaty and to renegotiate it. His motion proposed the elimination or alteration of almost every concession the treaty made to Britain.[21] But Burr's motion failed, 20 to 10.[22] If the vote held firm, it meant the Federalists had the two-thirds of the Senate necessary to advise and consent to the treaty without a vote to spare. The Republicans attempted to split the votes of the southern Federalists by moving to seek compensation for the Negroes, which failed by a more narrow margin of 15 to 12.[23] One final attempt to defeat the treaty failed and, after Article XII was suspended, the treaty itself was approved, 20 to 10. In a last gasp of protest the Republicans moved to renew discussions on compensation for the Negroes, but this was defeated by one vote, 14 to 15.[24]

Having failed to defeat the treaty in the Senate, the Republicans turned to the people. They hoped that popular disapproval would keep the president from ratifying it. The Federalists, however, sought to stall the campaign by making access to the terms of the treaty difficult. The Senate lifted its demand for secrecy, but the Federalists pushed through a ruling that no Senator would authorize or allow any copy of the treaty or of any article in it to be made. King and Hamilton both thought this ruling unwise, and King was successful in convincing Randolph and Washington that the treaty should be printed, since secrecy was doing the treaty more harm than good.[25] But they were too late. Senator Pierce Butler from South Carolina, who had recently been aboard an American revenue cutter when a British ship mistakenly fired upon it,[26] found his chance to retaliate by sending a copy of the treaty to Madison.[27] Another copy was smuggled out by Senator Mason. Consequently, on the same day that the government planned to make the treaty public, the Republican *Aurora* beat it to the punch by printing an abstract of the terms. A few days later, the *Aurora* published the entire text.[28] The Devil was loose.

Benjamin Franklin Bache, Republican editor of the *Aurora*, set off immediately for New England, distributing along the way copies of the treaty and accounts of Republican strictures of it in the Senate.[29] The outcry was immediate and violent. Evidently, few people had even one word of defense for the instrument. In Boston, a mob, believing a hapless little British vessel docked in the harbor to be one of the Bermuda privateers that had been preying upon American commerce, descended upon it and destroyed it.[30] "The flame I see is kindled in Boston and I doubt not will spread in spite of our ministerialists," reported R. R. Livingston.[31] Indeed, the flames did, and they lapped eagerly at effigies of Jay in many an American town. One of the Democratic-Republican societies decided not to take the time to burn Jay in effigy, but mused, "if the original were here—!"[32]

Taking advantage of the sentiment against Jay's treaty, Republicans in many cities organized meetings to condemn the treaty and to send petitions to the president urging him not to ratify it. Alexander Hamilton attempted to speak for the opposition in a meeting called in New York. But he was stoned from the podium, which one Federalist observed to be a prudent measure on the part of the Jacobins since by knocking out his brains they would "reduce him to an equality with themselves."[33]

Hamilton was involved in another ugly incident several days later. A chance meeting between himself, King, Edward Livingston, and several others led to a heated and personal exchange. While King and Livingston sought to separate the parties, Hamilton stepped forward and offered to fight all the Republicans there, one by one. Then, throwing up his arms, he said he would fight to whole detestable faction. A Republican arriving on the scene stepped up and told Hamilton he would fight him in half an hour

ton. "It is not the opinion of *those* who were determined (before it was
promulgated) to *support*, or *oppose* it, that I am sollicitous to obtain," he
wrote to Hamilton.[44] He believed the decision to be his alone, and that he
should resist public pressures, basing his decision only on the facts and the
good of the country.[45]

While Washington deliberated, news reached America that the British
were again seizing American vessels bound for France. "What can these
things mean?" cried the Republican *Argus*.[46] The new British order-in-
council of April 25, 1795, under which these captures were taking place,
instructed British commanders to bring in any neutral vessels bound for
French-controlled ports and carrying provisions that might be French property masquerading as neutral produce.[47] Grenville had received news from
Hammond that the final payments of the French debt had been made by the
United States, and that there had been inordinate purchases of provisions
since then.[48] He told the Danish minister to England two days before the
order was issued that the French were in desperate need of provisions, that
they were reaching France by the covering of enemy property with neutral
colors, and that the British government meant to stop them.[49]

Jonathan Trumbull, who had been Jay's secretary during the negotiations with Britain, believed that the British had other reasons for issuing
the order. He believed that the order was useless as a military measure, for
the French had begun a good harvest and in addition had received great
quantities of foreign grain. He attributed the order to a shortage of provisions in Britain itself, a shortage that did, in fact, lead to bread riots in
parts of England a few months later.[50]

The British order was in strict compliance with the doctrine of *con-
sueto del mare*. It directed the seizure only of enemy property aboard
neutral vessels. This practice, though condemned by the doctrine "free ships,
free goods," had been acquisced in by the American government since the
war had begun. The order did not condemn the grain on the grounds that
it was contraband, the practice that had raised such a storm of protest in the
United States earlier.

Nonetheless, the order was administered just as though grain were
contraband. The first lord of the Admiralty wrote to one of the British captains that "the Government did not wish them to be over nice or scrupulous
respecting the nature of the papers of those ships, as we know the greatest
deceptions are attempted to be put into practice, and the present circumstances both with respect to the enemy and to this country are such as to
justify a less degree of attention to those delicate points than at another
time."[51] The fact that the British paid for the cargoes—which they did not

wherever he pleased. Hamilton told him that he alre
his hands (a quarrel with a Commodore Nicholson)
with that he would call on him. Evidently, however, he

Most of the Federalist campaign was waged on a
Many Federalists were reluctant to send petitions to
violated their principle that the executive should deci
feelings and pressures of the people. Nonetheless, exp
they attempted to match the Republicans meeting for
petition.[36] Influential Federalists urged their friends t
the treaty and formed committees of correspondence i

Many Federalists resorted to the newspapers. '
influential of the editorialists was "Camillus," a result
tween Hamilton and King. Noah Webster as "Cur
mightily to the Federalist newspaper campaign.[38]

No Federalist attempted publicly to claim that
could be desired. Most Federalists, in fact, were kee
During the negotiations, Hamilton had expressed gr
several articles that became part of the treaty; and
Federalists, had been violently opposed to Article
inating all distinctions between British and Americ
ports and was unhappy over the extended contraband
expected, he and other Federalist publicists slid rath
the points about which they had reservations, extolli
instrument and mitigating all its shortcomings.[40] The
accurately reflect their most important conviction
because of America's comparative weakness, little
expected; in any case, the treaty was better than war

Robert R. Livingston as "Cato" led the Repu
paign. Madison preferred to make his influence felt
urging others to write in opposition to the treaty an
outline of the points to be covered.[41]

By letter, petition, and newspaper, advice po
He must have felt, as he had earlier, that "The affai
go *amiss*. There are *so many watchful guardians of*
guides, that one is at no loss for a director at every
petitions he replied that the Constitution gave t
Senate the power to make treaties. To others, he
letter book, "No answer given. The address too rude
indecent."[43]

The people's advice, however, seems to have

need to do if the provisions actually were French property, but which they were bound to do by terms of the Jay Treaty if they confiscated American provisions as contraband—is a further indication that the British were capturing every American ship laden with provisions they could get their hands on. The wording of the order of April 25 was merely a ruse, a cover for reasserting the practices of the orders of June 8, 1793, and January 8, 1794. The British sought thus to feed their own hungry people while starving the French.

The order was a very foolish move. The specifications of the instructions were kept secret by the British government,[52] so the United States was unaware that the British were not seizing foodstuffs as contraband. The only visible manifestation of the order was a resumption of the capture of American provision vessels, a practice that had ceased during the Jay-Grenville negotiations.[53] Americans assumed, with good reason, that this was a renewal of Britain's earlier practices. One of the most damaging charges being made against the treaty by the Republicans was that Jay, by agreeing that compensation should be paid for any provisions confiscated, had tacitly recognized foodstuffs to be contraband. This charge had been angrily rebutted by the proponents of the treaty. But now the new British captures seemed to prove that the British did indeed consider the treaty to have legalized this procedure.[54] Prior to the arrival of this news, Washington had evidently been inclined to ratify the treaty. His principal concern had been the proper procedure of ratifying it while suspending the operation of Article XII.[55] But the new British outrages made his decision more difficult.

In this crisis he turned to his secretary of state and long-time friend, Edmund Randolph. Randolph advised that the treaty should be ratified, but only if the new "provisions order" were removed. He also advised informing Hammond that ratification hinged entirely on the rescinding of the order-in-council.[56] Washington evidently thought the idea a good one and sent Randolph to tell Hammond of the president's sentiments. Hammond inquired if it would not be sufficient simply to remove the order until the treaty was ratified and then renew it, a singularly tactless remark. Randolph heatedly replied that the principle was the important thing. Hammond then wanted to know if the president were irrevocably determined not to ratify unless the provision order was rescinded. Randolph replied that he had not been instructed on that point. When Randolph related this conversation to Washington, the president exploded and said that Randolph might have told Hammond that he would never ratify unless the provision order were removed. He told the secretary of state to prepare a memorial on the matter to present to Hammond. In addition, Randolph was instructed to prepare the forms of ratification suspending Article XII and the instructions for the person who was to handle the affair in London.[57]

Leaving matters in this train, Washington set out for a holiday at Mount Vernon. Many Federalists were dismayed that he had left without first ratifying the treaty. If it should become known that ratification was delayed, opponents of the treaty would naturally credit their opposition with having forced the president to reconsider, and this would lead to increased ferment and a complete prostration of government, wailed Christopher Gore.[58] "If delay should terminate in refusal, we are ruined," wrote George Cabot to Oliver Wolcott. "The present system will have finished its destiny."[59]

Washington was still convinced of the correctness of his course on his arrival at Mount Vernon. He wrote Randolph on July 22 that

the conditional ratification (if the late order which we have heard of respecting provision Vessels is not in operation), may, on all fit occasions, be spoken of as my determination; unless from any thing you have heard, or met with since I left you, it should be thought more advisable to communicate further with me on the subject. My opinion respecting the treaty is the same now that it was: namely, not favorable to it, but that it is better to ratify it in the manner the Senate have advised (and with the reservation already mentioned), than to suffer matters to remain as they are, unsettled.[60]

He later received Randolph's memorial announcing to the British minister that unless the order were laid aside, the president would have to take ratification into further consideration, and he wrote back that "The memorial seems well designed, to answer the end proposed."[61]

Though Washington seems to have been convinced of the expediency of withholding ratification until repeal of the new British order-in-council, events were conspiring to change his mind. A British cruiser had captured the French ship *Jean Bart*, aboard which were several dispatches from Joseph Fauchet, the French minister to America. One of these dispatches was the infamous Dispatch No. 10, which spoke of "precious confessions" made by Secretary of State Randolph to Fauchet. The dispatch also seemed to imply that Randolph had requested money from Fauchet for nefarious purposes.

Upon receiving these dispatches, Grenville sent them to Hammond with instructions that they should be communicated to well-disposed persons in America.[62] Hammond received them while Washington was at Mount Vernon debating on his course of action with regard to the treaty and the provisions order, and the British minister wrote Grenville that he would make such use of them "as I hope will be productive of the most beneficial effects to the general interests of His Majesty's service."[63]

Hammond turned Dispatch No. 10 over to Oliver Wolcott, who had been appointed secretary of the treasury upon Hamilton's retirement. Wolcott shared his news with fellow Federalists, Secretary of War Timothy Pickering and Attorney General William Bradford. Then, without telling Randolph of their secret, the three conspirators got the secretary of state to write to Washington requesting his immediate return to the capitol.[64] Pickering also sent a private note to Washington, warning, "On the subject of the treaty I confess that I feel extreme solicitude; and for a *special reason* which can be communicated to you only in person." He asked Washington "to decide on no important political measure, in whatever form it may be presented to you."[65]

Gleefully, Wolcott wrote Hamilton that even though Randolph had so far succeeded in delaying ratification of the treaty, Hamilton should "Feel no concern . . . for I see a clue which will conduct us through every labyrinth, except that of war."[66] When Washington returned to Philadelphia on August 11, Pickering and Wolcott informed him of Randolph's supposed treachery. The following day, the president held a cabinet meeting to discuss ratification of the treaty. Despite Randolph's protests, Washington announced he would ratify, and he instructed Randolph to prepare the documents pursuant to that decision. While Washington withheld information of Fauchet's dispatch from him, Randolph was forced to deliver a memorial announcing ratification to a gloating Hammond.[67]

After Randolph had done what was required of him to give the treaty effect, Washington suddenly confronted him with Fauchet's dispatch in the presence of the rest of the cabinet. Randolph found the information in the dispatch vague and confusing, and replied that he had never made an improper communication to Fauchet, that he had never received money from him or made any overture to him for that purpose. He then indignantly resigned his office.[68]

Did Washington's belief that Randolph was corrupt or a traitor cause him to decide to ratify the treaty without first requiring withdrawal of the offensive order-in-council? Pickering said that Washington had ratified unconditionally because he was "manifestly convinced that the true interests of his country (the motive to all his actions) required the ratification."[69] Wolcott also denied that the Randolph affair had caused Washington to reverse his course, maintaining that the president had never really decided to withhold ratification.[70]

Yet the evidence seems clear that Washington had earlier decided conclusively to follow Randolph's plan. It also seems clear that loss of confidence in the veracity and loyalty of Randolph was the major cause of his reversal of that decision. Pickering and Wolcott, despite their protestations to the contrary, probably believed this to be the case. When Randolph applied to the office of the secretary of state for the letters that Washington had previously sent to him, Pickering withheld Washington's letter of July 22 that announced his decision to ratify the treaty unless the provisions order was in effect. When Randolph applied for this letter specifically, Pickering told his clerk to inform Randolph that it would be necessary first to consult Wolcott. A few days later, after applying again, Randolph received the reply that it was not necessary to his vindication, since it had nothing to do with Fauchet's letter, the criminal evidence in which was the sole cause of his resignation. Only a direct application to Washington was successful in finally prying the letter loose from Pickering and Wolcott.[71]

Pickering, in later life, related details of a conversation with Washington which also shows his belief that Washington had reversed his decision and that the Randolph affair had been the cause of it. According to Pickering, Washington had called him into his office immediately after the president had received Randolph's pamphlet defending his conduct. After regaling him with the story of his past relationship with Randolph, Washington angrily declared that Randolph had plotted with his opponents, conducted an intrigue with Fauchet in an attempt to overthrow the administration, received money from him for that purpose and solicited more, while "all this time I have had entire faith in him, and been led by that faith to pay deference to his representations to delay the ratification of the British treaty."[72] If the story is true, it shows that Washington admitted and Pickering believed that the Randolph affair had caused the president to reverse his decision; if false, it shows at least that Pickering believed such to have been the case.[73]

Yet Randolph was not the only man among Washington's advisers who supported withholding the ratification. Alexander Hamilton had advised much the same course. On August 10, 1795, Hamilton had written Oliver Wolcott that the president ought to ratify the treaty but instruct his agent in London not to exchange the ratification until the provisions order was rescinded. The United States could never give an implied sanction to the principle that provisions were contraband, he stated.[74] Since this advice closely paralleled the course of action Randolph had suggested, why should Washington reverse his position merely because Randolph seemed no longer trustworthy?

The reason may be that Hamilton's advice actually represented a retreat from an earlier position he had taken recommending withholding ratification rather than delaying the exchange of ratifications. Randolph had written Washington on July 24, 1795, while the President was still at Mount Vernon, that "the advice, given to you from New York, as to withholding of a ratification, until the order for seizing provisions was rescinded, does not appear to have been circulated among the particular friends of the gentleman, from whom the advice came."[75] This advice almost certainly had come from Hamilton.[76] Washington must have received this advice before he left for Mount Vernon, and it doubtless played a role in his decision to withhold ratification until the provisions order was rescinded. If this was the case, the plan that Hamilton communicated to Wolcott on August 10 was an abandonment in part of the ideas he had shared with Randolph. This may have shaken Washington's confidence, a confidence then completely destroyed by Fauchet's Dispatch No. 10.

It is ironic that a loss of confidence in Randolph's veracity and loyalty should have been such a great factor in Washington's decision. Randolph's pamphlet defending his conduct demonstrates quite clearly that, though he was foolish and indiscreet, he was not guilty of treason.[77] (For a full discussion of the Randolph affair, see Appendix II.)

Yet Randolph's pamphlet did him little good. Henry Lee wrote the President that "so far as I can hear it works very dully and will produce a different effect from the author's expectation."[78] A British consul informed Grenville that all men agreed Randolph's *Vindication* had served to confirm the disgrace of its author, and Sedgwick observed that "no one of the most violent of the democrats here wish to vindicate the author. He seems to be made the scape goat of the party."[79] James Madison concluded, "His greatest enemies will not easily persuade themselves that he was under a corrupt influence of France, and his best friends cant save him from the self-condemnation of his political career as explained by himself."[80]

If Randolph's pamphlet was of little service to his own reputation, it was of great service to the Republican party. A correspondent wrote to the *Aurora*, "Whatever merits Mr. Randolph's pamphlet may claim as a vindication of his conduct, it is certain, that for once at least, he has been useful to the friends of Republicanism in this country, by its publication; for it contains an inexhaustible fund fo[r] reflection and comment on the conduct of our executive administration."[81] The apparent reversal of the president in his ratification of the treaty as described in Randolph's pamphlet was the handle of a violent and bitter attack on Washington himself, by far the worst personal abuse he had endured. The *Aurora* declared that the presi-

dent had ratified the treaty "in a fit of bad humor occasioned by an enig-
matical intercepted letter."[82] One Republican confided to his diary, "Washington now defies the whole Sovereign that made him what he is—and can
unmake him again. Better his hand had been cut off when his glory was at
its height, before he blasted all his Laurels."[83]

Despite the publication of Randolph's *Vindication* and the personal
abuse of Washington, the country was growing more willing to accept the
treaty. The reaction against the treaty had begun to cool off even before
Washington ratified it. His signature gave even greater impetus to this cool-
ing process. John Jay wrote the president that by all accounts the public
mind was becoming more composed. The virulent publications of the Republicans had occasioned indignation with themselves rather than with the
conduct of Washington, he reported.[84] One New England lady observed,
"The Storm, which the business of the treaty threatened to raise, seems to
be blown over; at least appearances are less dark and alarming." But she
added significantly, "what the Demoniacks of Congress may bring forward
to excite new commotions on the subject we shall soon know."[85]

11. A HOUSE DIVIDED

The "Demoniacks of Congress" were indeed ready to excite new commotions on the subject of the Jay Treaty. Of course the House had no specific constitutional role in making treaties; but an appropriation of some $90,000 was necessary to pay the arbitral commissions set up by the treaty, and revenue measures had to originate in the lower chamber. This would give the Republicans one last chance to defeat the hated instrument of Federalist foreign policy.

But were the Republicans willing to go this far? Were they ready to defy the president and the Senate, thus bringing on a constitutional as well as an international crisis? Or did they merely seek to use the unpopular treaty as an issue around which to build a strong, unified Republican party in Congress and a broad, passionate popular following in the countryside? With the Presidential and congressional elections less than a year away and with the expectation that Washington would refuse to run again, the Republicans had a good chance to displace their rivals. A widely publicized fight against the treaty in the House could build a popular election platform for them.

Many of Madison's contemporaries thought that he and his followers meant to oppose the treaty in the House for purely partisan reasons. They believed the Republicans would fight the treaty but draw back from an outright defeat of it to avoid creating either a constitutional crisis or a new war crisis with England. Theodore Sedgwick reported that many people thought Madison did not wish for success in the Republican opposition to the treaty, but expected "to lay in a stock of party influence from discussions."[1] William Vans Murray wrote that Republican opposition "will be all talk and writing."[2] John Adams told his wife that the Republicans would lash and maul awhile and then do the needful. He supported his opinion by recounting a conversation over a dinner table with Republican Senator Aaron Burr, Speaker of the House Jonathan Dayton, and several other members of Congress. They had all agreed that the House would express some unfavorable opinions on the treaty but would finally carry it into effect.[3]

Surely party considerations were prominent in the fight. Joseph Charles has shown that in the House session that considered the treaty, only 7 percent of the members failed to vote at least two-thirds of the time with the same party. This was a dramatic increase in party regularity. In 1790, 42 percent had failed to vote two-thirds of the time with the same party; and in 1795, in the session immediately prior to the one that considered appropriations for the Jay Treaty, nearly 20 percent had failed to do so.[4] This increase in party regularity was certainly not accidental. Party organizing activity in Congress and among the general public was frantic during the Jay Treaty session.

But party development was only a by-product of the House fight over the Jay Treaty. The struggle was first and foremost a battle over foreign policy. The idea that Madison and the Republicans in the House were not determined to overthrow the treaty arose from a gross misinterpretation of Republican tactics in the congressional debates. A close examination of the House fight will demonstrate that Madison and the Republicans were dead serious in their attempt to destroy the treaty. Their conception of America's power vis-à-vis Great Britain's and their ideas on a proper foreign policy for the United States were paramount over party considerations throughout the Jay Treaty debates.

The Republicans laid the groundwork for the House fight by trying to get support for their position from various state legislatures. With Madison's approval, Virginia Republicans pushed through their state's legislature a series of proposed constitutional amendments that would make treaties subject to a majority vote in the House of Representatives, would increase public control over the Senate, and would prohibit federal judges from holding other federal appointments. Republicans did not expect the resolutions to pass the House of Representatives but did hope they would attract support in other states for the coming assault on the treaty.[5]

The Republican campaign backfired. South Carolina, Kentucky, and Georgia did pass resolutions similar to those of Virginia, but nine other states including Republican North Carolina rejected them.[6] The Federalists were elated. "That a great change has been brought in the public mind, with respect to this Treaty within the last two months, is apparent to every one," Washington wrote.[7]

When the House of Representatives reconvened in early December 1795, it expected to deal immediately with the treaty issue. But Washington announced that notice of British ratification had not yet arrived, and that he would not request appropriations for the treaty until it did.[8] Washington may or may not have designed this delay to allow the full swing of popular opinion to take effect, but his move certainly embarrassed the Republican strategists. William Branch Giles of Virginia, Madison's chief aide in the House, wrote Jefferson at Monticello that "every day of age, is a day of strength to the Treaty: not on account of the daily discovery of intrinsic merit but on account of the astonishing exertions and artifices employed to give it efficacy."[9] Federalist tactics, he admitted, were having an effect beyond all rational calculation.[10]

Yet the Republicans could think of no way to bring the treaty before the House without destroying their chances of defeating it. Giles and Madison thought they could get a majority to defeat a proposition approving the treaty, but they did not believe a majority would vote for a proposition condemning it. Thus, a great deal depended on the timing and content of the motion offered to the House. If the Republicans waited for the president to present the treaty to Congress, the Federalists would move to authorize funds to carry it into effect. In this form the Republican strategists thought they could defeat the treaty. But meanwhile public opinion would continue to rise against them. On the other hand, any attempt by the Republicans to force consideration of the treaty before the president had officially communicated it to the House would seem a censure on Washington. It would also involve a motion positively condemning the treaty. Under these circumstances, Madison and Giles feared their majority would disintegrate.[11]

The Republicans first hoped that the Federalists might be tempted to express approval of the treaty in the House's answer to Washington's opening address. But the Federalists avoided this trap.[12] The Republicans then asked Speaker of the House Jonathan Dayton, a Federalist but an opponent of the treaty, to sponsor a motion bringing it before the House. As an opponent of the treaty, he might do it; as a Federalist his motion might avoid the reaction that would result from the same action taken by a Republican. But Dayton proved elaborately noncommittal.[13] Some Republicans now began to express doubts as to the constitutionality of the House of Representatives mixing in the treaty-making province of the president and the Senate.[14] As the weeks wore on, Madison despairingly concluded that the clear majority who disapproved the treaty would dwindle under pressure.[15]

The Federalists happily agreed. The Republicans would have a majority on most questions, claimed William Vans Murray, "but this majority is composed of different materials. Ten or twelve of them will shrink from the precipice of war, when they are brought up to it."[16]

Theodore Sedgwick of Massachusetts took charge of the Federalist effort in the House to make this prophecy come true. Corpulent and self-important, he presented a striking contrast to Madison. The nature of his leadership was also quite different. Sedgwick owed his position primarily to the fact that he had the confidence of both Washington's cabinet and the Federalists in the Senate. While they devised the programs and general strategy for the party, Sedgwick operated as their House tactician.[17]

Sedgwick, well aware of the difficulties the Republicans faced in attempting to get the treaty before the House, rejoiced at rumors that Giles might attempt to force the House immediately to declare itself on the treaty: "I have no objection that the effort should be made, because I am confident it would now meat [sic] with defeat, and that the attempt will disgrace its authors."[18]

By late December, however, he was as anxious for the treaty to arrive as the Republicans. It would never find the House in a better temper, he said.[19] Yet when copies of the British ratification arrived in Philadelphia and Charleston in late January, Washington decided he must wait for the originals.[20] Sedgwick believed this to be a terrible mistake. Any further delay would work against the treaty, he thought, for the Republicans were endeavoring to impress on "weak minds" that the treaty was purposely withheld to give opportunity for the executive to fortify its position.[21] On the rumor that Giles would request Washington to lay the treaty before the House immediately, he commented, "No *decent* man will certainly assent to so *indecent* a proposition yet I confess that I should not lament its success."[22]

As January and then February elapsed, the growing antagonism in Congress toward the treaty and its delay was made apparent when the House refused to adjourn for half an hour to pay the annual compliments to Washington on his birthday. The vote showed 50 opposed to 38 in favor.[23] The preceding year only 13 had dared vote against the adjournment.[24]

The evidence of growing disaffection in the House finally seems to have determined Washington to wait no longer for the originals. He told Secretary of State Timothy Pickering that he intended to bring the treaty to the attention of the House immediately if it was agreeable to "our people." Pickering sounded Sedgwick on the subject and was told there should be no delay.[25] On February 29, Washington declared the treaty in effect, and on March 1 he laid it before Congress. But still he did not request funds to implement it.[26] As a consequence, the House referred the president's message to the Committee of the Whole for the State of the Union and proceeded with its regular business. Madison and the Republican leadership were undoubtedly stunned that the executive had not requested House action. This would have allowed the Republicans to oppose a measure favoring the treaty rather than vote for a measure disapproving it. Now they had to initiate a course of action on the treaty themselves, and they needed time to devise one that would command a majority of the antitreaty people.

But some Republicans had grown restive under the ultracautious leadership of Madison. One of the foremost of these youngbloods was freshman Representative Edward Livingston. Livingston's father, Robert R.

Livingston, had advised him to move slowly on the treaty. For the Congress "To take no notice of so disgraceful and unconstitutional an act is impossible and yet how to notice it [is] a question of much delicacy," he wrote his son. "I would advise you to form no plan till you get to Congress and then to advise with Madison and some of the most prudent members of Congress so as to act in concert."[27]

Edward Livingston abided by this advice, but found the experience very disconcerting. He bewailed the fact that the Republicans could not bring themselves to call for the treaty. "I am really placed by these political friends in a very painful situation," he wrote his father. "I am persuaded of the fatal effects of delay and of the injury our fear to meet the discussion has done to the republican interest throughout the Union—I am convinced that we once had and I believe Still have a majority who think rightly on the Subject but yet I dare not take the responsibility on myself in opposition to the opinion of older members whose opinions I respect."[28]

Edward Livingston held his peace as long as he could. Now, with the treaty before the Congress, he kicked over the traces. On the day following Washington's message to the House, Livingston suddenly rose and offered a resolution. Since it was generally understood that some important constitutional questions would be involved when the treaty came under consideration, he said, the president should be requested to lay before the House all the papers concerning that document.[29] The Republican leadership had obviously not been consulted on the move, for Madison considered Livingston's motion too abrupt. He wrote Jefferson that "The Policy of hazarding [the motion] is so questionable that he [Livingston] will probably let it sleep or withdraw it."[30] Yet while he opposed Livingston's tactics, Madison had not formulated an acceptable alternative. "Notice of direct propositions on the Treaty will probably be given tomorrow," he wrote Jefferson. "The purport and form of them create much diversity of ideas among the opponents of the Treaty. The state of the business as it now presents itself, with the uncertainty of the particular way of thinking in several quarters of the House, make it truly difficult to decide on the course most acceptable to the body of anti-treaty members."[31]

While debating his own course of action, Madison evidently made known his displeasure with the form and timing of Livingston's resolution; for on March 7, Livingston offered a modification of the motion "calculated to meet the suggestions of gentlemen to whose opinions he paid the highest respect."[32] He moved to exempt from the papers the president was requested to lay before Congress all those that might embarrass any existing negotiations.[33] Later Madison tried to soften the resolution even further by leaving

175

the choice of the papers entirely to the discretion of the president.[34] Obviously, the thing he most feared about the resolution was that it directly challenged the president. Surprisingly, Madison's amendment was defeated, 37 to 47.[35] By his hesitancy, he had lost his control of the Republican faction in the House of Representatives. The leadership had passed to more decisive and more headstrong men.

Though Madison considered Livingston's motion to have been a tactical error, evidently the Federalists thought it a clever move. Sedgwick was quite sure that the resolution would be carried because the information requested would gratify so much curiosity that a call for it would be irresistible. He thought that the Federalists should conserve their strength, not expending it here where they were sure to be beaten but on the treaty itself, where they had a better prospect of success. But by one vote, a Federalist caucus voted to attempt a sustained opposition to the motion. "I submited as I always do, but regreted the decision," wrote Sedgwick. "Those who concurred in opinion with me were generally those of most experience," he claimed, but noted that King and Ellsworth were of a different opinion.[36]

Sedgwick's comment is very revealing of the state of Federalist organization in Congress. It shows that the Federalists caucused regularly and that they may well have expected party discipline. The Federalist caucus obviously included Senate as well as House members, since King and Ellsworth belonged to the upper chamber.

Abiding by the caucus decision, the Federalists attacked Livingston's resolution. They argued that the House of Representatives constitutionally had no part in accepting or rejecting treaties, even when their consent to appropriations for carrying them into effect was required by the Constitution. Many Republicans were overjoyed that the Federalists had chosen to fight Livingston's motion, and that they had chosen this ground on which to oppose it. "The Treaty People have unnecessarily taken very untenable ground, from which we shall *most certainly* dislodge them," reported Edward Livingston to his father. On subsequent questions, this victory of the Republicans would surely operate very favorably, he chortled; "We shall after the production of the papers submit resolutions declaratory of our rights to Sanction or refuse treaties which contain Stipulations affecting any of the powers vested in Congress—expressive of our opinion of this Treaty and Containing a refusal to carry it into Effect."[37] Even Madison joined the Republican assault on the Federalists' constitutional doctrine, and Livingston's motion carried, 62 to 37.[38] Giles now thought the treaty more in jeopardy than at any other time during the session. The question of the right of the

House to pass on the treaty, which had been deterring some antitreaty men from all-out opposition, was now eliminated.[39]

The answer of the president jolted the Republicans from their mutual congratulations. He categorically refused to lay any of the papers before the House, declaring that there was a need for secrecy and that the treaty-making power lay entirely with the Senate and the executive.[40]

Federalists were jubilant over Washington's answer. Some were so enamored with his message that they were having it printed in white satin, framed, and glazed.[41] Sedgwick rejoiced that "It has given us some confidence, and in the same proportion, has dejected the other party."[42]

Some Republicans were indeed depressed. Giles had lost much of his recent optimism, and thought it doubtful that the treaty could be defeated against the weight of the "President, twenty Senators, funded gentry . . . and a gregarious tribe of sycophants and rum-mad speculators."[43] But Madison was affected very differently. His hesitancy turned to grim determination. "The effect of this reprehensible measure on the majority is not likely to correspond with . . . the calculations of its authors," he wrote Jefferson.[44] He proceeded to shape two resolutions upholding the rights of the House while avoiding as much as possible a direct challenge to the president.[45] Surprisingly, they both passed easily by a majority of twenty-two.[46]

The sturdiness of the Republican majority in the face of a direct challenge from Washington was a great shock to the Federalists. Until that vote they had felt confident that the Republicans would pass a few strictures on the treaty to build a Republican platform for future elections, and then retreat to allow the treaty to go into effect. Even when Sedgwick saw that the motion requesting the papers from Washington would pass by a majority of more than twenty, he consoled himself that this was no indication of the strength of the parties, and that notwithstanding this humiliation there was no reason to despair of executing the treaty. "I have not sufficient respect for the faction to suppose they dare to do an action so bold and adventurous," he wrote.[47]

Now the Federalists were frightened. As if the passage of Madison's resolutions in the face of Washington's challenge were not enough, Fisher Ames reported that in a private meeting, a majority of the House of Representatives, fifty-seven concurring, had resolved to refuse the appropriations.[48]

The meeting of which Ames spoke was in fact the first Republican caucus in the House of Representatives. It had met just before Madison introduced his resolutions challenging Washington. The accuracy of Ames's information was borne out by the fact that Madison's resolutions were supported by precisely the number Ames had mentioned, fifty-seven. The Republicans might have had even more votes had they required the party discipline that the Federalists did. But those who had voted in the minority in the Republican caucus were allowed to vote as they pleased on the floor of the House without being proscribed from the party.[49]

Even without such discipline, fifty-seven votes were sufficient to defeat the treaty. John Adams now reported to his wife that contrary to his former opinions, "The House of Representatives are determined to go all lengths."[50] He believed that this had come about because "A few outlandish men in the House have taken the lead, and Madison, Giles and Baldwin are humble followers."[51] Sedgwick too reported that prospects for implementing the treaty were poor, and that Albert Gallatin had become the leader of the Republicans.[52]

In all probability, the Federalists were wrong in asserting that Madison had lost control of the House Republicans and that things were proceeding in a way of which he disapproved. Madison had reasserted his leadership with the resolutions challenging Washington's refusal to lay the papers before the House of Representatives. On April 15, he made a long speech urging that the appropriations to implement the treaty be refused and proposed that the treaty then be renegotiated. It is probable that this was the proposition which he enclosed in a letter to Jefferson three days later and which he asserted would be carried "According to present calculation . . . by *nearly* the same majority as prevailed in the vote asserting the Rights of the House on the subject of Treaties."[53] That same day he wrote Monroe that the motion against the treaty should pass by a majority of twenty.[54] The Federalists had mistakenly attributed Madison's hesitancy in the early portions of the session to an unwillingness to defeat the treaty. It was actually only a result of his inability to unite his party in a single course of action. In his private correspondence he never complained about the extremism of any of the motions, including that of Livingston. His only complaint was that they might not be able to command a majority of the House. When he was sure of that majority, as he was between April 15 and April 18, he advocated outright defeat of the treaty.

With the Republicans now seemingly united and willing to destroy the treaty, the Federalists desperately fought back. They increased their activities to draw petitions from the people addressed to Congress and demanding the implementation of the treaty. Hamilton's father-in-law, Phillip Schuyler, prevailed on several "active and influential characters" to go to different parts of the country to inform the people of the pernicious consequences of a failure to implement the treaty.[55] In Virginia, John Marshall circulated petitions to counter those of the Republicans. James McHenry organized the Federalist effort in Maryland from his position in the War Office.* Two bank presidents in Philadelphia recruited signatures on Federalist petitions by hinting darkly to various persons that they would not get discounts at the bank if they did not sign.[56] "Scarce a merchant or trader but what depends on discounts, and at this moment there is a general pinch for money," wrote Madison to Jefferson. "Under such circumstances, A Bank Director soliciting subscriptions is like a Highwayman with a pistol demanding the purse."[57]

Madison also wrote Jefferson that the insurance companies in Philadelphia and New York had stopped business to alarm the public, and evidently this was at least partially true. John Fenno's *Gazette of the United States*, an ardently pro-Federalist newspaper, printed an extract of a letter from a respectable mercantile house in New York which stated that the political aspect of the country had almost totally arrested commerce and that the underwriters had refused to insure any more vessels until the treaty question had been settled. The *Gazette* also printed the resolution of a meeting of underwriters of New York that it would be inexpedient to underwrite in the present crisis. This resolution was subsequently mailed to other seaports.[58]

Doubtless the underwriters and merchants who refused to do business until the treaty was implemented were motivated in part by the fear that a refusal to put it into effect would mean war with Great Britain and the ruin of any voyages they undertook or underwrote.[59] This fear of war was used very effectively by the Federalists in their campaign for public support. With the cry of "war, war, no Insurance to be had, . . . no employment of the people," the Federalists "harry people into an opinion, that upon reflection,

---

* As was usual for him, McHenry bungled the job. He wrote Robert Oliver in Baltimore to call together their best friends for the purpose of influencing the vote of Samuel Smith, their congressman. He enclosed the substance of the instruction he wished given to Smith and advised that, to obtain consent of sufficient people to the instruction, "You must only communicate with those you can trust in the first instance, and fix upon persons to carry it round the different wards at one and the same hour. By these means a certain party will not have time to take any measures to defeat it." He begged that his own name be kept out of the maneuver, and closed melodramatically with "Fare wel [sic] my dear Oliver. It is for Baltimore to save the republic." Oliver followed McHenry's instructions, but the bumbling secretary of war had miscalculated. The instruction given to Smith *ordered* him to vote for the appropriations. Smith in fact had already been inclined to vote for the treaty, but this instruction so wounded his pride that the Federalists feared he would now oppose it to prove his independence. James McHenry to Robert Oliver, April 12, 1796, McHenry Papers, LC; King to Hamilton, April 20, 1796, Hamilton Papers, LC; Sedgwick to E. Williams, April 20, 1796, Sedgwick Papers, MHS.

they must condemn," reported Republican Senator John Langdon.[60] Desperately the Republicans tried to counter. Boston Republicans were told, "Beware! Beware! of British Influence. You will be told the mournful *worn-out* ditty of PEACE OR WAR!—Believe them not. The question is— *Will you again be connected with your greatest enemy—or will you remain free and independent.*"[61]

The contention of the Federalists that rejection of the treaty would mean war was given substance, however, when it became known that the British intended to withhold the western posts until the treaty was implemented by the House. The British cabinet had decided on this course of action on January 14, 1796, and dispatched orders to that effect.[62] When British chargé d'affaires Phineas Bond informed Secretary of State Timothy Pickering of this resolution, Pickering not only told the British representative that the action was proper, but plotted with him ways to make use of the threat to influence Congress toward a more favorable view of the treaty.[63] Evidently, the two conspirators discarded the idea of a public communication from Bond warning of the orders of the British cabinet. They feared this would unnecessarily stimulate the passions of the opposition.[64] So word of the British intentions was spread unofficially. They hoped to inform the people of the consequences of rejecting the treaty without stirring their passions.[65]

While using economic pressure and the fear of war to stir the populace, the Federalists were making use of still another effective weapon. A very favorable treaty with Spain had just been negotiated by Thomas Pinckney, opening the navigation of the Mississippi to Americans. The Federalists successfully convinced many that this treaty was tied irrevocably to the British treaty. The failure of one meant the failure of both, for both were based on similar constitutional principles, they asserted.[66] This gambit was very successful in stirring up petitions from the West in favor of the Jay Treaty.

Not only did the Federalists attempt to tie the Spanish and British treaties together in the minds of the naive westerners, but they tried much the same thing in Congress as well. In early April the President submitted the Pinckney Treaty to the House for appropriations. No sooner had the Committee of the Whole opened discussion on the implementation of the British treaty, than Sedgwick was on his feet moving that the Spanish Treaty, the British Treaty, and a treaty recently negotiated with the dey of Algiers be implemented.[67] Thus he tied all of the treaties up with the fate of the British instrument. Several members rose together in protest. But Sedgwick defended his parliamentary coup, reminding his listeners triumphantly that once in Committee of the Whole of the State of the Union "any man who got first possession of the floor had a right to make any proposition with regard to any subject before the Committee."[68]

It took the House all day and part of the next to finally separate the treaties, after which the Spanish treaty was quickly passed by the Committee of the Whole.[69] But the Federalists were not willing to let the Spanish treaty go so easily. Despite Alexander Hamilton's advice not to tie the other treaties up with the British treaty, the Federalists had decided that, if the House refused appropriations for the British treaty, the Federalist-dominated Senate would resist appropriations for the Spanish and Algerian treaties until those for the British were passed.[70] As Rufus King remarked to Hamilton, "We shall amend [the Pinckney Treaty] by adding a provision for the British Treaty—if the house disagree, we shall adhere, and they will lose the bill by refusing our amendment—we shall then add to the Algerine Bill on amendment providing for all the Treaties—this likewise they may reject—but my Belief is that the Opposition will give way before we have gone through this course."[71]

The Senate was prepared to go even further in its defense of the British treaty. Chauncy Goodrich wrote that the Senate would probably also refuse to pass the federal city loan bill, land office bill, perhaps the appropriation for the army, and then refuse to adjourn, arresting the whole government until the House implemented the treaty.[72]

While this political maneuvering was going on backstage, the Republicans and Federalists were belaboring one another on the floor of the House. The Republicans attacked the treaty's every provision, while the Federalists found no fault that was unmitigated. But the primary debate was not over the provisions; these had been examined ad nauseum in conversation and newspaper, and each speaker repeated the same tired criticisms or defenses that the preceding speaker had launched.

The main question that occupied the debaters was whether a rejection of the treaty would mean war with Great Britain. The Republicans argued that acceptance would be more likely to breed war than rejection. Acceptance would offend France and bring the possibility of war with her.[73] Acceptance would also raise the danger of war with Britain, for the treaty forbade the use of economic weapons such as debt sequestration and discriminatory duties against her. The only weapon that would remain in the hands of America to redress injuries inflicted on her by Great Britain was war itself, and war would be far less effective in coercing Great Britain than economic measures.[74]

At the same time, the Republicans deprecated the idea that rejection of the treaty would mean war. "The idea of war, as a consequence of refusing to give effect to the Treaty, was too visionary and incredible to be admitted into the question," said Madison. By rejecting it, America was merely protecting its own interests, which was no cause for war. Great Britain would not make war on its best customer in any case, he concluded.[75] Giles pointed out that Britain was now exhausted and desirous of peace. Prussia, Spain, and Holland had abandoned the British alliance and were on the brink of war with her, if not already engaged in it. Austria was almost exhausted, and Britain was in desperate need of provisions. Thus, he concluded, Britain would never go to war with the United States if it rejected the treaty.[76]

The Federalists disagreed. "Some gentlemen have thrown out an idea that Britain would not proceed to war against us, because [it would be] contrary to her interest. But it was well known from the whole conduct of that nation that they were far from dreading a war with us," said Zephaniah Swift. "At a time when we were discussing commercial regulations, which were to operate upon their fears to engage in a war with us, it was a fact that they were meditating war against this country."[77]

The Federalists did not claim that the outcome of a rejection of the treaty would be an immediate declaration of war against the United States by Britain. Instead, they pointed out that the British would refuse to give up the posts, would again turn the Indians against the United States, and would increase spoliations against American commerce and impressment of American seamen. Under these continual provocations, the United States itself would finally be driven into a declaration of war.[78]

To this assertion, the Republicans replied that British provocations would not result in war. "For my part," said William Cooper of New York, "should Britain never give up the posts, I would not vote for war, nor be at the expense of a single regiment to take them; nor would I go to war to recover losses sustained by spoliation." Instead, he said, if Congress rejected the treaty, the United States could make use of the nonintercourse proposition that the Senate had rejected in 1794.[79] This called forth the same debate which had taken place during the war crisis of 1794, with the Federalists maintaining that such economic retaliation would itself bring war, and the Republicans maintaining that it would bring British acquiescence instead.[80]

The Republicans were so sure that rejection of the treaty would not mean war that they regarded the Federalists' use of the issue as a complete fraud, mouthed solely to frighten the people and gain votes for the Federalist treaty. The cry of war and dissolution of the government if the treaty were rejected was "something like the tale of 'Rawhead and Bloody-bones,' designed to frighten children," remarked Republican Gabriel Christie of Maryland.[81] Many present-day historians seem to regard the matter in the same light.[82] They argue that a shortage of food in England would have deterred the British from challenging the United States. They point to the fact that Samuel Bayard, an American in London, was writing home in 1795 that "the lower class of the people are literally starving." Gouveneur Morris noted in his diary that bread was double the former price and still rising.[83] The Republicans were well aware of Britain's need for bread, and this no doubt increased their confidence that rejection of the treaty would not mean war.[84]

Yet, by the time Congress began discussing the treaty, the worst of the grain shortage was already over. Gouveneur Morris advised a friend from London that if he had speculated in wheat, he should sell it immediately. There would be a good harvest in England, he reported, and "the want in this Country is by no Means so great as is generally imagined."[85] John Quincy Adams also wrote in April from London that "The scarcity of provisions has suddenly disappeared both in France and in this Country."[86] In any case, the British reaction to a bread shortage had not been that of greater pliancy before American demands, but the sudden, secret, and stringent order-in-council of April 1795.

Despite the fact that the British were not starving, it is clear that the war was going badly for them and that they were not at all anxious to provoke an American war gratuitously. Thus, it is certain that rejection of the treaty would not have brought an immediate declaration of war from Britain. Still, the British were resolved to hold the posts in case the treaty was not implemented; and now that Wayne had defeated the Indians at Fallen Timbers, there was no buffer between British and American troops. The confrontation was direct, and it is difficult to conceive that peace could have been maintained there in the atmosphere that would have been created between the two countries had the treaty been rejected. Spoliations would doubtless have continued; and the treaty would not have been in effect, thereby allowing the British to take food as contraband without compensation. Even if the treaty had been submitted for renegotiation, it is doubtful that Britain would have given up much more than it already had, and the ill will created by delay and disappointment would have increased chances of a clash on the frontier or the ocean even while negotiations were pending. In short, the Federalists' contention that rejection of the treaty meant war certainly had more basis in fact than the Republicans and some present-day historians have realized.

The Federalists thought ratification of the treaty was absolutely necessary. Should it be rejected, there would probably be war, and war would be a disaster. "That a dissolution of the union would be the consequence of war with Great Britain, I think very probable," wrote John Quincy Adams.[87] His father agreed. "A prospect of foreign war and civil war in conjunction, is not very pleasant," he wrote gloomily. "We are a poor, divided nation, in the middle of all our prosperity. . . . If the House refuse to make the appropriations, it is difficult to see how we can avoid war, and . . . preserve this government from dissolution."[88]

The Adams theme was brilliantly played upon by Fisher Ames in his famous oration to the House of Representatives at the conclusion of the debates on the implementation of the treaty. Pale and cadaverous, sick and seemingly close to death, Ames mourned that if the treaty were not accepted, even he might outlive the Constitution and the existence of the nation. He told the House that rejecting the treaty after the president and Senate had ratified it was a breach of America's word. He made good use of Washington's name and influence, and finally he pulled out the Federalists' ultimate weapon, the fear of war: "In the day time, your path through the woods will be ambushed; the darkness of midnight will glitter with the blaze of your dwellings. You are a father; the blood of your sons shall fatten your corn-field! You are a mother: the war-whoop shall wake the sleep of the cradle! . . . By rejecting the posts, we light the savage fires—we bind the victims." He denounced the Republicans for treating the idea of war "as a bugbear" and found the levity unseasonable and unbecoming those who had brought it so near in 1794 and who would be among the foremost to bring it on were the posts refused to America after the treaty was rejected by the House.[89]

John Adams and Judge Iredell who heard the speech found themselves in tears and exclaiming, "God! how great he is." They saw no dry eye in the whole House save for "some of the jackasses who had occasioned the necessity of the oratory." These attempted to laugh, Adams reported, "but their visages grinned horrible ghastly smiles!"[90]

The Federalists, meanwhile, were putting strong personal pressure on doubtful members of the House. Months before the House debates on the treaty, Republican Frederick Muhlenberg of Pennsylvania had been sent an ultimatum from the Federalist father of the girl his son was courting. "If you do not give us your vote, your son shall not have my Polly," he was informed. Muhlenberg must have given evidence of a proper opinion, for the Federalist gave his consent to the marriage even before the congressional session opened.[91] When Phillip Van Cortlandt, representative from New York, returned home for a short time during the debates, Rufus King wrote Hamilton, "Would it not be well to prepare a Reception for him which may return him in favor of the Treaty—His Friends may be induced to act upon his Mind, which balances, so as to decide it."[92]

The Federalists also worked on Speaker Jonathan Dayton. Sedgwick conveyed to Dayton a warning from Dayton's own brother-in-law that the people of New Jersey "would tear any of their representatives to pieces who should vote against the treaty." Evidently this convinced Dayton not only to vote for the treaty, but to work actively for it. He asked Sedgwick what he could do, and Sedgwick told him to go to William Findley of Pennsylvania, who was hesitating on the treaty, and to "tell him that he and he alone would save his country from anarchy and probably civil war." Also, he was "To impress on one hand those considerations that would alarm his fears (Findley is a coward) and on the other those which would flatter his vanity and ambition."[93] The Federalists even delayed the business of the House "owing to the wish of Dayton who believes his influence will be able to procure a sufficient accession of strength."[94] But the efforts of individuals like Dayton, Sedgwick, and King were probably less influential than the torrent of petitions raining upon House members during the debates, the preponderance of which urged the implementation of the treaty. "The People are alarmed and Petitions are coming from all Quarters, mostly in favor of the Treaty," John Adams wrote his wife.[95]

As a result of Federalist efforts both in and out of Congress, Madison found it more and more difficult to hold his party in line. Republican Samuel Maclay suddenly introduced a resolution that it would be inexpedient to pass laws carrying the treaty into effect.[96] This, of course, was bringing the measure to a vote in precisely the form that Madison and Giles had been endeavoring to avoid. Madison opposed it as superfluous, since the question before the House was the passing of the appropriations.[97] Though successful in keeping the proposition in the form he wished, Madison still found his majority slipping away. "The majority has melted by changes and absence [from 20] to 8 or 9 votes," he reported to Jefferson on April 28. "Whether they will continue firm is more than I can decide."[98] Frantically, he strove to buoy up his faltering ranks. Five days later John Adams observed, "Mr. Madison looks worried to death. Pale, withered, haggard."[99] He also thought Livingston and Gallatin to be suffering, and he was probably right.[100]

Stephen Kurtz, the most careful student of these debates, claims that the pressure of popular opinion actually forced Madison, Gallatin, and Livingston to abandon their opposition to these propositions.[101] This is a great misinterpretation of their actions. To prove Madison's defection,

Kurtz cites his opposition to Maclay's resolution. Yet it is clear that Madison opposed it because it was bringing the measure to a vote in the form that would ensure a Republican defeat. In fact, Madison said the Maclay resolution would be perfectly proper once the resolution to carry the treaty into effect had been defeated.[102] Kurtz shows that Gallatin offered to vote for full appropriations and says this indicates his desertion. But Gallatin opposed the resolution to carry the treaty into effect immediately. He advocated defeating the proposition and holding the treaty in suspension until the British ceased interfering with American neutral trade.[103] Kurtz states that Edward Livingston surrendered by introducing a petition from New York with an admonition to the House that the members should act as they thought best with respect to the treaty. But this admonition seems to have been that of the petition rather than of Livingston. In any case, the statement actually expressed the hope "that the House of Representatives would act as they thought best . . . without being influenced by the efforts of any party." Most likely this was a plea to resist Federalist pressure.[104]

Madison and his followers were acting on their principles of foreign policy in these debates, not merely out of partisan political passions. There was no reason for them to surrender. Even while the Republican majority was being whittled away, all the members of the House seemed to expect that the provisions for carrying the treaty into effect would be defeated. Madison wrote his father on April 25, four days before the critical vote, that there would be a majority against the resolution at least on the first vote, before the Senate sent it back tied to the other treaties.[105] The Federalists also believed this would be the case. Senator George Cabot of Massachusetts thought the resolution would fail by a vote of 52 to 48, and Sedgwick estimated the same, adding that the Federalists were still confident of ultimate success when the Senate entered the fray.[106]

The desperate measures contemplated by the Federalists were never needed. On April 29, the vote was finally taken in the Committee of the Whole, and the House divided evenly, 49 to 49. The deciding vote was now in the hands of Frederick Muhlenberg, Chairman of the Committee of the Whole, who had been involved in the dispute with his son's prospective father-in-law. Muhlenberg hesitated, then cast his vote for the appropriations.

Frantically, the Republicans rallied to try to salvage something from the wreckage. The following day, before the House voted on the report from the Committee of the Whole, Henry Dearborn proposed a preamble to the measure which said that the House consented to the treaty even though it was objectionable. Muhlenberg was willing to accept this. But "several wrongheads" who were opponents of the treaty thought that as long as the treaty was to be implemented, it should not be hindered by such a censure. They voted against it.[107] This allowed the Federalists to defeat the preamble by one vote, 50 to 49.[108] The implementation of the treaty then was passed by a vote of 51 to 48.[109]

Evidently the Federalists' petitions, oratory, senatorial threats, and personal pressure had done much to change opinion in the House. Washington believed that the petitions had been instrumental in the victory.[110] Van Cortlandt, who had voted consistently with the Republicans during the session, was now found on the Federalist side. Perhaps the petitions and the reception planned for him by King and Hamilton had secured his vote.[111] Sherburne of New Hampshire, one of the few New Englanders who opposed the treaty, evidently had been so worried by sentiment in his state that he had simply remained in New Hampshire and refused to return to the House in time to vote on the treaty.[112] Dayton was surely influenced by these petitions, and his efforts combined with those of Sedgwick may have had some influence with Findley of Pennsylvania. When the final roll-call vote was taken in the House on the treaty, Findley was found to be out mailing a trunk.[113]

The Jay Treaty was now securely fastened upon the American people, willing and unwilling alike. A conflict between its provisions and those of the treaty negotiated between Wayne and the Indians concerning the right of British traders in the American Northwest was quickly ironed out, and the stage was set for a limited rapprochement between Britain and the United States. For the Federalists this meant salvation for the nation. As bad as the treaty was, it at least preserved the peace, and, as Washington wrote, "Twenty years peace with such an increase of population and resources as we have a right to expect; added to our remote situation from the jarring power, will in all probability enable us in a just cause, to bid defiance to any power on earth."[114] For the Republicans, the implications were quite different. The United States was already able to bid defiance to any power on earth, and peace could have been had without purchasing it at the price of humiliation. The United States had been shorn by the harlot England.[115]

Thus, while the Jay Treaty preserved peace between the United States and Great Britain for a while, it did not bring peace between rival political factions within the United States. The quarrel between these factions over America's proper goals and the extent of power necessary to implement them became institutionalized in the two parties the Jay Treaty crisis had done so much to create. The conflict that had developed out of differing concepts of the nature, the necessary extent, and the use of American power in foreign affairs sometimes was superseded by other party issues; but its subsiding was never more than temporary. The undeclared naval war with France kept it before the people through 1799. It then was allowed to lapse into the background for a few years until it burst back into prominence in 1805. From 1805 until 1812, the whole Jay Treaty drama was replayed, this time with Republican principles emerging victorious and leading not to British concessions, but to the war the Federalists had always predicted and feared.

Ironically, the party conflict over foreign policy ended only when one of the two parties that the conflict had helped to create, the Federalist party, destroyed itself by too vigorous an opposition to the war that had resulted from the failure of Republican foreign policy.

REFERENCE MATERIALS

APPENDIX I

The Indians and the Fur Trade as Causes for British Retention of the Frontier Posts

There is an important historical controversy over the relative importance of the fur trade and the Indian problem as factors in the decision of the British government to hold the posts. Samuel Flagg Bemis in his *Jay's Treaty* asserted that the fur trade was the "real reason" for Britain's policy (p. 6). A. L. Burt, in his work *The United States, Great Britain and British North America*, took up the cudgels to show that Britain was not motivated by so selfish a concern. He claims that Britain kept the posts because of an honorable desire to protect its Indian allies from American rapacity, and because of a fear of Indian reprisals if the posts were turned over to the United States.

Burt has strong evidence on his side. He shows that maintenance of the posts cost the British much more than they would have lost by relinquishing the fur trade. He asserts that the British would have lost only the profits on the trade and not the manufacture of the furs, because America was incapable of manufacturing them. He admits that the fur trade was mentioned in the correspondence leading to the initial decision to hold the posts temporarily, but suggests that it played no part in the subsequent decision to hold them indefinitely. As evidence, he points to a proposal of Governor Haldimand that Britain offer to allow American traders to operate along with the British in the Indian country between the Canadian border and the Ohio River in return for permission to keep the posts. Since Haldimand expressed a willingness to share the fur trade with the United States, Burt concludes that the trade was not an important factor in the decision to hold the posts indefinitely.

The British indeed must have been more influenced by the threat the Indians posed to the very existence of their colony than by the possible loss of part of their fur trade. Nevertheless, Burt underestimates the influence of that trade on Britain's decision to keep the posts. In the first place, Haldimand's reasoning was not necessarily that of the British government. Haldimand may well have been more concerned with the Indian problem than with the fur trade, but this was not necessarily the case with Sydney and Pitt. The cabinet ministers were much closer to the pressure of the fur traders and their agents in London than that of the Indians in Canada. Nor

191

does Haldimand's suggestion that Americans be allowed to trade along with the British if the posts were to be held show that the fur trade played little or no part in the motivation of that policy. Even if Haldimand's proposition had been accepted, it did not mean that Britain would give up any substantial share of the trade. The Indians would have given preference to the British merchants, their friends and allies, rather than to their recent enemies, the Americans. As a consequence, the furs would still have followed their old route to the Great Lakes and Montreal. In any case, there is no evidence that anyone but Haldimand favored the project.

Furthermore, Burt's calculation that the fur trade cost the British government more than it brought in is deceptive. The British would have had to maintain frontier forts on the Canadian side of the border even if the fur trade had been totally eliminated. Also, the value of the fur trade to Britain was not solely a matter of balancing accounts. As Bemis points out, it furnished employment to British shipping, and the protection of her shipping was almost solely responsible for Britain's momentous decision to keep the West Indies closed to American ships. Though Burt is right when he maintains that the furs would have ultimately found their way to British factories, many might have traveled aboard American ships rather than British had the posts been given up. Finally, the fur trade furnished profitable employment to many in Canada, and this was important to a sparsely settled land that wanted desperately to attract settlers in order to resist encroachments from its fast-growing southern neighbor.

APPENDIX II

The Randolph Affair

The "precious confessions" of Randolph, which Dispatch No. 10 said had been contained in Dispatch No. 3, turned out to be some comments by Randolph to the effect that Washington's advisers were trying to make a monarch of the president and to deceive him as to the true spirit of the people and the affairs of France. Fauchet also had included Randolph's presentation to Fauchet of the part of Jay's instructions forbidding him to make any agreement contrary to the French treaty as one of these "precious confessions."[1] This, of course, Randolph had done by the order of Washington himself.

The implications concerning the soliciting of a bribe were not so quickly and easily dealt with, but they do seem to have been rather innocuous. In Dispatch No. 10, Fauchet referred his government to Dispatch No. 6 for details. In Dispatch No. 6, Fauchet told how Randolph had come to see him and related the unhappy events surrounding the Whiskey Rebellion:

It is all over, he said to me. A civil war is about to ravage our unhappy country. Four men by their talents, their influence, and their energy may save it. But debtors of English merchants, they will be deprived of their liberty, if they make the smallest step. Could you lend them instantaneously funds, sufficient to shelter them from English persecution. This inquiry astonished me much. It was impossible for me to make a satisfactory answer. . . . I have never since heard of propositions of this nature.[2]

Randolph explained this episode in his *Vindication* by reminding Washington that there had been evidence that the British were helping foment the rebellion, and that he had had great fears that the attempted suppression of the rebels would drive them to seek aid of the British, which would in turn cut off supplies to Wayne's army. He reminded the president that Governor Mifflin, Attorney General Bradford, and Washington himself had feared British intervention. In Randolph's conversation with Fauchet concerning the rebellion, the British interference in the rebellion was connected by Fauchet with an attempt by Hammond and others to destroy the influence of Randolph, Governor Clinton, and the French Republic. Randolph then mentioned that Fauchet could aid in uncovering these conspiracies by applying to those merchants in New York with whom he had contracts to supply flour to the French government. Supposedly they were in a position to gain information on this nefarious British plan. Randolph then said that these men were likely to owe large debts to the British, and that some advance of money on the flour contracts might enable them to speak up without fear of the British using their debts to ruin them.[3] For what it was worth, Fauchet sent a certificate to Randolph verifying his story and asserting that Randolph had never made improper disclosures to him nor received money from him.[4]

The explanations of Randolph and Fauchet leave some tantalizing gaps, however. What did Fauchet mean when he said that Governor Mifflin and Secretary Dallas of Pennsylvania with Randolph at their head were balancing as to their parties? Fauchet said it meant that they wanted information on the degree of British involvement before they decided on the proper actions to be taken against the Whiskey rebels. If the British were involved, publication of the facts would automatically deflate support for the rebels. If they were not involved, suppression could take place without risk of driving the rebels into the hands of the British.[5] I do not find that explanation fully convincing.

Perhaps an even more vulnerable part of Randolph's story was that concerning the flour merchants. Fauchet spoke very definitely of "Four men who by their talents, their influence, and their energy" could save the country from civil war.[6] Yet Randolph later asserted that he had not the most distant idea of the names or number of the men involved, a fact that Fauchet later verified in his certificate. It is worthy of note, however, that Theodore Sedgwick, after seeing Randolph's *Vindication*, wrote to a friend, "the flour contractors, the men whose being out of a gaol depended on the indulgence of British Creditors, these men were John Vaughan and Cunningham and Nesbitt of this City and John Murray of New York exporters to and not Importers from Great Britain, who have constantly bills to fill and never want to purchase, and who perhaps never owed five pounds there in their lives."[7]

The whole idea of using flour contractors to uncover British conspiracies seems farfetched, and the disturbing inconsistencies in the stories of Randolph and Fauchet, coupled with Sedgwick's testimony, must raise some doubts about the whole episode. Still, Wolcott remembered years later that Randolph had mentioned the flour merchants when first confronted with Fauchet's Dispatch No. 10 by Washington, and Fauchet did write that these men were to save the country from civil war, not foment the war.[8]

Randolph and his two major modern defenders have suggested in fact that either George Hammond or Oliver Wolcott had in their possession Fauchet's Dispatch No. 6, which exonerated Randolph from the treason implied in No. 10, and that they deliberately withheld it to ruin Randolph and to secure immediate ratification of the Jay Treaty. Their evidence is rather impressive. Randolph claimed that he had been assured that a duplicate of No. 6 had accompanied No. 10 from Philadelphia.[9] Randolph's biographer Moncure Conway pointed out that despite Wolcott's statement that "I have never seen or been possessed of Mr. Fauchet's letter, numbered 3 or 6, or either of them in or out of cypher, and I have no knowledge whether they, or either of them, have been seen by Lord Grenville or Mr. Hammond," he had written in his notes of the "letters" read to him by Hammond.[10] Lately, Irving Brant has pointed out that Lord Grenville had written Hammond that he was enclosing "the original of the dispatches from the different ministers and agents of the French Convention in America which were found on board the French vessel, Jean Bart." Hammond had acknowledged "the several important papers which were inclosed" and which he hoped to use with beneficial effects. He had also written, "The originals of the French letters are peculiarly interesting and will I am persuaded, if properly treated, tend to effect an essential change in the public sentiment of this country with regard to the characters and principles of certain individuals and to the real motives of their political conduct."[11] From these comments Brant concludes that there was more than one letter to be used against Randolph, and that Hammond must have received both No. 6 and No. 10 or a dispatch on the same subject from one of the other commissioners. Since Randolph refused to confer with Fauchet in the presence of the other commissioners, he claims that the other dispatch had to be No. 6.[12]

Brant reinforces his case by pointing out that Pickering's translation of No. 10 tends to prove that he had seen No. 6. Dispatch No. 10 related that Randolph had arrived to see Fauchet "avec un air fort empressé." Pickering had translated this phrase to read "with a countenance expressive of much anxiety." The natural translation for one as little familiar with the language as Pickering would have been "with an air of anxiety" rather than "with a countenance expressive of much anxiety." Brant concludes that Pickering must have seen Dispatch No. 6 which, in describing Randolph's state, used the phrase "toute sa physionomie était douleur," which indeed might have been translated "with a countenance."[13] Either Wolcott and Pickering or Hammond thus seem convicted of ruining the reputation of a man they knew to be innocent in order to further their own partisan ends.

An investigation of the British records, however, indicates that Dispatch No. 6 was never seen by any of them. The originals of the French dispatches intercepted from the *Jean Bart* have disappeared; but attached to the letter to Hammond in which the originals were enclosed is a précis of them. It lists Fauchet's dispatches Nos. 9 through 17 inclusive along with numerous dispatches of the other French commissioners. It does not list Fauchet's Dispatch No. 6. Thus, in all probability, it was not seen by any of the British or Americans involved.[14]

NOTES

ABBREVIATIONS USED

AHA	American Historical Association
ASPFR	American State Papers, Foreign Relations
BM Add. Mss	British Museum, Additional Manuscripts
BT	Records of the British Board of Trade, preserved in the PRO
CO	Records of the British Colonial Office, preserved in the PRO
FO	Records of the British Foreign Office, preserved in the PRO
HMC	Historical Manuscripts Commission
LC	Library of Congress, Washington, D.C.
MHS	Massachusetts Historical Society, Boston
MPC	Michigan Pioneer and Historical Society Collections and Researches
NYHS	New York Historical Society, New York City
NYPL	New York Public Library, New York City
PRO	Public Record Office, London
WO	Records of the British War Office, preserved in the PRO

1. GREAT BRITAIN: FROM CONCILIATION TO CONFRONTATION

1. *Public Advertiser* (London), January 31, 1783.

2. *Ibid.*

3. See for instance *Morning Herald and Daily Advertiser*, February 15, 1783; *Public Advertiser*, January 31 and February 11, 1783.

4. *Public Advertiser*, February 8, 1783.

5. *Ibid.*, January 31, 1783.

6. *Ibid.*, February 3, 1783.

7. *The Parliamentary History of England*, 36 vols. (London, 1806–1820), XXIII, 453.

8. *Ibid.*, p. 468.

9. *Ibid.*, p. 377.

10. *Ibid.*, p. 354.

11. *London Chronicle*, January 30 and February 1, 1783.

12. Cobbett, *Parliamentary History*, XXIII, 398.

13. *Ibid.*, p. 400.

14. Vincent Todd Harlow, *The Founding of the Second British Empire, 1763–1793*, 2 vols. (London, 1952–1964), I, 431.

15. Cobbett, *Parliamentary History*, XXIII, 609–611.

16. Lucy Frances Horsfall, "The West Indian Trade," in *The Trade Winds, A Study of British Overseas Trade During the French Wars, 1793–1815*, ed. C. Northcote Parkinson (London, 1948), p. 164.

17. Cobbett, *Parliamentary History*, XXIII, 611 ff.; Sir George Pretyman Tomline, *Memoirs of the Life of the Right Honorable William Pitt*, 3 vols., 2nd ed. (London, 1821), I, 143–145.

18. *Morning Chronicle* (London), March 8, 1783; *Public Advertiser*, March 10 and March 12, 1783.

19. John B. Holroyd, Lord Sheffield, *Observations on the Commerce of the American States* (London, 1784).

20. *Ibid.*, p. 3.

21. *Ibid.*, p. 140.

22. *Ibid.*, pp. 151, 152.

23. *Ibid.*, pp. 185–200.

24. *Ibid.*, pp. 198–199.

25. This paragraph is based on Harlow, *Founding of the Second British Empire*, I, 459–477.

26. *Ibid.*

27. "Considerations of the West India Planters," November 26, 1783, FO 4/3.

28. See for instance John Stevenson, *An Address to Brian Edwards, Esq.* (London, 1784), pp. 21–22; G. Chalmers, *Opinions on Interesting Subjects of Public Law and Commercial Policy Arising from American Independence* (London, 1784). Chalmers was a close associate of David Jenkinson, later Lord Hawkesbury, and was one of his secretaries on the Committee on Trade.

29. *Morning Herald* (London), January 3, 1784.

30. Harlow, *Founding of the Second British Empire*, I, 482.

31. "Report of the Committee on Trade of the Privy Council," May 31, 1784, BT 5/1.

32. *London Chronicle*, July 27–29, 1784.

33. *Journal of the House of Commons*, XL, 429. The bill passed the House of Commons on August 13, 1784.

34. Michigan Pioneer and Historical Society, *Collections and Researches* (Lansing, 1895–1912), XX, 139. Hereafter cited as MPC.

35. Alfred LeRoy Burt, *The United States, Great Britain, and British North America from the Revolution to the Establishment of Peace After the War of 1812* (New Haven, 1940), pp. 94–95. The treaty stipulated only that the posts were to be evacuated "with all convenient speed."

36. Haldimand to Carlton, September 18, 1782, MPC, XX, 57.

37. For example, see the comment of General Haldimand, quoted in Burt, *The United States*, p. 92.

38. Quoted in *ibid.*, p. 88.

39. *Ibid.*

40. See the speeches of the British Indian agents Johnson and McKee, MPC, XX, 177.

41. MPC, XX, 177, 124.

42. Burt, *The United States*, p. 103.

43. Abigail Adams to Jefferson, June 6, 1785, Julian P. Boyd, ed., *The Papers of Thomas Jefferson* (Princeton, 1950—), VIII, 179. Hereafter, Jefferson, *Papers* (Boyd).

44. John Adams to John Jay, June 2, 1785, Charles Francis Adams, ed., *The Works of John Adams*, 10 vols. (Boston, 1850–1856), VIII, 255–259. Hereafter, Adams, *Works*. Adams to Jefferson, October 3, 1785, Jefferson, *Papers* (Boyd), VIII, 577.

45. Adams, *Works*, VIII, 302–314.

46. Vernon G. Setser, *The Commercial Reciprocity Policy of the United States, 1774–1829* (Philadelphia, 1937), p. 4; Max Savelle, "The American Balance of Power and European Diplomacy, 1713–1778," *The Era of the American Revolution*, edited by Richard B. Morris (New York, 1939), pp. 168–169.

47. *Ibid.*

48. Setser, *Commercial Reciprocity Policy*, p. 53 and *passim*.

2. THE UNITY OF THE AMERICAN RESPONSE

1. Samuel Flagg Bemis, *Pinckney's Treaty: A Study of America's Advantage from Europe's Distress*, rev. ed. (New Haven, 1960).

2. Harold C. Syrett, ed., *The Papers of Alexander Hamilton* (New York, 1961—), III, 295. Hereafter, Hamilton, *Papers* (Syrett).

3. *Ibid.*, IV, 420.

4. Hamilton to Washington, March 17, 1783, Henry Cabot Lodge, ed., *The Works of Alexander Hamilton*, 12 vols., federal edition (New York, 1904), IX, 324. Hereafter, Hamilton, *Works* (Lodge).

5. Jay to Jefferson, January 19, 1786, Jefferson, *Papers* (Boyd), IX, 185–186.

6. Jay to Robert R. Livingston, April 22, 1783, Henry P. Johnston, ed., *The Correspondence and Public Papers of John Jay*, 4 vols. (New York, 1890–1893), III, 42.

7. Jay to Robert R. Livingston, December 14, 1782, *ibid.*, p. 7.

8. For example, see his address to the people of Great Britain, quoted in Frank Monaghan, *John Jay* (New York, 1935), p. 10.

9. *Ibid.*, p. 274.

10. Jay to Jefferson, September 8, 1787, Jefferson, *Papers* (Boyd), XII, 106.

11. Jay to Jefferson, July 14, 1786, *ibid.*, X, 135.

12. John Adams to Jay, August 10, 1785, Adams, *Works*, VIII, 299.

13. John Adams to Jay, April 13, 1785, *ibid.*, p. 235–236.

14. John Adams to Jefferson, October 3, 1785, Jefferson, *Papers* (Boyd), VIII, 577.

15. John Adams to Jay, October 15, 1785, Adams, *Works*, VIII, 321.

16. Jefferson to John Randolph, August 25, 1775, Jefferson, *Papers* (Boyd), I, 242.

17. Jefferson expounded on British conduct in the South in a letter to William Gordon, July 16, 1788, *ibid.*, XIII, 362–364.

18. Jefferson to William Carmichael, December 17, 1787, *ibid.*, XII, 424.

19. Jefferson to Abigail Adams, June 21, 1785, *ibid.*, VIII, 239.

20. Jefferson to Jay, August 14, 1785, *ibid.*, p. 373–374.

21. Jefferson to John Adams, September 24, 1785, *ibid.*, p. 545.

22. Jefferson to Jay, November 3, 1787, *ibid.*, XII, 310. France was perfectly aware of Jefferson's feelings and accurately gauged his motivations. La Luzerne wrote to his government in 1784 that Jefferson "is full of honor and sincerity and loves his country greatly, but is too philosophic and tranquil to hate or love any other nation unless it is for the interest of the United States to do so. He has a principle that it is for the happiness and welfare of the United States to hold itself as much aloof from England as a peaceful state of affairs permits, that as a consequence of this system it becomes them to attach themselves particularly to France, even that Congress ought as quickly as possible to direct the affection of the people toward us in order to balance the penchant and numerous causes continually attracting them toward England." Quoted in Samuel Flagg Bemis, ed., *American Secretaries of State and Their Diplomacy*, 10 vols. (New York, 1927–1929), vol. 2, Samuel Flagg Bemis, *Thomas Jefferson*, p. 7.

23. James Madison to Phillip Mazzei, July 7, 1781, Gaillard Hunt, ed., *The Writings of James Madison*, 9 vols. (New York, 1900–1910), I, 146. Hereafter, Madison, *Writings*.

24. Irving Brant, *James Madison*, 6 vols. (Indianapolis and New York, 1941–1961), II, 160–161.

25. Fisher Ames to George Richards Minot, May 3, 1789, Seth Ames, ed., *The Works of Fisher Ames*, 2 vols. (Boston, 1854), I, 35.

26. [James Madison], "North American II," *William and Mary Quarterly*, 3rd Ser., III (1946), 584, 586.

27. George Washington to Henry Knox, December 26, 1786, John C. Fitzpatrick, ed., *The Writings of George Washington*, 39 vols. (Washington, D.C., 1931–1944), XXIX, 124. Hereafter, Washington, *Writings*.

28. Washington to Henry Laurens, November 14, 1778, *ibid.*, XIII, 254.

29. Jefferson to William Carmichael, December 15, 1787, Jefferson, *Papers* (Boyd), XII, 424.

30. Jefferson to Jay, May 23, 1786, *ibid.*, X, 569.

31. Hamilton, *Papers* (Syrett), III, 552.

32. See Washington to La Luzerne, August 1, 1786, Washington, *Writings*, XXVIII, 601; Adams to Jefferson, January 19, 1786, Jefferson, *Papers* (Boyd), IX, 181; Jefferson to Ralph Izard, November 18, 1786, *ibid.*, X, 541.

33. Alexander Hamilton and William Floyd to George Clinton, March 24, 1783, Hamilton, *Papers* (Syrett), III, 303.

34. John Adams to Rufus King, June 14, 1786, Charles Ray King, ed., *The Life and Correspondence of Rufus King*, 6 vols. (New York, 1894–1900), I, 185. Hereafter, King, *Life and Correspondence*.

35. See above, Chapter 1, p. 11.

36. Dorset to the American Commissioners, March 26, 1785, Jefferson, *Papers* (Boyd), VIII, 55–56.

37. John Adams to Jay, February 14, 1788, Adams, *Works*, VIII, 475.

38. Washington to Lafayette, August 15, 1786, Washington, *Writings*, XXVIII, 521; Jay to Congress, October 20, 1785, *Papers of the Continental Congress, 1774–1789*, Item 81, Vol. I (microfilm Reel 107), 456; Jefferson to Monroe, November 11, 1784, Jefferson, *Papers* (Boyd), VII, 511; John Adams to Jefferson, July 31, 1786, *ibid.*, X, 176–177.

39. Jefferson to Monroe, February, 1785, *ibid.*, VII, 638–640. Hamilton expressed the same idea in Federalist No. 11. See Hamilton, *Papers* (Syrett), IV, 341.

40. Madison to Jefferson, October 3, 1785, Madison, *Writings*, II, 180.

41. Jefferson to Monroe, August 11, 1786, Jefferson, *Papers* (Boyd), X, 225.

42. Jefferson to Madison, July 31, 1788, *ibid.*, XIII, 443. Jefferson also favored a provision in the Bill of Rights barring a standing army. Jefferson to Monroe, August 9, 1788, *ibid.*, p. 490.

43. Richard B. Morris, ed., *Alexander Hamilton and the Founding of the Nation* (New York, 1957), p. 80. Washington, however, was not sanguine about the adequacy of militia troops. Washington to the President of Congress, September 24, 1776, Washington, *Writings*, VI, 112.

44. Jefferson, *Papers* (Boyd), I, 46; Paul Leicester Ford, ed., *The Writings of Thomas Jefferson*, 10 vols. (New York, 1892–1899), I, 418, n. 3. Hereafter, Jefferson *Writings* (Ford).

45. Page Smith, *John Adams*, 2 vols. (Garden City, New York, 1962), I, 162–187; Monaghan, *John Jay*, p. 63.

46. Madison, *Writings*, I, 26, 28; Alexander Hamilton, "Full Vindication" and "The Farmer Refuted," Hamilton, *Papers* (Syrett), I, 45–79, 81–165.

47. Adams to Jefferson, September 4, 1785, Jefferson, *Papers* (Boyd), VIII, 477.

48. Jay to Charles Thomson, November 14, 1783, Johnston, *Correspondence of John Jay*, III, 96.

49. Madison to Monroe, August 7, 1785, Madison, *Writings*, II, 156–157.

50. Washington to Charles Vaughan, November 18, 1785, Washington, *Writings*, XXVIII, 316.

51. "A Full Vindication," and "The Farmer Refuted," in Hamilton, *Papers* (Syrett), I, 45–79, 81–165. See also Federalist No. 11, *ibid.*, IV, 340.

52. *Ibid.*

53. *Ibid.*, 230.

54. Samuel Flagg Bemis, *Jay's Treaty: A Study in Commerce and Diplomacy*, rev. ed. (New Haven, 1962), p. 49; American State Papers, *Commerce and Navigation*, I, 34–35.

55. Anne Cornelia Clauder, *American Commerce as Affected by the Wars of the French Revolution and Napoleon, 1793–1812* (Philadelphia, 1932), p. 16.

56. Jefferson to Count de Moustier, October 9, 1787, Jefferson, *Papers* (Boyd), XII, 225.

57. See the table printed in Bemis, *Jay's Treaty*, pp. 46–47.

58. *Ibid.*

59. Adams to Jay, August 8, 1785, Adams, *Works*, VIII, 297.

60. Jefferson to Monroe, April 15, 1785, Jefferson, *Papers* (Boyd), VIII, 88–89.

61. Alexander Hamilton, "A Full Vindication," Hamilton, *Papers* (Syrett), I, 57.

62. Adams to Jay, March 9, 1785, Adams, *Works*, VIII, 228.

63. Jay to Robert R. Livingston, September 12, 1783, Johnston, *Correspondence of John Jay*, III, 79.

64. For the reaction to the Sheffield pamphlet, see Madison to Edmund Randolph, August 30, 1783, Madison, *Writings*, II, 11.

65. Jefferson to John Langdon, September 11, 1785, Jefferson, *Papers* (Boyd), VIII, 512–513.

66. Jay to Adams, September 6, 1785, Johnston, *Correspondence of John Jay*, III, 164–165.

67. Adams to Jefferson, March 1, 1787, Jefferson, *Papers* (Boyd), XI, 189.

68. Washington to William Carmichael, June 10, 1785, Washington, *Writings*, XXVIII, 161.

69. Max Farrand, *Records of the Federal Convention of 1787*, 4 vols., rev. ed. (New Haven, 1966), I, 19.

70. *Ibid.*, II, 29, 389; III, 273, 286.

3. ALEXANDER HAMILTON AND THE HEROIC STATE

1. Joseph Gales, comp., *Debates and Proceedings in the Congress of the United States, 1789–1824*, 42 vols. (Washington, 1834–1856), I, 237. Hereafter cited as *Annals of Congress*.

2. *Ibid.*, pp. 183, 188.

3. *Ibid.*, p. 200.

4. *Ibid.*, pp. 201–202.

5. Madison to Edmond Pendleton, Madison, *Writings*, V, 361.

6. *Ibid.*

7. The vote was 25–27. *Annals of Congress*, I, 590.

8. *Ibid.*, pp. 608–610, 618–619; Fisher Ames to George Minot, July 2, 1789, Seth Ames, *Works of Fisher Ames*, I, 57. For the text of the provision concerning rum, see *Annals of Congress*, II, 2129.

9. Fisher Ames to George Minot, May 27, 1789, Ames, *Works of Fisher Ames*, I, 45–46. Although overt discrimination was eliminated from the bill, Vernon Setser points out that rum, a product primarily of the British West Indies, was more heavily taxed than brandy, which of course was primarily a product of the French. Also madeira was more heavily taxed than any other wine. Setser, *Commercial Reciprocity Policy*, p. 107. Despite this subtle discrimination, however, the bill must be regarded essentially as a pro-British measure, for, as Professor Alexander DeConde points out,

it left the major part of America's trade in the hands of the British. Alexander DeConde, *Entangling Alliance: Politics and Diplomacy Under George Washington* (Durham, North Carolina, 1958), pp. 40, 74.

10. Washington to David Stuart, July 26, 1789, Washington, *Writings*, XXX, 363.

11. *Annals of Congress*, I, 45, 49, 57; ASPFR, I, 6; Setser, *Commercial Reciprocity Policy*, p. 106.

12. Douglas Brymner, ed., *Report on the Canadian Archives, 1890* (Ottawa, 1891), p. 128.

13. Madison to Jefferson, May 9, 1789, Madison, *Writings*, V, 355; Charles A. Beard, ed., *The Journal of William Maclay* (New York, 1927), p. 94; Setser, *Commercial Reciprocity Policy*, p. 106.

14. Hamilton to Edward Stevens, November 11, 1769, Hamilton, *Papers* (Syrett), I, 4.

15. John C. Miller, *Alexander Hamilton: Portrait in Paradox* (New York, 1959), *passim.*

16. For an account of Hamilton's activities during the French crisis, see *ibid.*, also Broadus Mitchell, *Alexander Hamilton*, 2 vols. (New York, 1957–1962), II, *passim.* For Hamilton's admiration of Caesar, see Jefferson to Benjamin Rush, January 16, 1811, Andrew A. Lipscomb and Albert E. Bergh, eds. *Writings of Thomas Jefferson,* 20 vols. (Washington, 1903–1904), XIII, 4. Hereafter, Jefferson, *Writings* (Memorial Edition).

17. Federalist No. 11, Jacob E. Cooke, ed., *The Federalist* (Middletown, Conn., 1961), p. 72.

18. *Ibid.*, pp. 72–73.

19. Federalist No. 6, *ibid.*, p. 28.

20. Hamilton, speech to the Constitutional Convention (Yates's version) in Max Farrand, *Records of the Federal Convention of 1787*, I, 381.

21. *Ibid.*, p. 299.

22. *Ibid.*, p. 381.

23. *Ibid.*, p. 299.

24. Hamilton, speech to the Constitutional Convention (Madison's version), *ibid.*, pp. 288–289.

25. Adrienne Koch, *Power, Morals and the Founding Fathers* (Ithaca, 1961), p. 60.

26. This question has been asked and answered in a brilliant and searching but slightly different way than below by Cecilia M. Kenyon in "Alexander Hamilton: Rousseau of the Right," *Political Science Quarterly*, LXXIII, No. 2 (June 1958).

27. See Hamilton to Lafayette, October 6, 1789, Hamilton, *Papers* (Syrett), V, 425–426.

28. Hamilton's conversation with Beckwith, October, 1789, *ibid.*, 482–488.

29. *Ibid.*, p. 483.

30. See *ibid.*, IV, 230, 240, quoted above, pp. 24–25.

31. Adam Seybert, *Statistical Annals* (Philadelphia, 1818), p. 750.

32. Edward Stanwood, *American Tariff Controversies in the Nineteenth Century,* 2 vols. (Boston, 1903), I, 74.

33. Hamilton to Jefferson, January 13, 1791, Hamilton, *Works* (Lodge), IV, 348.

34. "Report on Manufactures," *ibid.*, 136.

35. See, for example, William Appleman Williams, *Contours of American History* (Cleveland, 1961), p. 155.

36. *Ibid.*, p. 163.

37. *Ibid.*, pp. 153–167.

38. Hamilton to Congress, April 22, 1790, Hamilton, *Works* (Lodge), II, 293.

39. Stanwood, *American Tariff Controversies*, I, 100–101.

40. Federalist No. 35, Cooke, *The Federalist*, p. 216.

41. "Report on Public Credit," Hamilton, *Papers* (Syrett), VI, 70–71.
42. "Report on Manufactures," Hamilton, *Works* (Lodge), IV, 70–198.
43. Hamilton, *Papers* (Syrett), V, 488.
44. *Ibid.*
45. Hamilton to Jefferson, January 13, 1791, Hamilton, *Works* (Lodge), IV, 348.
46. Hamilton to Colonel Edward Carrington, May 26, 1792, *ibid.*, IX, 527.
47. Federalist No. 34, Cooke, *The Federalist*, p. 212.
48. Federalist No. 15, *ibid.*, p. 94.
49. Federalist No. 6, *ibid.*, pp. 31–32.
50. *Ibid.*, p. 32.
51. Federalist No. 11, *ibid.*, pp. 67–68.
52. Federalist No. 34, *ibid.*, p. 211.
53. Federalist No. 11, *ibid.*, pp. 68–69.
54. *Ibid.*, p. 68.
55. *Ibid.*
56. *Ibid.*
57. *Ibid.*, pp. 72–73.
58. Federalist No. 25, *ibid.*, p. 162.
59. Federalist No. 8, *ibid.*, pp. 44–45.
60. *Ibid.*, p. 49.
61. *Ibid.*, p. 45.
62. *Ibid.*
63. Hamilton, *Papers* (Syrett), V, 484.

4. HAMILTON, WASHINGTON, ADAMS, AND JAY: HEROISM *VERSUS* RESPECTABILITY

1. "The Public Conduct and Character of John Adams, Esq.," in Richard B. Morris, ed., *Alexander Hamilton and the Founding of the Nation*, p. 399.
2. Federalist No. 24, Hamilton, *Papers* (Syrett), IV, 420.
3. Conversation with Beckwith, October, 1789, *ibid.*, V, 484.
4. For a convenient account of Beckwith's status and an account of the Beckwith-Hamilton conversations, see Julian Boyd, *Number 7: Alexander Hamilton's Secret Attempts to Control American Foreign Policy* (Princeton, 1964), pp. 6–13.
5. See Felix Gilbert, *To the Farewell Address: Ideas of Early American Foreign Policy* (Princeton, 1961).
6. See John Adams to Jefferson, October 3, 1785, Jefferson, *Papers* (Boyd), VIII, 577; Gouverneur Morris got the same impression on his informal mission to England. G. Morris to Washington, September 18, 1790; Jared Sparks, *The Life of Gouverneur Morris*, 3 vols. (Boston, 1832), II, 46. See also John C. Fitzpatrick, ed., *The Diaries of George Washington, 1748–1799*, 4 vols. (Boston, 1925), IV, 139.
7. Hamilton, *Papers* (Syrett), V, 483.
8. *Ibid.*, p. 484. (Italics mine.)
9. *Ibid.*, pp. 484, 488.
10. Madison to Jefferson, May 27, 1789, Madison, *Writings*, V, 371.
11. *Annals of Congress*, II, 1570.
12. *Ibid.*, p. 1572.
13. *Ibid.*, p. 1573.
14. *Ibid.*, p. 1581.
15. *Ibid.*
16. Jefferson, *Papers* (Boyd), XVI, 513–523.
17. Jefferson to Thomas Mann Randolph, Jr., May 30, 1790, *ibid.*, p. 450.
18. *Annals of Congress*, II, 1653, 1655–1656.
19. Lord Dorchester to Major George Beckwith, June 27, 1790, printed in Boyd, *Number 7*, pp. 143–144.
20. Memorandum from the Secretary of the Treasury to the President, July 8, 1790, printed in *ibid.*, pp. 146–147.
21. *Ibid.*, p. 147.
22. For conflicting discussions of the Morris mission, see Bemis, *Jay's Treaty*, pp. 66–85, and Julian Boyd, *Number 7*, pp. 66–72.
23. *Ibid.*, p. 66 ff.
24. Dorchester urged an eventual alliance with the United States, although in

guarded terms. Boyd believes him to have been urging an alliance with Vermont to seduce it from the United States, but his interpretation does not seem justified. Dorchester to Grenville, March 8, 1790, No. 18 in Douglas Brymner, *Report on the Canadian Archives for 1890* (Ottawa, 1891), p. 242. Same to same, July 21, 1790, No. 43, *ibid.*, p. 255. Also, extracts printed in Boyd, *Number 7*, p. 142. Beckwith urged concessions to American commerce soon after this incident of which Boyd writes, and it seems likely that the British agent favored this course of action even before he wrote of it. Beckwith to Grenville, January 23, 1791. FO 4/12.

25. Boyd, *Number 7*, pp. 140–143.

26. Dorchester to Beckwith, June 27, 1790, printed in *ibid.*, p. 145.

27. Both documents are printed in *ibid.*, pp. 153–158.

28. *Ibid.*, pp. 156–158.

29. Hamilton, *Papers* (Syrett), VI, 496, n. 1, 493–497.

30. Quoted in Miller, *Alexander Hamilton*, p. 234.

31. *Ibid.*, p. 514; see also p. 154. 32. Hamilton, *Works* (Lodge), IV, 329.

33. *Ibid.*, p. 339. 34. *Ibid.*

35. *Ibid.*, p. 325. 36. *Ibid.*, pp. 333–342.

37. *Ibid.*, p. 331. 38. *Ibid.*, p. 340.

39. Conversation of Senator Johnson of Connecticut with Beckwith in Brymner, *Report on the Canadian Archives, 1890*, p. 146.

40. Beckwith to Lord Grenville, January 23, 1791, FO 4/12.

41. *Ibid.*

42. Jefferson, *Writings* (Ford), V, 261–263.

43. *Annals of Congress*, II, 1962 ff.

44. Beckwith conversation with Hamilton, February 16, 1791, FO 4/12.

45. Jefferson's "Anas," Jefferson, *Writings* (Ford), I, 186–187.

46. *Ibid.*, pp. 206–207.

47. Adams to Pickering, October 31, 1797, Adams, *Works*, VIII, 560.

48. For Washington, see Jefferson, *Writings* (Ford), I, 199; for Adams, see John R. Howe, *The Changing Political Thought of John Adams* (Princeton, 1966), pp. 34, 134, 185; for John Jay, see Monaghan, *John Jay*, p. 278.

49. See Howe, *Changing Political Thought of John Adams*, p. 185.

50. Washington chastised the Democratic-Republican clubs as dangerous "self-created" societies. For Adams, see *ibid.*, p. 185.

51. Jay to Adams, July 4, 1787, Johnston, *Correspondence of John Jay*, III, 248–249.

52. Adams to Jefferson, October 9, 1787, Jefferson, *Papers* (Boyd), XII, 221.

53. Jay to Washington, January 7, 1787, Johnston, *Correspondence of John Jay*, III, 227.

54. For Jay, see Monaghan, *John Jay*, pp. 342–347; for Adams, see Page Smith, *John Adams*, 2 vols. (Garden City, New York, 1962), II, 796–797.

55. Washington, notes of February, 1792, in Washington, *Writings*, XXXI, 493.

56. Jay to Washington, August 28, 1790, in Boyd, *Number 7*, pp. 113–116.

57. Adams to Washington, August 29, 1790, *ibid.*, pp. 116–119.

58. Adams to Jefferson, August 7, 1785, Jefferson, *Papers* (Boyd), VIII, 354–355.

59. Jefferson to Adams, November 19, 1785, *ibid.*, IX, 43.

60. Adams to Jefferson, November 5, 1785, *ibid.*, p. 21.

61. Fisher Ames to George Minot, May 16, 1789, Ames, *Works of Fisher Ames*, I, 38.

62. Such at least is the conclusion I draw from the fact that Hamilton thought it important to note that the British Privy Council regarded the South rather than the North as the center of opposition to commercial discrimination. Notes on the Report of the Committee of the Privy Council for 1791, Hamilton Papers, LC, XXIII, 3241.

5. JEFFERSON AND MADISON: A FOREIGN
POLICY IN PURSUIT OF HAPPINESS

1. Jefferson to ——, December 31, 1797, Jefferson, *Writings* (Memorial Edition), II, 92 fn; Madison, *Writings*, VI, 69.
2. Madison to Jefferson, October 17, 1788, Madison, *Writings*, V, 274.
3. Federalist No. 48, Cooke, *The Federalist*, p. 332.
4. Hamilton, Federalist No. 8, *ibid.*, p. 45; Madison, Federalist No. 43, *ibid.*, p. 297.
5. Madison, *Writings*, VI, 92.
6. *Ibid.*, p. 122.
7. Adrienne Koch, *Power, Morals and the Founding Fathers*, p. 39.
8. Federalist No. 55, Cooke, *The Federalist*, p. 378.
9. Jefferson, "Notes on Virginia," Jefferson, *Writings* (Memorial Edition), II. 165.
10. Madison, *Writings*, VI, 96–99.
11. Jefferson, "Notes on Virginia," Jefferson, *Writings* (Memorial Edition), II, 229.
12. Jefferson to Washington, August 14, 1787, Jefferson, *Papers* (Boyd), XII, 38.
13. *Ibid.*
14. Jefferson, "Notes on Virginia," Jefferson, *Writings* (Memorial Edition), II, 229.
15. *Ibid.*
16. Jefferson to Jay, August 23, 1785, Jefferson, *Papers* (Boyd), VIII, 426.
17. Jefferson, "Notes on Virginia," Jefferson, *Writings* (Memorial Edition), II, 177.
18. Madison, *Writings*, VI, 86.
19. Jefferson, "Notes on Virginia," Jefferson, *Writings* (Memorial Edition), II, 205.
20. Jefferson to Monroe, March 18, 1785, Jefferson, *Papers* (Boyd), VIII, 42; see also Jefferson to Madame d'Enville, April 2, 1790, *ibid.*, XVI, 291.
21. Jefferson, "Notes on Virginia," Jefferson, *Writings* (Memorial Edition), II, 163.
22. Federalist No. 10, Cooke, *The Federalist*, pp. 55–65.
23. Douglas Adair, "David Hume, James Madison, and the Tenth *Federalist*," *Huntington Library Quarterly*, XX (August 1957), 343–360.
24. Federalist No. 51, Cooke, *The Federalist*, p. 351.
25. Madison, *Writings*, VI, 90.
26. Federalist No. 51, Cooke, *The Federalist*, p. 352.
27. Jefferson, "Notes on Virginia," Jefferson, *Writings* (Ford), III, 279.
28. Jefferson to Madame d'Enville, April 2, 1790, Jefferson, *Papers* (Boyd), XVI, 291.
29. Madison, "Address to the States," Madison, *Writings*, I, 459–460.
30. Jefferson to Madison, September 6, 1789, Jefferson, *Writings* (Ford), V, 123; for Madison's agreement, see Madison "On Perpetual Peace," Madison, *Writings*, VI, 88–90.
31. Madison, "On Perpetual Peace," *ibid.*, p. 90; for Jefferson's agreement, see Jefferson to Madison, September 6, 1789, Jefferson, *Writings* (Ford), V, 120–123.
32. Jefferson to Jay, August 23, 1785, Jefferson, *Papers* (Boyd), VIII, 427.
33. Jefferson to Monroe, February, 1785, *ibid.*, VII, 640.
34. Jefferson to Jay, August 23, 1785, *ibid.*, VIII, 427.
35. *Annals of Congress*, I, 235.
36. Madison, "North American #1," *William and Mary Quarterly*, 3rd ser., III (October 1946), 579–580; for Jefferson's agreement, see Adrienne Koch, *The Philosophy of Thomas Jefferson* (New York, 1943), p. 146.
37. Jefferson to Madison, March 18, 1785, Jefferson, *Papers* (Boyd), VIII, 40.
38. Madison, "North American #2," *William and Mary Quarterly*, 3rd ser., III (October 1946), 581–582.

39. Jefferson to Madison, March 8, 1785, Jefferson, *Papers* (Boyd), VIII, 40.
40. Madison, "North American #2," p. 583.
41. Jefferson to Madison, July 31, 1788, Jefferson, *Papers* (Boyd), XIII, 443.
42. Madison to Jefferson, August 20, 1784, Madison, *Writings,* II, 69; Jefferson to Archibald Stuart, January 25, 1786, Jefferson, *Papers* (Boyd), IX, 218.
43. Jefferson to John Brown, May 26, 1788, Jefferson, *Writings* (Ford), V, 17.
44. Madison to Jefferson, August 20, 1784, Madison, *Writings,* II, 68–70.
45. Jefferson to Archibald Stuart, March 14, 1792, Jefferson, *Writings* (Ford), V, 454.
46. Jefferson, "Anas," March 9, 1792, Jefferson, *Writings* (Ford), I, 181.
47. Jefferson to Thomas Walker, June 23, 1790, Jefferson, *Papers* (Boyd), XVI, 562.
48. Jefferson to Jay, August 23, 1785, *ibid.,* VIII, 426–427.
49. Jefferson to G. K. van Hogendorp, October 13, 1785, *ibid.,* p. 633.
50. Jefferson to Washington, August 14, 1787, *ibid.,* XII, 38.
51. Jefferson to Jay, August 23, 1785, *ibid.,* VIII, 426; Jefferson to Washington, March 15, 1784, *ibid.,* VII, 26.
52. Jefferson to Washington, August 14, 1787, *ibid.,* XII, 38.
53. For exposition of these ideas, see Felix Gilbert, *To The Farewell Address: Ideas of Early American Foreign Policy.*
54. Quoted in *ibid.,* p. 71.
55. Madison to Monroe, August 7, 1785, Madison, *Writings,* II, 156.
56. *Ibid.*
57. Jefferson to John Langdon, September 11, 1785, Jefferson, *Papers* (Boyd), VIII, 512–513.
58. *Annals of Congress,* I, 205.
59. *Ibid.,* pp. 205, 237. He made it clear in this speech that he was counting on the dependence of the British West Indies on provisions supplied by the United States.
60. Jefferson to Thomas Pleasants, May 8, 1786, Jefferson, *Papers* (Boyd), IX, 472.
61. *Ibid.,* p. 473.
62. Madison to Jefferson, March 18, 1786, Madison, *Writings,* II, 229.
63. Jefferson to Nathaniel Tracy, August 17, 1785, Jefferson, *Papers* (Boyd), VIII, 398.
64. *Annals of Congress,* I, 181–182.
65. Madison to Edmund Pendleton, January 9, 1787, Madison, *Writings,* II, 306; Jefferson, "Notes on Virginia," Jefferson, *Writings* (Memorial Edition), II, 230; see also Jefferson to Elbridge Gerry, May 7, 1786, Jefferson, *Papers* (Boyd), IX, 468.
66. Jefferson, "Notes on Commercial Policy towards Great Britain," (1792), Jefferson, *Writings* (Ford), V, 451–452; Jefferson to Madison, March 18, 1785, Jefferson, *Papers* (Boyd), VIII, 40; Jefferson to Monroe, November 11, 1784, *ibid.,* VII, 511.
67. Jefferson to Monroe, June 17, 1785, *ibid.,* VIII, 232.
68. Jefferson to Washington, November 4, 1788, *ibid.,* XIV, 328.
69. Jefferson to David Ross, May 8, 1786, *ibid.,* IX, 475.
70. Madison to Edmund Pendleton, January 9, 1787, Madison, *Writings,* II, 307.
71. *Ibid.;* Jefferson to John Brown, May 26, 1788, Jefferson, *Writings* (Ford), V, 18.
72. Madison to Jefferson, October 3, 1785, Madison, *Writings,* II, 180; Jefferson to Monroe, August 11, 1786, Jefferson, *Papers* (Boyd), X, 225.
73. April 21, 1789, *Annals of Congress,* I, 189.
74. Jefferson to Monroe, February, 1785, Jefferson, *Papers* (Boyd), VII, 639.
75. Jefferson, "Notes on Virginia," Jefferson, *Writings* (Memorial Edition), II, 243.
76. *Ibid.,* pp. 242–243.
77. May 13, 1790, *Annals of Congress,* II, 1571.

78. Jefferson to Francis Kinloch, November 26, 1790, Jefferson, *Writings* (Ford), V, 249; Jefferson to Gouverneur Morris, August 12, 1790, *ibid.*, 224–225; Jefferson to Thomas Walker, June 23, 1790, Jefferson, *Papers* (Boyd), XVI, 562.

79. Jefferson to Gouverneur Morris, August 12, 1790, Jefferson, *Writings* (Ford), V, 224–225.

80. *Ibid.*, p. 225.

81. "Heads of Proposals on the Nootka Crisis," July 12, 1790, *ibid.*, p. 200.

82. Cabinet Opinion on Nootka Crisis, August 28, 1790, *ibid.*, p. 238.

83. "Heads of Proposals on the Nootka Crisis," July 12, 1790, *ibid.*, p. 201.

84. "Heads of Proposals on the Nootka Crisis," July 12, 1790, *ibid.*, pp. 200–202; Cabinet Opinion on the Nootka Crisis, August 28, 1790, *ibid.*, p. 238–239.

85. Cabinet Opinion on the Nootka Crisis, August 28, 1790, *ibid.*, p. 239.

86. *Ibid.*

87. Irving Brant, *James Madison,* 6 vols. (Indianapolis and New York, 1941–1961), II, 160–161; Dumas Malone, *Thomas Jefferson and His Times,* 3 vols. (Boston, 1948—), I, 292.

88. William Hill, *The First Stages of the Tariff Policy of the United States* (Baltimore, 1893), p. 97.

89. See B. Lincoln to Rufus King, February 11, 1786, Charles Ray King ed., *The Life and Correspondence of Rufus King,* 6 vols. (New York, 1894–1900), I, 157–158, for the varying interests of the states. See Rufus King to John Adams, November 2, 1785, *ibid.*, 112–113, for the concern caused by southern reluctance to pass a national navigation law. See also Madison to Jefferson, August 20, 1785, Madison, *Writings,* II, 161–162; and Madison to Jefferson, January 22, 1786, *ibid.*, 218.

90. F. A. Ogg, "Jay's Treaty and the Slavery Interests of the United States," AHA Annual Report for 1901, I, (Washington, 1902), 275–298.

91. FO 4/14. Fisher Ames thought mistakenly that Madison's actions stemmed from the pressures of his Virginia constitutents for discrimination against Britain rather than his own convictions. Ames to George Minot, July 2, 1789, Seth Ames, ed., *The Works of Fisher Ames,* I, 58.

92. Madison to Jefferson, October 3, 1785, Madison, *Writings,* II, 181.

93. Madison to Monroe, August 7, 1785, *ibid.*, p. 159.

94. Alice B. Keith, "Relaxations in the British Restrictions on the American Trade with the British West Indies, 1783–1802," *Journal of Modern History,* XX (March 1948), 4.

95. Jefferson's Report on Commerce in 1791, Jefferson, *Writings* (Ford), V, 411–413.

96. The problems of the West India trade were discussed in 1806 by Jacob Corwinshield in a letter to James Madison, printed in *William and Mary Quarterly,* 3rd ser., XVI (January 1959), 83–118.

6. GREAT BRITAIN HOLDS THE LINE

1. See for example, *World, Fashionable Advertiser,* November 19, 1787; Adams to Jay, February 14, 1788, Adams, *Works,* VIII, 475.

2. *Public Advertiser,* November 21, 1787; for other newspaper comment in the same vein, see *World, Fashionable Advertiser,* November 18, 1787.

3. *Public Advertiser,* November 21, 1787.

4. John Brown Cutting to Jefferson, March 1790, Jefferson, *Papers* (Boyd), XVI, 252.

5. Report on the Newfoundland Fishery, 1786, BT 5/3, p. 489.

6. Lowell Joseph Ragatz, *The Fall of the Planter Class in the British Caribbean, 1763–1833* (New York, 1928), pp. 184, 186.

7. Report of the Committee of the Privy Council on trade between the British dominions and America (1791), in *Collection of Interesting and Important Reports and Papers on Navigation and Trade* (London, 1807), pp. 77–78. Hereafter cited as *Interesting and Important Reports.*

8. *Ibid.,* p. 76.

9. *Ibid.,* p. 82.

10. *Ibid.,* p. 85.

11. Phineas Bond to Lord Carmarthen, January 4, 1789, J. Franklin Jameson ed., "Letters of Phineas Bond," AHA Annual Report for *1896,* I (Washington, 1897), 591; this letter was read (undoubtedly with much satisfaction) in the Committee on Trade on February 5, 1789, BT 4/4, p. 190; for a comparison of British and foreign tonnage engaged in the American trade, see Committee of the Privy Council Report (1791) in *Interesting and Important Reports,* p. 91.

12. Minutes of the Committee on Trade, March 1, 1786, BT 5/3, pp. 189–191.

13. *The Times* (London), August 6, 1791, quoting a New York report of May 10, 1791.

14. Phineas Bond to Grenville, September 10, 1791, Jameson, ed., "The Letters of Phineas Bond," I, 486.

15. Committee of the Privy Council Report (1791), in *Interesting and Important Reports,* pp. 66–69; for the American statistics of Anglo-American balance of trade see Timothy Pitkin, *A Statistical View of the Commerce of the United States of America,* 2d ed. (New York, 1817), p. 38.

16. Minutes of the Committee on Trade, January 16, 1790, BT 5/6, pp. 13–15. See also Hawkesbury to Harry Wickens, January 25, 1790, Liverpool Papers, BM, Add. Mss, 38,310, f. 47.

17. Hawkesbury to Mr. Ryder (a fellow member of the committee on Trade), no date, but Ryder's answer is dated February 19, 1793, Liverpool Papers, BM, Add. Mss, 28,338, f. 324.

18. Minutes of the Committee on Trade, February 12, 1789, BT 5/5, p. 203.

19. Beckwith to Grenville, January 23, 1791, FO 4/12; same to same, March 3, 1791, FO 4/12; Minutes of the Committee on Trade, March 6, 1792, BT 5/6, pp. 390–391.

20. My italics. Grenville to Hawkesbury, January 14, 1791, Liverpool Papers, BM Add. Mss, 38,226.

21. Anna L. Lingelbach, "The Inception of the British Board of Trade," *American Historical Review,* XXX (July 1925), 701–727.

22. Bernard Mayo, "Instructions to the British Ministers to the United States, 1791–1812," AHA Annual Report for *1936,* III (Washington, 1941), 5–9. FO 4/10. Hawkesbury was somewhat less authoritative in trade policy concerning Europe, with which Pitt concerned himself. Hawkesbury wrote to Joseph Banks, "I endeavoured last year to check the Importation of Oats from Holland and East Friesland by making it necessary to import them in British Vessels only. . . . But Mr. Pitt influenced by Political Motives obliged me to relinquish this Design." Hawkesbury to Joseph Banks, May 19, 1790, Liverpool Papers, BM, Add. Mss, 38,310, f. 53.

23. Hawkesbury's draft of instructions to Hammond, Mayo, "Instructions to the British Ministers to the United States," III, 9–12. The pilotage and lighthouse duties and various other fees charged American ships in British ports amounted to slightly more than the 50 cents per ton charged on foreign ships in American ports. See Committee of the Privy Council Report (1791), in *Interesting and Important Reports,* Appendix A, iii. In fact, the American tonnage duties were evidently set purposely to correspond approximately to these British fees. The 10 percent extra duty charged on goods imported in foreign ships, however, Hamilton admitted was not an equivalent

duty, telling Beckwith that it was part of a plan to encourage American over foreign shipping, and was "confessedly in our favor." Beckwith to Grenville, January 23, 1791, FO 4/12.

24. Grenville's instructions to Hammond, September 1, 1791, No. 2, Mayo, "Instructions to the British Ministers to the United States," III, 17–18.

25. In fact, Britain would probably have applied the alien duties, from which America was then exempt, immediately after the conclusion of the treaty allowing her to do so. This she did immediately after the ratification of the Jay Treaty.

26. Jefferson, "Anas," October 31, 1792, Jefferson, *Writings* (Ford), I, 207.

27. See Bemis, *Jay's Treaty*, pp. 22–27; Burt, *The United States*, pp. 104–105; Brymner, *Report on the Canadian Archives, 1890*, pp. 99, 100, 107.

28. Burt, *The United States*, pp. 102–104; Bemis, *Jay's Treaty*, p. 21.

29. Douglas Brymner, ed., "Vermont Negotiations," *Report on the Canadian Archives, 1889* (Ottawa, 1890), pp. 53–58.

30. Burt, *The United States*, pp. 102–104.

31. Samuel Flagg Bemis, "Relations Between the Vermont Separatists and Great Britain, 1789–1791," *American Historical Review*, XXI (April 1916), 554.

32. Committee of Privy Council for Trade to Grenville, April 17, 1790, Chatham Papers, PRO 30/8/343.

33. Brymner, *Report on the Canadian Archives, 1890*, Note E, p. 132.

34. *Ibid.*, pp. 131–133.

35. Burt, *The United States*, pp. 111–113; Bemis, *Jay's Treaty*, pp. 77–78.

36. For Bowles's history see Elisha P. Douglass, "The Adventurer Bowles," *William and Mary Quarterly*, 3rd ser., VI, (January 1949), 3–23.

37. Bowles to Grenville, January 13, 1791, printed in Frederick Jackson Turner, ed., "English Policy Toward America in 1790–91," *American Historical Review*, VII (1901–1902), 729.

38. *Ibid.*, pp. 730–732.

39. *Ibid.*, p. 732.

40. Grenville to Hawkesbury, January 14, 1791, Liverpool Papers, BM, Add. Mss. 38,226, ff. 42–43.

41. Brymner, *Report on the Canadian Archives, 1890*, xliii.

42. Grenville to Hammond, January 3, 1792, FO 115/1. Mayo, *Instructions to British Ministers*, III, 20–21.

43. Grenville to Hammond, September 1, 1791, No. 1, FO 115/1.

44. Grenville to Hammond, March 17, 1792, No. 8, FO 115/1.

45. *Ibid.*

46. Grenville to Hammond, April 25, 1792, No. 9, FO 115/1. For a map of the proposed Indian border state, see Bemis, *Jay's Treaty*, p. 152.

47. Brymner, *Report on the Canadian Archives, 1890*, p. 168.

48. *Ibid.*, p. 171.

49. Hammond to Grenville, December 19, 1791, FO 4/11.

50. Grenville to Hammond, March 17, 1792, No. 8, FO 115/1.

51. Grenville to Hammond, April 25, 1792, No. 9, FO 115/1.

52. Hammond to Grenville, June 8, 1792, No. 23, FO 4/15.

53. Grenville to Hammond, August 4, 1792, No. 13, Mayo, *Instructions to British Ministers*, III, 30–31.

54. Hammond to Simcoe, April 21, 1792, Ernest Cruikshank, ed., *The Correspondence of Lieutenant Governor John Graves Simcoe*, 5 vols. (Toronto, 1923–1931), I, 130–131. Hereafter cited as Cruikshank, *Simcoe Correspondence*.

55. Simcoe to Alexander McKee, August 30, 1792, CO 42/417; MPC XXIV, 483–501.

56. Jefferson, "Anas," December 10 and 12, 1792, Jefferson, *Writings* (Ford), I, 210–211.

57. Hammond to Simcoe, April 21, 1792, Cruikshank, *Simcoe Correspondence,* I, 130–131; Simcoe to Hammond, September 27, 1792, CO 42/317.

58. Jefferson, "Anas," October 31, 1792, Jefferson, *Writings* (Ford), I, 207.

59. Jefferson, "Anas," February 26, 1793, *ibid.*, pp. 218–219.

60. *Ibid.*

61. Once, however, Jefferson did recommend building a post at Presqu'Isle on land recently purchased from the Indians, and there beginning naval preparations on the Great Lakes. This, Hamilton said, would bring on war. Jefferson, "Anas," March 9, 1792, *ibid.*, I, 181.

62. BT 5/6, p. 63.

63. P. Colquhoun to Grenville, July 29, 1791, the Manuscripts of J. B. Fortescue, Esq., Preserved at Dropmore, Publications of the Historical Manuscripts Commission of Great Britain, II, 145; hereafter cited as *Dropmore Papers,* HMC. Colquhoun to Grenville, August 5, 1791, *ibid.*, p. 157.

64. P. Colquhoun to Grenville, July 29, 1791, *ibid.*, p. 145.

65. Grenville to Hammond, September 1, 1791, No. 2, FO 4/11.

66. *Ibid.*; Jefferson to Hammond, November 29, 1791, FO 4/11; Hammond to Jefferson, November 30, 1791, *ibid.*; Hammond to Jefferson, December 6, 1791, *ibid.*

67. Grenville to Hammond, September 1, 1791, No. 2, FO 4/11.

68. Committee of the Privy Council Report (1791), in *Interesting and Important Reports,* p. 126.

69. *Ibid.*, p. 127.

70. *Ibid.*, pp. 127–130.

71. *Ibid.*, p. 138.

72. Hawkesbury to Henry Wilckens, September 23, 1789, Liverpool Papers, BM Add. Mss, 38,310, ff. 42–43.

73. *Ibid.*, BM Add. Mss, 38,255, ff. 106–107.

74. The American government had in its possession a copy of the Committee of the Privy Council's Report for 1791, and so both Jefferson and Hamilton must have been aware of this probability. Copies of the report may be found in both the Washington Papers, LC and the Jefferson Papers, LC.

75. John Adams to Jefferson, August 4, 1785, Jefferson, *Papers* (Boyd), VIII, 341–342.

7. THE STRUCTURE OF AMERICAN NEUTRALITY

1. Jefferson to Washington, April 1, 1793, Washington Papers, LC, Ser. 2, XXIX, 178–179.

2. Hamilton to Washington, April 5, 1793, Hamilton Papers, LC; Hamilton to Washington, April 8, 1793, *ibid.*

3. For a good outline of the state of American opinion on the eve of the war, see Tobias Lear to Washington, April 8, 1793, Washington Papers, LC, Ser. 4, CCLIX, 73 A and B.

4. The Treaty of Amity and Commerce and the Treaty of Alliance are in David Hunter Miller, ed., *Treaties and Other International Acts of the United States of America,* 8 vols. (Washington, 1931), I, 5–40. French possessions at this time included the French islands in the West Indies and the two small islands of St. Pierre and Miquelon in the Gulf of St. Lawrence. Samuel Flagg Bemis, *John Quincy Adams and the Foundations of American Foreign Policy* (New York, 1949), p. 33.

5. Charles S. Hyneman, "Neutrality During the European Wars of 1792–1815," *American Journal of International Law,* XXIV (April 1930), 285–286.

6. Hamilton to ——, May, 1793, Hamilton Papers, LC.

7. Jefferson to Brissot, May 8, 1793, Jefferson Papers, LC; Jefferson to H. Innes, May 23, 1793, *ibid.*

8. "Pacificus III," Hamilton, *Works* (Lodge), IV, 458, 456.

9. "Pacificus VI," *ibid., p.* 477–478.

10. Hamilton, *Works* (Lodge), IV, 370, 388.

11. *Ibid., p.* 375.

12. *Ibid., p.* 377.

13. *Ibid., p.* 397.

14. *Ibid., p.* 390.

15. "Pacificus III," *ibid., p.* 457.

16. Jefferson to Mr. Donald, March 5, 1793, Jefferson Papers, LC; Jefferson to William Short, March 23, 1793, *ibid.*, Jefferson to Washington, April 7, 1793, Jefferson, *Writings* (Ford), VI, 212.

17. Jefferson to James Monroe, May 5, 1793, Jefferson Papers, LC.

18. Jefferson to Madison, June 23, 1793, Madison Papers, LC.

19. Jefferson to Madison, June 29, 1793, Madison Papers, LC.

20. Jefferson to Doctor Gilmer, June 28, 1793, Jefferson Papers, LC; see also Jefferson to Monroe, June 28, 1793, *ibid.*

21. Jefferson to Madison, March 24, 1793, *ibid.*; same to same, September 1, 1793, Madison Papers, LC.

22. Jefferson to Mr. Murray, May 21, 1793, Jefferson Papers, LC.

23. Jefferson to Madison, March 24, 1793, Jefferson Papers, LC.

24. Jefferson notes, July 5, 1793, Jefferson Papers, LC.

25. Later, when Jefferson was out of office, he did tell Madison that he had "no doubt but that we ought to interpose at a proper time, and declare both to England and France that those islands are to rest with France, and that we will make common cause with the latter for that object." Jefferson to Madison, April 3, 1794, Madison Papers, LC. But even here Jefferson was careful to say "at a proper time," and his statements when he was no longer responsible for the action of the government were generally more radical than when he was in office. While in office Jefferson explored many ways of abiding by the guarantee without bringing war. He had spoken for an insertion into the Proclamation of Neutrality of a determination on the part of America to follow the laws of nations as determined by *modern* usage. Modern usage of international law he interpreted to mean that all property on neutral ships save contraband would be immune from seizure, and such a law would allow America to carry supplies for either of the belligerents. Thus he proposed to insert the phrase *modern usage* "to open upon [England] the idea that we should require acquiescence in that principle as the condition of our remaining in peace. It was thought desirable by the other gentlemen, but having no expectation of any effect from it they acquiesced in the insertion of the word mainly to gratify me.—I had another view, which I did not mention to them, because I apprehended it would occasion the loss of the word. By the ancient law of nations, e.g. in the time of the Romans, the furnishing a limited aid of troops, tho' stipulated [by treaty], was deemed a cause of war. In latter times it is admitted not to be a cause of war. This is one of the improvements in the law of nations. I thought we might conclude by parity of reasoning that the guaranteeing a limited portion of territory, in a stipulated case, might not by the *modern* law of nations be a cause of war. I therefore meant by the introduction of that word to lay the foundation of the execution of our guarantee by way of negociation with England." Jefferson note, [1793], Jefferson Papers, LC.

26. Jefferson to Madison, May 19, 1793, Madison Papers, LC.

27. Helvidius V, Madison, *Writings,* VI, 186.

28. See for instance, Jefferson's cabinet opinion, May 16, 1793, Jefferson Papers, LC; notes on cabinet meeting, August 3, 1793, *ibid.*

29. Jefferson to Thomas Randolph, June 24, 1793, Jefferson Papers, LC.

30. Jefferson to Washington, October 3, 1793, Washington Papers, LC, Ser. 2, XXIX, 295–296.

31. See Gerald Stourzh, *Benjamin Franklin and American Foreign Policy* (Chicago, 1954), p. 185.

32. Notes on cabinet conference, April 18, 1793, Jefferson Papers, LC.

33. Madison to Jefferson, December 21, 1793, Madison, *Writings*, VI, 229–230.

34. John Adams to Abigail Adams, December 5, 1793, Charles Francis Adams, ed., *Letters of John Adams, Addressed to His Wife*, 2 vols. (Boston, 1841), II, 131.

35. Jefferson to Madison, February 14, 1783, Jefferson, *Papers* (Boyd), VI, 241.

36. Notes on cabinet meeting, 1793, Jefferson Papers, LC.

37. Randolph's opinion on receiving Genet, May 6, 1793, Washington Papers, LC, Ser. 4, CCLX, 16–32.

38. Jefferson to Madison, 1793, Madison Papers, LC.

39. Washington to Governor Thomas Sim Lee of Maryland, October 13, 1793, Washington, *Writings*, XXXIII, 119.

40. For Washington's sympathy for France and her cause, see Jefferson's Anas, December 27, 1792, Jefferson, *Writings* (Ford), I, 212; also notes on cabinet conference, August 20, 1793, Jefferson Papers, LC; for qualifications on this support, see Washington to Governor Henry Lee of Virginia, May 6, 1793, Washington, *Writings*, XXXII, 450. Washington's remarks on James Monroe's *View of the Conduct of the Executive* also make clear Washington's sympathy for the French cause. See Jared Sparks, ed., *The Writings of George Washington*, 12 vols. (Boston, 1834–1837), XI, 505.

41. Washington to Governor Henry Lee, August 26, 1794, Washington, *Writings*, XXXIII, 479.

42. Washington to Hamilton, May 7, 1793, *ibid.*, XXXII, 451.

43. Edward Livingston to Robert R. Livingston, May 15, 1793, Robert R. Livingston Papers, NYHS. The manuscript is mutilated in several spots.

44. *Gazette of the United States*, May 22 and 25, 1793.

45. Jefferson to Madison, July 7, 1793, Madison Papers, LC.

46. Robert R. Livingston to Edward Livingston, August 19, 1793, Robert R. Livingston Papers, NYHS.

47. Ulrich B. Phillips, "The South Carolina Federalists," *American Historical Review*, XIV, No. 4 (July 1909), 733.

48. Jefferson to Madison, August 11, 1793, Madison Papers, LC; Madison to Jefferson, September 2, 1793, Madison, *Writings*, VI, 191.

49. Madison, *Writings*, VI, 191–193; see also Madison to Jefferson, August 27, 1793, *ibid.*, p. 179 n.; for what is evidently a typical letter from Madison to a county leader, see Madison to Archibald Stuart, September 1, 1793, *ibid.*, 188.

50. R. Troup to Rufus King, January 1, 1794, King, *Life and Correspondence*, I, 540; William S. Smith to Hamilton, August 22, 1793, Hamilton Papers, LC.

51. George Cabot to Rufus King, August 2, 1793, Lodge, *Life of Cabot*, p. 74; Ames to Hamilton, August 31, 1793, Hamilton Papers, LC.

8. THE WEAPONS OF AMERICAN NEUTRALITY

1. Marshall Smelser, *The Congress Founds the Navy, 1787–1798* (Notre Dame, 1959), pp. 60–61, n. 38.

2. *Ibid.*

3. See Jefferson's report to the President, December 1793, Jefferson Papers, LC.

4. John Alsop to King, December 12, 1793, King Papers, NYHS.

5. Fifth Annual Address to Congress, December 3, 1793, Washington, *Writings,* XXXIII, 165–169.

6. Jefferson's Report on Commerce, Jefferson, *Writings* (Ford), VI, 472–483.

7. *Annals of Congress,* IV, 156.

8. This point is well brought out by Broadus Mitchell, *Alexander Hamilton,* 2 vols. (New York, 1957–1962), II, 292.

9. *Annals of Congress,* IV, 174–210.

10. Fisher Ames to Christopher Gore, January 28, 1794, Ames, *Works of Fisher Ames,* I, 133.

11. Fisher Ames to Thomas Dwight, January 17, 1794, *ibid.*

12. *Annals of Congress,* IV, 198–208.

13. *Ibid.,* p. 302.

14. *Ibid.,* pp. 229–230.

15. *Ibid.,* pp. 245–246.

16. Americanus I and II, February 1 and 8, 1794, Hamilton *Works* (Lodge), V, 74ff.

17. *Annals of Congress,* IV, 418–419, 425.

18. *Ibid.,* p. 429.

19. Madison to Jefferson, March 2, 1794, Madison Papers, LC.

20. *Annals of Congress,* IV, 431–432.

21. Christopher Gore to Rufus King, March 3, 1794, King, *Life and Correspondence,* I, 547.

22. Sedgwick to E. Williams, February 18, 1794, Sedgwick Papers, MHS.

23. Madison to Jefferson, March 2, 1794, Madison Papers, LC.

24. Fisher Ames to Christopher Gore, Ames, *Works of Fisher Ames,* I, 135.

25. For Madison's suspicions, see Madison to Jefferson, March 9, 1794, Madison Papers, LC.

26. ASPFR, I, 429.

27. Sedgwick to ——, March 3, 1794, Sedgwick Papers, MHS.

28. Madison to Jefferson, March 9, 1794, Madison Papers, LC.

29. *General Advertiser,* March 22, 1794.

30. *Annals of Congress,* IV, 529; ASPFR, I, 428.

31. Dorchester's Speech to the Indians, printed in Cruikshank, *Correspondence of Lieutenant Governor Simcoe,* II, 149 ff.

32. *Annals of Congress,* IV, 529–530; Ames to Christopher Gore, March 5, 1794, Ames, *Works of Fisher Ames,* I, 138. Ames's discussion of the laying of the embargo was obviously added to the letter on March 25 or 26.

33. For Federalist reservations, see Ames to Christopher Gore, March 5, 1794, *ibid.,* pp. 138–139; John Adams to Abigail Adams, April 1, 1794, C. F. Adams, ed., *Letters of John Adams Addressed to His Wife,* II, 148.

34. William Barry Grove (representative from North Carolina) to James Hogg, April 3, 1794, Kemp L. Battle, *Letters of Nathaniel Macon, John Steele and William Barry Grove* (Chapel Hill, North Carolina, 1902), pp. 94–95.

35. Sedgwick to E. Williams, March 28, 1794, Sedgwick Papers, MHS.

36. Sedgwick to Williams, March 29, 1794, *ibid.*; John Adams to Abigail Adams, March 31, 1794, *Adams Papers* (microfilm), Reel 377.

37. Madison to Jefferson, April 14, 1794, Madison Papers, LC; Bemis asserts mistakenly in his *Jay's Treaty,* p. 268, that Dayton's proposition passed the Committee of the Whole on March 31. It did not, however. See *Annals of Congress,* IV, 556–557.

38. *Ibid.*, p. 596.
39. See, for instance, Sedgwick to Dwight Foster, January 12, 1794, Miscellaneous Bound Papers, MHS; John Adams to Abigail Adams, March 27, 1794, *Adams Papers* (microfilm), Reel 377.
40. Ames to Christopher Gore, February 25, 1794, Ames, *Works of Fisher Ames,* I, 136.
41. Rufus King to Jay, March 2, 1794, Jay Papers, Iselin Collection, Columbia University; see also Fisher Ames to Christopher Gore, February 25, 1794, Ames, *Works of Fisher Ames,* I, 135.
42. Sedgwick to E. Williams, April 18, 1794, Sedgwick Papers, MHS; John Adams to Abigail Adams, April 5, 1794, Adams, *Letters of John Adams to His Wife,* II, 152.
43. Hamilton to Washington, March 8, 1794, Hamilton, *Works* (Lodge), X, 63–65.
44. Sedgwick to E. Williams, March 10, 1794, Sedgwick Papers, MHS.
45. See letters in *General Advertiser,* December 27, 1793, and January 3, 1794.
46. *Annals of Congress,* IV, 488–491.
47. Madison to Madison Sr., February 21, 1794, Madison Papers, LC.
48. Henry Tazewell to Monroe, March, 1794, Monroe Papers, LC. Even to John Adams, these arguments seemed valid. He thought it would be better to buy off the Algerians. "Build a few Frigates if you will but expect they will be useless because unmanned," he wrote his wife. John to Abigail Adams, February 10, 1794, *Adams Papers* (microfilm), Reel 377.
49. *General Advertiser,* February 12, 1794.
50. *Annals of Congress,* IV, 497–498.
51. Lyman and Dearborn of Massachusetts and Gilman of New Hampshire. *Ibid.,* p. 459.
52. Madison to Jefferson, March 9, 1794, Madison Papers, LC.
53. Knox to Washington, December 4, 1793, Washington Papers, LC, Ser. 4, CCLVIV, 18.
54. *Annals of Congress,* IV, 501–504.
55. *Ibid.,* pp. 556–557.
56. *Ibid.,* p. 558.
57. Sedgwick to E. Williams, April 7, 1794, Sedgwick Papers, MHS.
58. Christopher Gore to Rufus King, March 15, 1794, King, *Life and Correspondence,* I, 552.
59. Randolph to Washington, April 6, 1794, Washington Papers, LC, Ser. 2, XXX, 16–20.
60. King, *Life and Correspondence,* I, 523.
61. This is reconstructed from notes by Rufus King in *ibid.,* p. 517, and an account in the Ellsworth Papers, Bancroft Transcripts, NYPL.
62. Ellsworth Papers, Bancroft Transcripts, NYPL.
63. King, *Life and Correspondence,* I, 518.
64. Washington to Governor Clinton, March 31, 1794, Washington, *Writings,* XXXIII, 310–311.
65. Washington to William Pearce, April 6, 1794, *ibid.,* pp. 314–315.
66. King, *Life and Correspondence,* I, 524.
67. Monroe to Washington, April 8 and 11, 1794, Washington Papers, LC, Ser. 4, CCLXVI, 76, 87–88; John Nicholas to Washington, April 6, 1794, *ibid.,* pp. 56–57. Since Edmund Randolph had also objected to Hamilton's name, Washington evidently suspected that the letters from James Monroe and John Nicholas, both friends of Randolph, had been inspired by his own secretary of state. Randolph denied this. See Randolph to Washington, April 9, 1794, *ibid.,* p. 80.
68. Hamilton to Washington, April 14, 1794, Hamilton, *Works* (Lodge), V, 97–

114; for Washington's doubts concerning Hamilton, see King, *Life and Correspondence*, I, 518.

69. *Ibid.*, p. 520.

70. Washington to Edmund Randolph, April 15, 1794, Washington, *Writings*, XXXIII, 329. Italics in original.

71. King, *Life and Correspondence*, I, 522; see also Madison to Jefferson, April 28, 1794, Madison, *Writings*, VI, 211–212.

72. *Annals of Congress*, IV, 602–603.

73. Sedgwick to E. Williams, April 22, 1794, Sedgwick Papers, MHS.

74. Madison to Madison Sr., April 29, 1794, Madison Papers, LC.

75. *Annals of Congress*, IV, 90, 605–606.

76. John Adams to Abigail Adams, February 9, 1794, Adams, *Letters of John Adams to His Wife*, II, 141.

77. John Adams to Abigail Adams, March 31, 1794, *Adams Papers* (microfilm), Reel 377.

78. John Adams to Abigail Adams, April 15, 1794, Adams, *Letters of John Adams to His Wife*, II, 155.

79. *Annals of Congress*, IV, p. 90.

80. Jefferson to Madison, September 21, 1795, Jefferson, *Writings* (Memorial Edition), VII, 33.

81. Madison to Jefferson, March 14, 1794, Madison Papers, LC.

82. Jefferson to Monroe, April 24, 1794, Jefferson Papers, LC.

83. Judge Innes to Monroe, March 11, 1794, Monroe Papers, NYPL.

84. Madison to Horatio Gates, March 24, 1794, Madison, *Writings*, VI, 209.

85. Jefferson to Tenche Coxe, May 1, 1794, Jefferson Papers, LC; see also Madison to Jefferson, March 14, 1794, Madison Papers, LC, for evidence that Madison believed that war with England was a possibility even if America retaliated commercially.

86. *Argus*, May 12, 1795.

87. Robert R. Livingston to Monroe, March 10, 1794, Robert R. Livingston Papers, NYHS; *Annals of Congress*, IV, 486–492.

88. Joseph Jones to Monroe, March 22, 1794, Monroe Papers, LC, Ser. I.

89. Jefferson to Martha Randolph, December 22, 1793, Jefferson Papers, LC; Robert R. Livingston to Monroe, March 10, 1794, Robert R. Livingston Papers, NYHS; same to same, March 13, 1794, Monroe Papers, LC, Ser. I; same to same, April 8, 1794, *ibid.*

90. *General Advertiser*, January 8, 1794.

91. Hamilton to Washington, April 14, 1794, Hamilton, *Works* (Lodge), V, 105.

92. *Gazette of the United States*, April 17, 1794.

93. Americanus I, Hamilton, *Works* (Lodge), V, 84; John Adams to Abigail Adams, March 15, 1794, *Adams Papers* (microfilm), Reel 377.

94. Hamilton to Washington, April 14, 1794, Hamilton, *Works* (Lodge), V, 109.

95. Americanus I, *ibid.*, pp. 84–85.

96. Hamilton to Governor Clinton, October 3, 1793, *ibid.*, IX, 393; Pacificus VI, *ibid.*, IV, 478; John Adams to Jay, May 8, 1795, Adams, *Works*, VIII, 246.

97. Americanus I, Hamilton, *Works* (Lodge), V, 79–84.

98. Hamilton to Governor Clinton, October 3, 1783, *ibid.*, IX, 393.

99. Hamilton to Washington, April 14, 1794, *ibid.*, V, 111.

100. Timothy Dwight to Oliver Wolcott, 1793, George Gibbs, ed., *Memoirs of the Administrations of Washington and John Adams, Edited from the Papers of Oliver Wolcott, Secretary of the Treasury*, 2 vols. (New York, 1846), I, 107. Hereafter, Gibbs, *Memoirs of Administrations*.

101. John Quincy Adams to John Adams, January 5, 1794, *Adams Papers* (micro-

film), Reel 377; John Adams to Thomas Boylston Adams, March 19, 1794, *ibid.*

102. Fisher Ames to Christopher Gore, March 26, 1794, Ames, *Works of Fisher Ames,* I, 140.

103. Jefferson to Tenche Coxe, May 1, 1794, Jefferson Papers, LC.

104. Asher Robbins to Benjamin Bourne, March 6, 1794, Robbins Letters, Clements Library, University of Michigan.

105. Ames to Christopher Gore, February 25, 1794, Ames, *Works of Fisher Ames,* I, 136.

106. See for instance Hamilton to Washington, June 22, 1794, Hamilton, *Works* (Lodge), V, 134.

107. Alexander DeConde, *Entangling Alliance,* p. 101.

108. Ames to Christopher Gore, March 26, 1794, Ames, *Works of Fisher Ames,* I, 140.

109. John Adams to Abigail Adams, April 19, 1794, Adams, *Letters of John Adams to His Wife,* II, 157.

110. Sedgwick to E. Williams, March 6, 1794, Sedgwick Papers, MHS.

111. Ames to Christopher Gore, March 26, 1794, Ames, *Works of Fisher Ames,* I, 140.

112. George Cabot to Samuel Phillips, March 10, 1794, Henry Cabot Lodge, ed., *The Life and Letters of George Cabot* (Boston, 1877), p. 77.

113. Hamilton to Washington, April 14, 1794, Hamilton, *Works* (Lodge), V, 110.

114. *Ibid.,* pp. 105–106.

115. *Ibid.,* p. 105.

116. King, *Life and Correspondence,* I, 520.

117. Hamilton to Washington, April 23, 1794, Hamilton, *Works* (Lodge), V, 115–118; Hamilton to Jay, May 6, 1794, *ibid.,* pp. 124–125.

118. Adams to Jefferson, May 11, 1794, Jefferson Papers, LC.

119. See Washington's letter to Richard Henry Lee, dated April 15, 1794, the day before he sent Jay's nomination to the Senate, in Washington, *Writings,* XXXIII, 331.

120. Madison to Jefferson, May 11, 1794, Madison Papers, LC.

121. *Ibid.*

122. John Adams to Abigail Adams, May 10, 1794, Adams, *Letters of John Adams to His Wife,* II, 159; see also the account of Rufus King, in King, *Life and Correspondence,* I, 525–527.

123. *Annals of Congress,* IV, 683.

124. *Ibid.,* pp. 715–716.

125. *Ibid.,* p. 709.

126. Monroe to Jefferson, May 26, 1794, Jefferson Papers, LC; *Annals of Congress,* IV, 738; Madison to Jefferson, June 1, 1794, Madison, *Writings,* VI, 217–218.

127. *Annals of Congress,* IV, 761–767.

128. Hamilton to Jay, June 4, 1794, Hamilton, *Works* (Lodge), X, 66–67.

129. Ames to Christopher Gore, May 2, 1794, Ames, *Works of Fisher Ames,* I, 142.

130. Madison to Jefferson, May 25, 1794, Madison, *Writings,* VI, 217.

9. NEGOTIATIONS

1. Grenville to Hammond, February 8, 1793, No. 3, FO 115/2.

2. See for instance, *The Times* (London), May 7 and 17, 1793.

3. *The Times,* September 7 and 19, 1793; *Morning Chronicle,* June 7, 1793; *St. James's Chronicle or British Evening-Post,* October 8–19, 1793.

4. Opposition newspapers regularly praised Washington. However, they praised all things American primarily as a means of attacking the ministers and their policies toward France and America. But the ministerial newspapers also praised Washing-

ton. *St. James's Chronicle or British Evening-Post,* September 14–17 and October 8–10, 1793. Even Hawkesbury had a good word for him. Hawkesbury to Phineas Bond, January 14, 1796, Liverpool Papers, BM, Add. Mss, 38,310, ff. 147–148. Jay's comment is in Jay to Tenche Coxe, December 18, 1794, Johnston, *Correspondence of John Jay,* IV, 153.

5. Grenville to Hammond, January 11, 1794, No. 1, FO 115/3.

6. *Ibid.*

7. Hammond to Grenville, March 7, 1793, No. 6, FO 5/1.

8. Grenville to Hammond, November 20, 1794, FO 5/5.

9. Henry Dundas to Lt. Governor Clarke of Canada, May 1, 1793, CO 42/97.

10. Report of Governor Dorchester, enclosed in Dorchester to Dundas, October 25, 1793, No. 3, CO 42/97.

11. *Ibid.*

12. Benjamin Fisher to Lt. Governor Clarke, May 3, 1793, enclosed in Clarke to Dundas, October 25, 1793, No. 95, CO 42/97.

13. Simcoe to Dorchester, March 14, 1795, Cruikshank, *Simcoe Correspondence,* II, 179.

14. Report of Governor Dorchester, enclosed in Dorchester to Dundas, October 25, 1793, No. 3, CO 42/97.

15. Simcoe to Dundas, September 20, 1793, No. 18, CO 42/317.

16. Dorchester to Dundas, October 25, 1793, No. 3, CO 42/97.

17. Simcoe to Dundas, September 20, 1793, No. 18, CO 42/317.

18. Dorchester to Dundas, January 18, 1794, No. 11, CO 42/98; same to same, February 24, 1794, No. 18, CO 42/98.

19. Dundas to Dorchester, January 8, 1794, No. 1, CO 42/98.

20. Grenville to Hammond, March 12, 1793, No. 6, FO 115/2.

21. Hammond to Grenville, May 17, 1793, No. 14, FO 5/1.

22. Hammond to Grenville, July 7, 1793, No. 16, FO 5/1.

23. Grenville to Hammond, March 12, 1793, No. 6, FO 115/2.

24. *Morning Chronicle,* May 17, 1793.

25. Anne Cornelia Clauder, *American Commerce as Affected by the Wars of the French Revolution and Napoleon, 1793–1812* (Philadelphia, 1932), p. 64.

26. Hammond to Grenville, September 17, 1793, No. 19, FO 5/1.

27. ASPFR, I, 429.

28. John Stanley, writing from St. Christopher's, to Henry Dundas, June 27, 1793. This letter was transmitted from Dundas to Grenville, August 19, 1793, less than twenty days before the order of November 6 was issued. FO 5/3.

29. *St. James's Chronicle or British Evening Post,* August 20–22, 1793.

30. Phillips and Reed, *Neutrality,* II, 43–45; *Morning Chronicle,* August 16, 1793; Minutes of the Committee on Trade, January 6, 1794, BT 5/9.

31. Foreign Office Journal of J. B. Burges, December 28, 1793, *Dropmore Papers,* HMC, II, 488–489.

32. Grenville to Hammond, January 10, 1794, Mayo, *Instructions to the British Ministers,* p. 48.

33. Minutes of the Committee on Trade, January 6, 1794, BT 5/9.

34. Grenville to Hammond, January 11, 1794, Nos. 4 and 5, FO 4/5.

35. Tobias Lear, Washington's former secretary, wrote Washington from London that this was the main assumption of all Britain's policy toward America. Lear to Washington, February (?), 1794, Washington Papers, LC, Ser. 4, CCLXV, 96.

36. Dundas to Simcoe, March 16, 1794, No. 3, CO 42/318.

37. *Morning Chronicle,* April 26, 1794.

38. *Ibid.,* April 29, 1794; *World,* April 30, 1794.

39. *St. James's Chronicle or British Evening-Post*, April 29–May 1, 1794; *Sun*, May 7, 1794.

40. *St. James's Chronicle or British Evening-Post*, May 13–15, 1794.

41. *World*, May 20, 1794.

42. *Ibid.*, May 21, 1794.

43. *The Times*, May 23, 1794; *St. James's Chronicle or British Evening-Post*, May 20–22, 1794; *Sun*, May 24, 1794.

44. *World*, May 24, 1794.

45. *The Times*, May 27, 1794.

46. *Morning Chronicle*, May 26, 1794.

47. *Oracle and Public Advertiser*, May 27, 1794.

48. *Morning Chronicle*, May 26, 1794.

49. *World*, June 11, 1794.

50. *Ibid.*

51. *World*, June 12 and 13, 1794; *Sun*, June 11, 1794; *Morning Chronicle*, June 11 and 12, 1794; *St. James's Chronicle or British Evening-Post*, June 10–12 and 12–14, 1794; *The Times*, June 12, 1794.

52. Hammond to Grenville, April 17, 1794, No. 15, FO 5/4.

53. Bemis, *Jay's Treaty*, p. 300.

54. Dundas to Dorchester, July 5, 1794, No. 2, CO 42/98.

55. *World*, April 28, 1794; *St. James's Chronicle or British Evening-Post*, April 24–26, 1794; *Oracle and Public Advertiser*, April 28, 1794.

56. Bemis, *Jay's Treaty*, p. 316.

57. Hammond to Grenville, March 12, 1794, No. 7, FO 5/4.

58. Lt. Governor Bruce to Dundas, March 29, 1794. Received April 22, 1794, CO 71/26.

59. Phineas Bond to Grenville, April 28, 1794, J. Franklin Jameson, ed., "The Letters of Phineas Bond, British Consul at Philadelphia, to the Foreign Office of Great Britain, 1790–1794," AHA Annual Report for 1897 (Washington, 1898), p. 552.

60. See for instance CO 28/64; CO 260/12; CO 152/72.

61. The correspondence of Sir Charles Grey is in CO 319/5.

62. Stephen Fuller to John King, August 27, 1794, CO 137/93. From the account of this incident in Bemis, *Jay's Treaty*, one might derive the implication that bread was so scarce as to render two-ounce loaves a curiosity in the West Indies. The correspondence cited by Bemis for this statement indicated that Fuller's letter was the basis for it, and Fuller's letter speaks of loaves from five and one-half to seven and one-half ounces, not two ounces. The letter also states that the loaves would be a curiosity in England, not in the West Indies. The situation was bad, but not quite as bad as Bemis implies.

63. John King to Stephen Fuller, August 29, 1794, CO 137/93.

64. Lt. Governor Home to Dundas, August 1, 1794, CO 101/33; Lt. Governor Williamson to Dundas, June 11, 1794, CO 137/93. King must have been mistaken in asserting that Williamson's last letter had been dated June 28. No dispatch bearing that date is now to be found, and the dispatch bearing news of the shortage was dated two weeks before June 28, although it did not arrive until September 18. King probably was referring to Williamson's dispatch of April 28, 1794, which of course did not mention the shortage.

65. Governor Hamilton to Dundas, June 3, 1794, postscript dated June 21, 1794, CO 37/44.

66. Grenville to Hammond, August 8, 1794, FO 115/3, Pt. I.

67. Dundas to Dorchester, July 5, 1794, CO 52/98.

68. Portland to Dorchester, October 4, 1794, No. 5, CO 42/100; see also same to same, August 14, 1794, No. 2, CO 42/99.

69. See for instance Simcoe to Dundas, February 23, 1794, CO 42/318.

70. Grenville to Hammond, May 10, 1794, No. 13, FO 115/3, Pt. I.

71. *St. James's Chronicle or British Evening-Post*, April 24–26, 1794; *Oracle and Public Advertiser*, April 28, 1794.

72. Grenville to Hammond, May 10, 1794, No. 13, FO 115/3, Pt. I.

73. Jay to Hamilton, September 17, 1794, Johnston, *Correspondence of John Jay*, IV, 115.

74. Jay to Hamilton, September 17, 1794, *ibid.*; same to same, August 17, 1794, *Jay Papers*, Iselin Collection (microfilm), Reel 1.

75. Jay to Hamilton, July 11, 1794, Johnston, *Correspondence of John Jay*, IV, 30.

76. *Ibid.*

77. Jay to Randolph, June 23, 1794, *ibid.*, p. 29.

78. Jay to Washington, August 11, 1794, Washington Papers, LC, Ser. 4, CCLXVIII, 70.

79. Jay to Hamilton, September 8, 1792, Johnston, *Correspondence of John Jay*, III, 448.

80. Jay to Washington, September 13, 1794, *ibid.*, IV, 58; Jay to Hamilton, April 11, 1783, Hamilton Papers, LC.

81. Brymner, *Report on the Canadian Archives, 1890*, p. 140.

82. Jay to Randolph, June 23, 1794, Johnston, *Correspondence of John Jay*, IV, 29; Jay to Washington, September 13, 1794, *ibid.*, p. 59; Jay to Hamilton, July 11, 1794, *ibid.*, p. 30.

83. Jay to Robert Goodloe Harper, January 19, 1795, *ibid.*, p. 202.

84. John Temple to the Marquis of Carmarthen, December 7, 1786, FO 4/4.

85. Lord Auckland to Lord Grenville, June 22, 1794, *Dropmore Papers*, HMC, II, 578.

86. Jay to Washington, July 21, 1794, Johnston, *Correspondence of John Jay*, IV, 34.

87. Theodore Sizer, ed., *The Autobiography of Colonel John Trumbull* (New Haven, Conn., 1953), p. 181.

88. Hamilton, *Works* (Lodge), V, 136.

89. Jay to Randolph, November 19, 1794, ASPFR, I, 503.

90. Grenville to John Nutt and William Molleson, 1794, FO 95/512.

91. Jay to Grenville, September 4, 1794, ASPFR, I, 492; Grenville to John Nutt and William Molleson, July 23, 1794, FO 95/512.

92. Jay to Randolph, November 19, 1794, ASPFR, I, 503.

93. Randolph's Instructions to Jay, May 6, 1794, *ibid.*, p. 473.

94. Jay to Randolph, November 19, 1794, *ibid.*, p. 503.

95. *Ibid.*

96. Jay to Randolph, June 1, 1795, *ibid.*, p. 520.

97. George Chalmers to Hawkesbury, July 27, 1794, Liverpool Papers, BM, Add. Mss, 38,229, ff. 307–310; same to same, no date, *ibid.*, ff. 327–328.

98. Chalmers to Hawkesbury, July 27, 1794, *ibid.*, ff, 307–310; same to same, August 2, 1794, *ibid.*, ff. 331–334; same to same, August 5, 1794, *ibid.*, ff. 335–336.

99. Hawkesbury's draft of a memorandum, *ibid.*, BM, Add. Mss, 38,352, ff. 381–389; a shortened and less strongly worded appeal against the opening of the West Indies to American ships is in BM Add. Mss, 38,354, and has been printed by Bradford Perkins, ed., "Lord Hawkesbury and the Jay-Grenville Negotiations," *Mississippi Valley Historical Review*, XL (1953–1954), 291–304.

100. Hawkesbury to Grenville, October 17, 1794, Chatham Papers, PRO, CLII.

101. Jay to Randolph, September 13, 1794, ASPFR, I, 486.
102. Grenville to Hammond, March 17, 1792, FO 115/1.
103. ASPFR, I, 492, 493.
104. James Fulton Zimmerman, *Impressment of American Seamen* (New York, 1925), p. 45.
105. Henry Knox to Washington, April 15, 1794, *Washington Papers*, LC, Ser. 4, CCLXVI, 10.
106. *Morning Chronicle*, July 13, 1793.
107. For a comprehensive treatment of this subject, see Samuel Flagg Bemis, "Jay's Treaty and the Northwest Boundary Gap," *American Historical Review*, XXVII, No. 3 (April 1922), 405–484.
108. Jay's draft of September 30 is printed in Bemis, *Jay's Treaty*, pp. 391–433.
109. Bemis, *Jay's Treaty*, pp. 337–345.
110. Bemis has noted this, and does not claim that Hamilton's communication to Hammond affected this portion of the draft. See *ibid.*, pp. 368–370.
111. Simcoe to Dundas, August 30, 1794, No. 34, WO 1/14. This was received on October 15, 1794.
112. Grenville to Hammond, November 20, 1794, No. 21, FO 115/3.
113. Charles Francis Adams, ed., *Memoirs of John Quincy Adams*, 12 vols. (Boston, 1874–1877), I, 48.
114. Jay to William Short, November 24, 1794, Jay Papers, Monaghan Collection, Columbia University; Jay to Randolph, November 19, 1794, ASPFR, I, 503.

10. RATIFICATION

1. Monroe to Madison, December 18, 1794, Madison Papers, LC.
2. Theodore Sedgwick to E. Williams, December 9, December 12, 1794, Sedgwick Papers, MHS.
3. Josiah Parker to Thomas Smith, December 28, 1794, Josiah Parker Papers, NYPL.
4. Madison to Jefferson, March 11, 1795, Madison Papers, LC.
5. See for instance, William Barry Grove to James Hogg, January 21, 1795, printed in Henry McGilbert Wagstaff, *Federalism in North Carolina* (Chapel Hill, North Carolina, 1910), p. 55.
6. Josiah Parker to Thomas Smith, December 28, 1794, Josiah Parker Papers, NYPL.
7. Madison to Jefferson, March 11, 1795, Madison Papers, LC.
8. Fisher Ames to Thomas Dwight, February 3, 1795, Ames, *Works of Fisher Ames*, I, 166.
9. See, for instance, Robert R. Livingston to Madison, January 30, 1795, Madison Papers, LC.
10. Madison to Jefferson, February 15, 1795, *ibid.*
11. *Ibid.*
12. John Adams to Abigail Adams, February 10, 1795, *Adams Papers* (microfilm), Reel 379.
13. David Blaney to John Jay, September 20, 1795, Jay Papers, Iselin Collection (microfilm), Reel 1.
14. *Argus*, June 20, 1795.
15. Edmund Randolph to John Adams, April 2, 1795, *Adams Papers* (microfilm), Reel 379.

16. *Annals of Congress*, IV, 858.
17. *Argus*, June 24, 1795.
18. *Argus*, June 23, 1795.
19. *Aurora*, June 20, 1795.
20. *Annals of Congress*, IV, 859.
21. *Ibid.*, pp. 860–861.
22. *Ibid.*
23. *Ibid.*, pp. 861–862.

24. *Ibid.*, p. 865.

25. King, *Life and Correspondence*, II, 10, 11, 15; John Miller, *Alexander Hamilton: Portrait in Paradox*, p. 423.

26. Captain Beresford to Captain Cochran, April 23, 1795, FO 5/9.

27. Pierce Butler to Madison, June 12, 1795, Madison Papers, LC.

28. King, *Life and Correspondence*, II, 10; Bernard Fay, *The Two Franklins* (Boston, 1933), pp. 239–240.

29. Stephen Higginson to Timothy Pickering, July 14, 1795, J. Franklin Jameson, ed., *Letters of Stephen Higginson*, AHA Annual Report for 1896 (Washington, 1897), p. 787.

30. Daniel Sargent Jr. to John Quincy Adams, July 20, 1795, *Adams Papers* (microfilm), Reel 380.

31. Robert R. Livingston to Edward Livingston, July 19, 1795, Robert R. Livingston Papers, NYHS.

32. Quoted in Eugene Perry Link, *Democratic-Republican Societies, 1790–1800* (New York, 1942), pp. 132–133.

33. George Cabot to Rufus King, July 27, 1795, Lodge, *Life and Letters of Cabot*, p. 83.

34. Douglas Southall Freeman, *George Washington* (completed by John Alexander Carroll and Mary Wells Ashworth), 7 vols. (New York, 1948–1957), VII, 270, n. 27.

35. Edward Livingston to Margaret Beekman Livingston, July 20, 1795, Robert R. Livingston Papers, NYPL.

36. Stephen Higginson to Timothy Pickering, August 13, 1795, Jameson, *Letters of Stephen Higginson*, p. 789.

37. *Ibid.*; Christopher Gore to Rufus King, September 13, 1795; King, *Life and Correspondence*, II, 31.

38. Jefferson mistakenly attributed "Curtius" to Hamilton, this being the series of articles which occasioned his remark that Hamilton "is really a collossus to the anti-republican party. Without numbers, he is an host within himself." Jefferson to Madison, September 21, 1795, Madison Papers, LC.

39. See Hamilton to Washington, September 4, 1795, Hamilton, *Works* (Lodge), VI, 202–204; same to same, July 9, 1795, *ibid.*, V, 140–179.

40. For a particular instance, see "Camillus" in Hamilton, *Works* (Lodge), VI, 62–63, in which Hamilton slides over the matter of eliminating the distinctions between British and American ships in American harbors. Although this particular essay was evidently written by Rufus King, Hamilton read and approved it, for he has a notation on it. See also Lodge's footnote on p. 140.

41. Madison to——, August 23, 1795, Madison, *Writings*, VI, 238 ff.

42. Washington to G. Morris, June 25, 1794, Washington, *Writings*, XXXIII, 414.

43. *Ibid.*, XXXIV, 252–254.

44. Washington to Hamilton, July 3, 1795, *ibid.*, p. 226.

45. Washington to Randolph, July 29, 1795, *ibid.*, p. 256.

46. *Argus*, July 1, 1795.

47. Josiah T. Newcomb, "New Light on Jay's Treaty," *American Journal of International Law*, XXXVIII, No. 4 (October 1934), 685–692.

48. *Ibid.*, p. 692.

49. Minutes of Conference with Count Wedel of Denmark, April 23, 1795, *Dropmore Papers*, HMC, III, 59.

50. Trumbull to Jay, July 23, 1795, Johnston, *Correspondence of John Jay*, IV, 179–181.

51. Earl Spencer to Captain Sidney Smith, June 7, 1795, quoted in Bradford Perkins, *The First Rapprochement: England and the United States, 1795–1805* (Philadelphia, 1955), p. 35.

52. Newcomb, "New Light on Jay's Treaty," p. 688.

53. *Ibid.*, p. 686, n. 4.

54. The controversy over the order-in-council of April 25, 1795, is comprehensively discussed in *ibid.*

55. Freeman, *George Washington*, VII, 262, n. 133. Randolph later wrote that, before Washington submitted the treaty to the Senate, he had said he would not separate from the Senate. Edmund Randolph, *A Vindication of Edmund Randolph, Written by Himself and Published in 1795*, ed. Peter V. Daniel, Jr. (Richmond, Virginia, 1855), pp. 18–19. Hereafter cited as Randolph, *Vindication*.

56. Randolph to Washington, July 12, 1795, Worthington C. Ford, ed., "Edmund Randolph on the British Treaty, 1795," *American Historical Review*, XII, No. 3 (April 1907), 587–599.

57. Randolph, *Vindication*, p. 21.

58. Christopher Gore to Rufus King, August 7 and 14, 1795, Rufus King Papers, NYHS.

59. George Cabot to Oliver Wolcott, August 13, 1795, Gibbs, *Memoirs of the Administrations*, I, 225.

60. Washington to Randolph, July 22, 1795, Washington, *Writings*, XXXIV, 244.

61. Washington to Randolph, July 31, 1795, *ibid.*, p. 267. The memorial draft is in Randolph, *Vindication*, p. 23, and the contents of it were revealed by Randolph in a letter to Jay, August 16, 1795, Washington, *Writings*, XXXIV, 255, n. 67.

62. Grenville to Hammond, May 9, 1795, No. 8, June 4, 1795, No. 12, FO 5/9.

63. Hammond to Grenville, July 27, 1795, No. 28, FO 5/9.

64. Gibbs, *Memoirs of Administrations*, I, 233.

65. Timothy Pickering to Washington, July 31, 1795, Washington, *Writings*, XXXIV, 265, n. 81.

66. Oliver Wolcott to Hamilton, July 28, 1795, Gibbs, *Memoirs of Administrations*, I, 220.

67. Wolcott to John Marshall, June 9, 1806, *ibid.*, p. 241 ff; Pickering to Paine Wingate, November 21, 1795, Octavius Pickering and Charles W. Upham, *The Life of Timothy Pickering*, 4 vols. (Boston, 1867–1873), II, 189; Hammond to Grenville, August 14, 1795, No. 33, FO 5/9; Randolph, *Vindication*, pp. 1–4.

68. Wolcott to Marshall, June 9, 1806, Gibbs, *Memoirs of Administrations*, I, 245–246.

69. Timothy Pickering to Paine Wingate, November 21, 1795, Pickering and Upham, *Life of Pickering*, II, 189.

70. Wolcott to John Marshall, June 9, 1806, Gibbs, *Memoirs of Administration*, I, 245–246.

71. Randolph to Washington, October 8, 1795, *Washington Papers*, LC, Ser. 4, CCLXXV, 110; George Taylor to Randolph, October 6, 1795, Pickering Papers, MHS, XXXV, No. 288.

72. Pickering and Upham, *Life of Pickering*, II, 225.

73. Randolph's biographer points out that Pickering's account may well have been a myth, for Washington well knew that Randolph had not in fact received any money from Fauchet, the French minister having written that France did not purchase men to do their duty. Moncure Daniel Conway, *Omitted Chapters of History Disclosed in the Life and Papers of Edmund Randolph* (New York, 1888), p. 345. Hereafter cited as Conway, *Randolph*.

74. Hamilton to Oliver Wolcott, August 10, 1795, Hamilton, *Works* (Lodge), X, 113.

75. Randolph to Washington, July 24, 1795, Washington Papers, LC, Ser. 4, CCLXXIII, 127.

76. There are three letters from Hamilton to Washington dated July 6, 13, and 14 which have been lost, and whose existence is known only by the fact that Washington acknowledged them. See Freeman, *Washington*, VII, 260, n. 129; also p. 262, n. 137.

77. Randolph, *Vindication*. See also Irving Brant, "Edmund Randolph, Not Guilty," *William and Mary Quarterly*, 3rd ser., VII (April 1950), 179–198.

78. Henry Lee to Washington, January 3, 1796, Washington Papers, LC, Ser. 4, CCLXXVII, 18.

79. Phineas Bond to Grenville, January 22, 1796, FO 5/13; Sedgwick to Loring Andrews, December 18, 1795, Norton Papers, MHS.

80. Madison to Monroe, January 26, 1796, Madison Papers, LC.

81. *Aurora*, January 16, 1796.

82. *Ibid.*, January 5, 1796.

83. Charles Warren, *Jacobin and Junto or Early American Politics as Viewed in the Diary of Dr. Nathaniel Ames, 1758–1822* (Cambridge, 1931), p. 63.

84. Jay to Washington, December 14, 1795, Washington Papers, LC, Ser. 4, CCLXXVI, 92.

85. Miss Rachel Bradford to Samuel Bayard, November 26, 1795, J. J. Boudinot, ed., *The Life Public Services, Addresses and Letters of Elias Boudinot*, 2 vols. (Boston, 1896), II, 114.

11. A HOUSE DIVIDED

1. Sedgwick to ——, January 14, 1796, Norton Papers, MHS.

2. William Vans Murray to Wolcott, October 2, 1795, George Gibbs, ed., *Memoirs of Administrations*, I, 249.

3. John Adams to Abigail Adams, March 19, 1796, C. F. Adams, ed., *Letters of John Adams to His Wife*, II, 212–213; same to same, March 12, 1796, *ibid.*, p. 207.

4. Joseph Charles, *The Origins of the American Party System*, pp. 93–95.

5. Stephen G. Kurtz, *The Presidency of John Adams* (Philadelphia, 1957), pp. 20–30.

6. *Ibid.*; Rufus King to Judge Laurence, December 20, 1795, Rufus King Papers, NYHS.

7. Washington to G. Morris, March 4, 1796, Washington, *Writings*, XXXIV, 483.

8. Speech to Congress, December 8, 1795, *ibid.*, p. 388.

9. William B. Giles to Jefferson, December 20, 1795, Jefferson Papers, LC.

10. *Ibid.*

11. Giles to Jefferson, December 9, 1795, *ibid.;* Madison to Jefferson, December 27, 1795, Madison Papers, LC.

12. Madison to Monroe, December 20, 1795, *ibid.*; Giles to Jefferson, December 20, 1795, *ibid.*; Sedgwick to E. Williams, December 11, 1795, Sedgewick Papers, MHS; same to same, December 14, 1795, *ibid.*; same to same, December 16, 1795, *ibid.*; same to same, December 17, 1795, *ibid.*

13. Giles to Jefferson, December 20, 1795, Jefferson Papers, LC. In fact, Dayton was just as noncommittal to the Federalists. He wrote Hamilton in his long-winded, fence-straddling way, "Our session has hitherto been remarkably tranquil, but we can have no security that it will continue so, much longer. *That Instrument,* the cause of so much pleasure to some & of displeasure to others—*that Compact* which has already drawn forth so many pens & occasioned so much warmth—The Treaty, (as ratified) has for some time been impatiently expected, and will, when it arrives & is laid before the House, produce, or I err exceedingly, agitations, collisions & opposi-

tions, the extent of which cannot be foreseen or calculated." Jonathan Dayton to Hamilton, January 15, 1796, Hamilton Papers, LC.

14. Madison to Jefferson, December 13, 1795, Madison Papers, LC.

15. Madison to Monroe, December 20, 1795, *ibid.*

16. William Vans Murray to Wolcott, October 2, 1795, Gibbs, *Memoirs of Administrations*, I, 249.

17. When confronted with the Anglo-American war crisis which occasioned the Jay mission in the first place, Hamilton had laid out general guidelines for Federalist action and Sedgwick had introduced bills in the House which exactly implemented that strategy. See Hamilton to Washington, March 8, 1794, Hamilton, *Works* (Lodge), X, 63–65; and Theodore Sedgwick to Ephraim Williams, March 10, 1794, Sedgwick Papers, MHS. A good biography of Sedgwick is Richard E. Welch, *Theodore Sedgwick, Federalist* (Middletown, Conn., 1965).

18. Sedgwick to E. Williams, December 25, 1795, Sedgwick Papers, MHS.

19. Sedgwick to ——, December 28, 1795, Norton Papers, MHS.

20. Henry Tazewell to ——, January 24, 1796, Tazewell Papers, LC; Giles to Jefferson, March 26, 1796, Jefferson Papers, LC; Timothy Pickering to William Deas, February 27, 1796, Pickering Papers, MHS, XXXVI, No. 27.

21. Sedgwick to E. Williams, January 30, 1796, Sedgwick Papers, MHS.

22. Sedgwick to Loring Andrews, January 27, 1796, Norton Papers, MHS.

23. Freeman, *Washington*, VII, 343, n. 157.

24. Madison to Jefferson, February 29, 1796, Madison Papers, LC.

25. Sedgwick to E. Williams, February 27, 1796, Sedgwick Papers, MHS.

26. Freeman, *Washington*, VII, 348; *Annals of Congress*, V, 394.

27. Robert R. Livingston to Edward Livingston, October 30, 1795, Robert R. Livingston Papers, NYHS.

28. Edward Livingston to Robert R. Livingston, February 1, 1796, *ibid.*

29. *Annals of Congress*, V, 400–401.

30. Madison to Jefferson, March 6, 1796, Madison Papers, LC; same to same, March 13, 1796, *ibid.*

31. Madison to Jefferson, March 6, 1796, *ibid.*

32. *Annals of Congress*, V, 426.

33. *Ibid.*

34. *Ibid.*, p. 438.

35. *Ibid.*

36. Sedgwick to E. Williams, March 18, 1796, Sedgwick Papers, MHS; Sedgwick to ——, March 16, 1796, *ibid.*

37. Edward Livingston to Robert R. Livingston, March 15, 1796, Robert R. Livingston Papers, NYHS.

38. *Annals of Congress*, V, 759–760.

39. Giles to Jefferson, March 26, 1796, Jefferson Papers, LC. He still thought the treaty would pass, however.

40. *Annals of Congress*, V, 760–761.

41. Rufus King, *Life and Correspondence*, II, 58.

42. Sedgwick to ——, April 1, 1796, Sedgwick Papers, MHS.

43. Giles to Jefferson, April 6, 1796, Jefferson Papers, LC.

44. Madison to Jefferson, April 4, 1796, *ibid.*

45. *Ibid.*; see also Madison, *Writings*, VI, 264; and *Annals of Congress*, V, 771–772.

46. *Ibid.*, p. 782–783.

47. Sedgwick to Loring Andrews, March 23, 1796, Norton Papers, MHS; Sedgwick to Williams, March 26, 1796, Sedgwick Papers, MHS.

48. Hamilton to Rufus King, April 15, 1796, Hamilton, *Works* (Lodge), X, 157.

49. Henry Adams, ed., *The Writings of Albert Gallatin,* 3 vols. (Philadelphia, 1879), III, 553.

50. John Adams to Abigail Adams, April 16, 1796, Adams, *Letters of John Adams to His Wife,* II, 220.

51. *Ibid.*

52. Sedgwick to E. Williams, April 13, 1796, Sedgwick Papers, MHS.

53. Madison to Jefferson, April 18, 1796, Madison Papers, LC.

54. Madison to Monroe, April 18, 1796, *ibid.*

55. Phillip Schuyler to Rufus King, April 25, 1796, Rufus King Papers, NYHS.

56. Pierce Butler to Madison, August 21, 1795, Madison Papers, LC.

57. Madison to Jefferson, April 22, 1796, *ibid.*

58. *Gazette of the United States,* April 20, 1796. With King's interest in New York underwriting, it is not likely that he was totally uninvolved in this campaign.

59. See, for example, *Gazette of the United States,* April 13, 1796.

60. John Langdon to Madison, April 20, 1796, Madison Papers, LC.

61. *Gazette of the United States,* April 30, 1796.

62. Minutes of Cabinet Meeting, January 14, 1796, FO 5/16; Grenville to Bond, January 1796, No. 7, *ibid.*

63. Phineas Bond to Grenville, March 31, 1796, No. 17, FO 5/13; Bond to Grenville, April 17, 1796, No. 25, *ibid.*

64. Bond to Grenville, April 17, 1796, No. 25, *ibid.*

65. The information was current among informed people in Philadelphia at least as early as April 9. See Chauncey Goodrich to Wolcott, Sr., April 9, 1796, Gibbs, *Memoirs of the Administrations,* I, 326.

66. Alexander Addison to Albert Gallatin, May 4, 1796, Gallatin Papers, NYHS.

67. *Annals of Congress,* V, 940.

68. *Ibid.,* p. 941.

69. *Ibid.,* p. 969.

70. Chauncey Goodrich to Oliver Wolcott, Sr., April 20, 1796, Gibbs, *Memoirs of the Administrations,* I, 330; for Hamilton's advice against this course of action, see Hamilton to King, April 15, 1796, Hamilton, *Works* (Lodge), X, 159.

71. King to Hamilton, April 20, 1796, Hamilton Papers, LC.

72. Chauncey Goodrich to Wolcott, Sr., April 23, 1796, Gibbs, *Memoirs of the Administrations,* I, 331; see also John Adams to Abigail Adams, March 16, 1796, *Adams Papers* (microfilm), Reel 381.

73. *Annals of Congress,* V, 1100.

74. *Ibid.,* pp. 1014–1015.

75. *Ibid.,* pp. 986–987.

76. *Ibid.,* pp. 1050–1051.

77. *Ibid.,* p. 1024.

78. *Ibid.;* also pp. 1151–1152.

79. *Ibid.,* p. 1098.

80. *Ibid.,* pp. 1151–1152.

81. *Ibid.,* p. 1280.

82. See particularly Charles, *The Origins of the American Party System,* pp. 118–120; Alexander DeConde, *Entangling Alliance,* p. 138.

83. David L. Sterling, "A Federalist Opposes the Jay Treaty: The Letters of Samuel Bayard," *William and Mary Quarterly,* 3rd ser., XVIII, No. 3 (July 1961), 413–415; see also Samuel Bayard to James Monroe, October 18, 1795, Monroe Papers, LC, Ser. I. Anne C. Morris, ed., *The Diary and Letters of Gouverneur Morris,* 2 vols. (New York, 1888), II, 102.

84. Madison to Madison Sr., January 17, 1796, Madison Papers, LC.

85. G. Morris to John Parish, January 29, 1796, Gouverneur Morris Papers, LC, Letters, III.

86. John Quincy Adams to Abigail Adams, April 24, 1796, *Adams Papers* (microfilm), Reel 381.

87. John Quincy Adams to Charles Adams, June 9, 1796, Worthington Chauncey Ford, ed., *Writings of John Quincy Adams*, 7 vols. (Boston, 1913–1917), I, 493. Hereafter cited as J. Q. Adams, *Writings*.

88. John Adams to Abigail Adams, April 19, 1796, Adams, *Letters of John Adams to His Wife*, II, 222–223.

89. *Annals of Congress*, V, 1239–1263.

90. John Adams to Abigail Adams, April 30, 1796, Adams, *Letters of John Adams to His Wife*, II, 226–227.

91. Paul A. W. Wallace, *The Muhlenbergs of Pennsylvania* (Philadelphia, 1950), pp. 285–287.

92. King to Hamilton, April 17, 1796, Hamilton Papers, LC.

93. Sedgwick to Loring Andrews, April 5, 1796, Sedgwick Papers, MHS.

94. Sedgwick to E. Williams, April 9, 1796, *ibid.*

95. John Adams to Abigail Adams, April 28, 1796, *Adams Papers* (microfilm), Reel 381.

96. *Annals of Congress*, V, 970–971.

97. *Ibid.*, p. 976.

98. Madison to Jefferson, April 23, 1796, Madison Papers, LC.

99. John Adams to Abigail Adams, April 28, 1796, *Adams Papers* (microfilm), Reel 381.

100. *Ibid.*

101. Kurtz, *The Presidency of John Adams*, pp. 67–69.

102. *Annals of Congress*, V, 976.

103. *Ibid.*, pp. 1183–1202.

104. *Ibid.*, p. 1228.

105. Madison to Madison Sr., April 25, 1796, Madison Papers, LC.

106. George Cabot to Caleb Strong, April 27, 1796, Henry Cabot Lodge, ed., *Life and Letters of George Cabot*, p. 95; Sedgwick to ——, April 22, 1796, Sedgwick Papers, MHS.

107. Madison to Jefferson, May 1, 1796, Madison Papers, LC.

108. *Annals of Congress*, V, 1280.

109. *Ibid.*, p. 1291.

110. Washington to Thomas Pinckney, May 22, 1796, Washington, *Writings*, XXXV, 62.

111. In an open letter to his constituents, Van Cortlandt stated that he had not been fully convinced that the treaty was beneficial, "yet as it appeared . . . to be the general wish of the people of the northern and eastern states, that it ought to be carried into effect . . . I . . . conceived it most advisable to give an affirmative vote on the occasion." Van Cortlandt–Van Wyck Papers, NYPL.

112. William Plumer to Jeremiah Smith, May 11, 1796, William Plumer Papers, LC.

113. *Annals of Congress*, V, 1291; Kurtz, *The Presidency of John Adams*, p. 71.

114. Washington to Charles Carroll, May 1, 1796, Washington, *Writings*, XXXV, 30–31.

115. The phrase is Jefferson's and was used in a slightly different context, although it did refer primarily to the Jay Treaty. Jefferson to Phillip Mazzei, April 24, 1796, Jefferson Papers, LC.

APPENDIX II. THE RANDOLPH AFFAIR

1. Edmund Randolph, *A Vindication of Edmund Randolph, Written by Himself and Published in 1795*, ed. Peter V. Daniel Jr. (Richmond, Va., 1855). See also Irving

Brant, "Edmund Randolph, Not Guilty," *William and Mary Quarte* (April 1950), 179–198.

2. Fauchet's Dispatch No. 6, Randolph, *Vindication*, pp. 11–12.

3. *Ibid.*, pp. 62–66.

4. *Ibid.*, pp. 7–10.

5. See Fauchet's certificate, *ibid.*, pp. 9–10.

6. Fauchet's Dispatch No. 6, *ibid.*, pp. 11–12.

7. Theodore Sedgwick to E. Williams, December 23, 1795, Sedgwi

8. See Wolcott to Hamilton, November 16, 1795, George Gibbs, *Administrations*, I, 265, in which he states merely that Randolph Fauchet could get proof of the conspiracy since he had the resource government at his hand. In his letter to John Marshall, June 9, 18(mentions definitely the flour merchants. *Ibid.*, p. 245.

9. Randolph, *Vindication*, p. 37.

10. Wolcott to Randolph, October 2, 1795, *ibid.*, p. 14; Moncure 1 *Edmond Randolph*, p. 329.

11. Brant, "Edmund Randolph, Not Guilty," p. 194, n. 17.

12. *Ibid.*

13. *Ibid.*, p. 194.

14. The precis is attached to Grenville's letter to Hammond, dated No. 12, FO 115/4, ff. 77–104.

BIBLIOGRAPHY

MANUSCRIPTS

BRITISH

Public Record Office
Admiralty Papers
Board of Trade Minutes
Board of Trade Reports
Chatham Papers, Second Series
Colonial Office Papers
Foreign Office Papers
War Office Papers

British Museum
Liverpool Papers
Melville Papers
Pelham Papers
Rose Papers
Windham Papers

Clements Library, University of Michigan
Letters of George III (transcripts)
Melville Papers
Pitt Papers
Wedderburn Papers

Others
Boconnoc Papers. These are the papers of William Wyndham Grenville, Lord Grenville, formerly preserved at Dropmore, and now in the possession of George Grenville Fortescue at Boconnoc, Lostwithiel, Cornwall.

AMERICAN

Library of Congress
Elbridge Gerry Papers
Robert Goodloe Harper Papers
Alexander Hamilton Papers
Thomas Jefferson Papers
James McHenry Papers
James Madison Papers
John Marshall Papers
James Monroe Papers
Gouverneur Morris Papers
William Vans Murray Papers
William Plumer Papers
William Loughton Smith Papers

Henry Tazewell Papers
John Trumbull Papers
George Washington Papers
New-York Historical Society
  Albert Gallatin Papers
  Rufus King Papers
  Robert R. Livingston Papers
New York Public Library
  Oliver Ellsworth Papers
  John Jay Papers (photostat)
  Jay-Bancroft Correspondence
  Livingston Family Papers
  James Monroe Papers
  Josiah Parker Papers
  Edmund Randolph Papers
  Van Cortlandt–Van Wyck Papers
  Oliver Wolcott Papers (transcripts)
Columbia University
  Alexander Hamilton Papers
  John Jay Papers, Iselin Collection (microfilm), Monaghan Collection
  Gouverneur Morris Papers
Massachusetts Historical Society
  Thomas Jefferson Papers
  Henry Knox Papers
  Norton Papers
  Timothy Pickering Papers
  Theodore Sedgwick Papers
Clements Library
  Haskall Papers
  Members of Congress Papers
  Robbins Letters
Other
  Adams Papers (microfilm)

NEWSPAPERS

BRITISH
  London
    Morning Chronicle
    Annual Register
    Morning Herald
    Sun
    The Times
    St. James's Chronicle or British Evening-Post

BIBLIOGRAPHY

Star Evening Advertiser (variously, *Stuart's Star Evening Advertiser, Morning Star*, the *Star*)

Oracle, Bell's New World (variously, the *Oracle*, and, after March 1, 1794, becomes the *Oracle, Public Advertiser*)

Public Advertiser (becomes the *Public Advertiser, or Political and Literary Diary*, January 1, 1794, and the *Oracle and Public Advertiser*, on March 1, 1794)

London Gazette

London Chronicle

World, Fashionable Advertiser (on July 1, 1794, becomes *Morning Post and Fashionable World*)

True-Briton

AMERICAN

Philadelphia

Gazette of the United States

National Gazette

General Advertiser

Aurora

Philadelphia Gazette

New York

American Minerva (becomes the *Commercial Advertiser*)

Argus and Greenleaf's New Daily Advertiser

Halifax, North Carolina

North-Carolina Journal

Boston

Independent Chronicle

Columbian Centinal

Annapolis

Maryland Gazette

Richmond

Virginia Gazette, General Advertiser

Charleston

City Gazette and Daily Advertiser

Savannah

Georgia Gazette

PRINTED PRIMARY SOURCES

Adams, Charles Francis, ed. *Letters of Mrs. Adams.* Boston, 1841.

———. *Letters of John Adams Addressed to His Wife.* 2 vols. Boston, 1841.

———. *Memoirs of John Quincy Adams.* 12 vols. Boston, 1874–1877.

———. *The Works of John Adams.* 10 vols. Boston, 1850–1856. Cited as Adams, *Works.*

Adams, Henry, ed. *The Writings of Albert Gallatin.* 3 vols. Philadelphia, 1879.

American State Papers. *Foreign Relations, Indian Affairs, Military Affairs, Commerce and Navigation.* Washington, 1832–1834.

Ames, Seth, ed. *Works of Fisher Ames.* 2 vols. Boston, 1854.

Aspinall, Arthur, ed. *The Later Correspondence of George III.* 2 vols. Cambridge, England, 1962–1963.

Ballagh, James C., ed. *The Letters of Richard Henry Lee.* 2 vols. New York, 1911–1914.

Baring, Cecilia A., ed., *The Diary of the Right Hon. William Windham.* London, 1866.

Battle, Kemp L. *Letters of Nathaniel Macon, John Steele and William Barry Grove.* University of North Carolina, James Sprunt Historical Monographs, No. 3. Chapel Hill, 1902.

Beard, Charles A., ed. *The Journal of William Maclay.* New York, 1927.

Bentley, William. *The Diary of William Bentley, D. D.* 4 vols. Gloucester, Mass., 1962.

Boudinot, J. J., ed. *The Life, Public Services, Addresses and Letters of Elias Boudinot.* 2 vols. Boston, 1896.

Boyd, Julian P., ed. *The Papers of Thomas Jefferson.* 17 vols. Princeton, 1950—. Cited as Jefferson, *Papers* (Boyd).

Brown, Stuart Gerry, ed. *The Autobiography of James Monroe.* Syracuse, 1959.

Brymner, Douglas, Arthur C. Doughty, and Gustave Lanctot, eds. *Report on the Canadian Archives.* Ottawa, 1872—.

Burnett, Edmund C. *Letters of Members of the Continental Congress.* 8 vols. Washington, 1921–1936.

Butterfield, L. H., ed. *Diary and Autobiography of John Adams.* 4 vols. Cambridge, Mass., 1961.

————. *The Letters of Benjamin Rush.* 2 vols. Princeton, 1951.

Cappon, Lester J., ed. *The Adams-Jefferson Letters.* 2 vols. Chapel Hill, 1959.

Carey, Matthew, ed. *The American Remembrancer. . . .* 3 vols. Philadelphia, 1795.

Chalmers, George. *Opinions on Interesting Subjects of Public Law and Commercial Policy Arising from American Independence.* London, 1784.

Cobbett, William. *Porcupine's Works.* 12 vols. London, 1801.

Collection of Interesting and Important Reports and Papers on Navigation and Trade. London, 1807.

Colonial Office Records, Michigan Pioneer and Historical Society Collections and Researches, Vols. XX, XXIV, XXV. Lansing, 1912, 1895, 1896.

Considerations on the Present State of the Intercourse Between His Majesty's Sugar Colonies and the Dominions of the United States of America. Distributed by a meeting of West India planters, James Allen, Secretary. London, 1784.

Conway, Moncure Daniel. *Omitted Chapters of History Disclosed in the Life and Papers of Edmund Randolph.* New York, 1888.

Cooke, Jacob E., ed. *The Federalist.* Middletown, Conn., 1961.

Coxe, Tench. *A View of the United States of America.* . . . Dublin, 1795.

Cruikshank, Brig.-Gen. Ernest A., ed. *The Correspondence of Lieutenant Governor John Graves Simcoe.* 5 vols. Toronto, 1923–1931.

Cushing, Harry Alonzo, ed. *The Writings of Samuel Adams.* 4 vols. New York, 1904–1908.

Dallas, George Mifflin, ed. *Life and Writings of Alexander James Dallas.* Philadelphia, 1871.

Daniel, Peter V. Jr., ed. *A Vindication of Edmond Randolph, Written by Himself and Published in 1795.* Richmond, 1855.

Donnan, Elizabeth, ed. *Papers of James A. Bayard, 1796–1815.* American Historical Association Annual Report for 1913, Vol. II. Washington, 1915.

Drake, Francis S. *Life and Correspondence of Henry Knox.* Boston, 1873.

Eden, Robert John, Lord Auckland, Bishop of Bath and Wells, ed. *The Journal and Correspondence of William, Lord Auckland.* 4 vols. London, 1861–1862.

Edwards, Brian. *Thoughts on the Late Proceedings of Government.* . . . Second Edition. London, 1784.

Farrand, Max. *Records of the Federal Convention of 1787.* 4 vols. Rev. ed. New Haven, 1966.

Fitzpatrick, John C., ed. *The Diaries of George Washington, 1748–1799.* 4 vols. Boston, 1925.

———. *The Writings of George Washington.* 39 vols. Washington, 1931–1944.

Fitzpatrick, Walter, ed. *Report on the Manuscripts of J. B. Fortescue, Esq., Preserved at Dropmore.* Historical Manuscripts Commission, Vols. I–III. London, 1892–1899. Cited as *Dropmore Papers,* HMC.

Ford, Emily Ellsworth Fowler, compiler. *Notes on the Life of Noah Webster.* 2 vols. New York, 1912.

Ford, Paul Leicester, ed. *The Writings of Thomas Jefferson.* 10 vols. New York, 1892–1899. Cited as Jefferson, *Writings* (Ford).

Ford, Worthington C., ed. "Edmund Randolph on the British Treaty, 1795." *American Historical Review,* XII (1906–1907), 587–599.

———. *Writings of John Quincy Adams.* 7 vols. Boston, 1913–1917.

——— et al., eds. *Journals of the Continental Congress, 1774–1789.* 34 vols. Washington, 1904–1937.

Gales, Joseph, compiler. *Debates and Proceedings in the Congress of the United States, 1789–1824.* 42 vols. Washington, 1834–1856. Cited as the *Annals of Congress.*

Gibbs, George, ed. *Memoirs of the Administrations of Washington and John Adams, Edited from the Papers of Oliver Wolcott, Secretary of the Treasury.* 2 vols. New York, 1846.

Grant, W. L., James Munro, and A. W. Fitzroy, eds. *Acts of the Privy Council of England, Colonial Series.* 6 vols. Hereford, 1908–1912.

Greely, A. W., ed. *Public Documents of the Early Congresses.* American Historical Association Annual Report for 1896. Washington, 1897.

Grenville, Richard Plantagenet Temple Nugent Brydges Chandos, Duke of Buckingham and Chandos. *Memoirs of the Court and Cabinets of George the III.* 4 vols. London, 1853–1858.

Hamilton, John C., ed. *The Works of Alexander Hamilton.* 7 vols. New York, 1850–1851.

Hamilton, Stanislaus Murray. *The Writings of James Monroe.* 7 vols. New York, 1898–1903.

Harcourt, Leveson V., ed. *The Diaries and Correspondence of the Right Hon. George Rose.* 2 vols. London, 1860.

Harper, Robert Goodloe. *Address to His Constituents, Containing His Reasons for Approving the Treaty.* Philadelphia, 1796.

Holroyd, John B., Lord Sheffield. *Observations on the Commerce of the American States.* London, 1784.

Hunt, Gaillard, ed. *The Writings of James Madison.* 9 vols. New York, 1900–1910. Cited as Madison, *Writings.*

Hutchinson, William T. and William M. E. Rachal, eds. *Papers of James Madison.* 4 vols. Chicago, 1962—. Cited as Madison, *Papers* (Hutchinson).

Jameson, J. Franklin, ed. *Letters of Phineas Bond, British Consul at Philadelphia . . . , 1787, 1788, 1789.* American Historical Association Annual Report for 1896, Vol. I. Washington, 1897.

———. *Letters of Phineas Bond, British Consul at Philadelphia . . . , 1790–1794.* American Historical Association Annual Report for 1897. Washington, 1898.

———. *Letters of Stephen Higginson, 1783–1804.* American Historical Association Annual Report for 1896, Vol. I. Washington, 1897.

Jefferson, Thomas. *Notes on Virginia.* Richmond, 1853.

Johnston, Henry P., ed. *The Correspondence and Public Papers of John Jay.* 4 vols. New York, 1890–1893.

Journal of the Executive Proceedings of the Senate of the United States. 3 vols. Washington, 1828.

Journal of the House of Representatives of the United States. 9 vols. Philadelphia, 1826.

Journals of the House of Commons.

Kenneys, J. G. *A Free and Candid Review of a Tract, Entitled "Observations on the Commerce of the American States. . . ."* London, 1784.

King, Charles Ray, ed. *The Life and Correspondence of Rufus King.* 6 vols. New York, 1894–1900.

Lipscomb, Andrew A. and Albert E. Bergh, eds. *Writings of Thomas Jefferson.* 20 vols. Washington, 1903–1904. Cited as Jefferson, *Writings* (Memorial Edition).

Lodge, Henry Cabot, ed. *Life and Letters of George Cabot.* Boston, 1877.

———. *The Works of Alexander Hamilton.* 12 vols. Federal Edition. New York, 1904. Cited as Hamilton, *Works* (Lodge).

Manning, William R., ed. *Diplomatic Correspondence of the United States: Canadian Relations, 1794–1860.* Vol. I. Washington, 1940.

Mayo, Bernard, ed. *Instructions to the British Ministers to the United States, 1791–1812.* American Historical Association Annual Report for 1936, Vol. III. Washington, 1941.

Miller, David Hunter, ed. *Treaties and Other International Acts of the United States of America.* 8 vols. Washington, 1931.

Mitchell, Stewart, ed. *New Letters of Abigail Adams.* Boston, 1947.

Monaghan, Frank, ed. *Unpublished Correspondence of William Livingston and John Jay.* Newark, New Jersey, 1934.

Monroe, James. *A View of the Conduct of the Executive.* . . . Philadelphia, 1797.

Morris, Anne C., ed. *The Diary and Letters of Gouverneur Morris.* 2 vols. New York, 1888.

Morris, Richard B., ed. *Alexander Hamilton and the Founding of the Nation.* New York, 1957.

Papers of the Continental Congress, 1774–1789. Microfilm Edition.

The Parliamentary History of England. 36 vols. London, 1806–1820.

Ragatz, Lowell Joseph, ed. *Statistics for the Study of British Caribbean Economic History, 1763–1833.* London [1928].

Robertson, John Ross, ed. *The Diary of Mrs. John Graves Simcoe.* Toronto, 1911.

Russell, Lord John, ed. *Memorials and Correspondence of Charles James Fox.* 4 vols. London, 1853–1857.

Sizer, Theodore, ed. *The Autobiography of Colonel John Trumbull.* New Haven, Conn., 1953.

Sparks, Jared, ed. *The Writings of George Washington.* 12 vols. Boston, 1834–1837.

Steiner, Bernard C., ed. *The Life and Correspondence of James McHenry.* Cleveland, 1907.

Sterling, David L. "A Federalist Opposes the Jay Treaty: The Letters of Samuel Bayard." *William and Mary Quarterly,* 3rd ser., XVIII (1961), 404–428.

Stevenson, John. *An Address to Brian Edwards, Esq.* London, 1784.

Syrett, Harold C., ed. *The Papers of Alexander Hamilton.* 13 vols. New York, 1961—. Cited as Hamilton, *Papers* (Syrett).

Trumbull, John. *Autobiography, Reminiscences and Letters of John Trumbull.* New Haven, 1841.

Turner, Frederick J., ed. "English Policy Toward America in 1790–91." *American Historical Review,* VII (1901–1902), 706–735.

Wagstaff, H. M., ed. *The Papers of John Steele.* 2 vols. Raleigh, North Carolina, 1924.

Warren, Charles. *Jacobin and Junto, or Early American Politics as Viewed in the Diary of Dr. Nathaniel Ames, 1758–1822.* Cambridge, Mass., 1931.

Wharton, Francis. *Revolutionary Diplomatic Correspondence of the United States.* 6 vols. Washington, 1889.

Wilson, J. G. "Judge Bayard of New Jersey, and His London Diary of 1795–96." *New Jersey Historical Society Proceedings*, 2nd ser., VIII (1884).

SECONDARY WORKS

Adair, Douglass. "David Hume, James Madison, and the Tenth Federalist." *Huntington Library Quarterly*, XX (August 1957), 343–360.

Adams, Ephraim Douglass. *The Influence of Grenville on Pitt's Foreign Policy, 1787–1798*. Carnegie Institution of Washington, Publication No. 13, Washington, 1904.

Adams, Henry. *The Life of Albert Gallatin*. Philadelphia, 1880.

Ammon, Harry. "The Formation of the Republican Party in Virginia, 1789–1796." *Journal of Southern History*, XIX (August 1953), 283–310.

Amory, Thomas C. *Life of James Sullivan*. 2 vols. Boston, 1859.

Anderson, Dice Robins. *Edmund Randolph*. Vol. II, *The American Secretaries of State and Their Diplomacy*, edited by Samuel Flagg Bemis. New York, 1927.

———. *William Branch Giles: A Study in the Politics of Virginia and the Nation from 1790 to 1830*. Menasha, Wis., 1914.

Aspinall, Arthur. *Politics and the Press, 1780–1850*. London, 1949.

Barnes, Donald Grove. *George III and William Pitt, 1783–1806*. Stanford University, 1939.

Bassett, John Spencer. *The Federalist System*. Vol. XI, *The American Nation*, edited by Albert Bushnell Hart. New York, 1906.

Beard, Charles A. *Economic Origins of Jeffersonian Democracy*. New York, 1915.

Beardsley, Eben E. *Life and Times of William Samuel Johnson*. New York, 1876.

Bell, H. C. "British Commercial Policy in the West Indies, 1783–1793." *English Historical Review*, XXXI (1916), 429–441.

Bemis, George. *Precedents of American Neutrality*. Boston, 1864.

Bemis, Samuel Flagg. "Alexander Hamilton and the Limitation of Armaments." *Pacific Review*, II (1922), 587–602.

———. "Jay's Treaty and the Northwest Boundary Gap." *American Historical Review*, XXVII (1922), 465–484.

———. *Jay's Treaty: A Study in Commerce and Diplomacy*. Revised Edition. New Haven, 1962.

———. *John Quincy Adams and the Foundations of American Foreign Policy*. New York, 1949.

———. "The London Mission of Thomas Pinckney, 1792–1796." *American Historical Review*, XXVIII (1923), 228–247.

———. *Pinckney's Treaty: A Study of America's Advantage from Europe's Distress, 1783–1800*. Revised Edition. New Haven, 1960.

———. "Relations Between the Vermont Separatists and Great Britain, 1789–1791," *American Historical Review*, XXI (1916), 547–560.

――――. *Thomas Jefferson.* Vol. II, *The American Secretaries of State and Their Diplomacy,* edited by Samuel Flagg Bemis. New York, 1927.

――――. "The United States and the Abortive Armed Neutrality of 1794." *American Historical Review,* XXIV (1918), 26–47.

Bernard, Winfred E. A. *Fisher Ames, Federalist and Statesman, 1758–1808.* Chapel Hill, 1965.

Bernado, C. J. and E. H. Bacon. *American Military Policy: Its Development Since 1775.* Harrisburg, Pa., 1955.

Boorstin, Daniel J. *The Lost World of Thomas Jefferson.* New York, 1948.

Booth, David A. "The Constitutional and Political Aspects of the Jay Treaty, 1794–1796." Doctoral dissertation, University of Virginia, 1957. University Microfilm, Ann Arbor, No. 22,884.

Bourne, H. R. Fox. *English Newspapers.* 2 vols. London, 1887.

Bowers, Claude G. *Jefferson and Hamilton: The Struggle for Democracy in America.* Boston, 1925.

Boyd, Julian P. *Number 7: Alexander Hamilton's Secret Attempts to Control American Foreign Policy.* Princeton, 1964.

Bradley, Arthur Granville. *Lord Dorchester.* In *The Makers of Canada,* edited by Duncan Campbell Scott, Pelham Edgar, and William Dawson Le Sueur. London, 1907.

Brant, Irving. "Edmund Randolph, Not Guilty!" *William and Mary Quarterly,* Third Series, VII (April 1950), 179–198.

――――. *James Madison.* 6 vols. Indianapolis and New York, 1941–1961.

Brebner, John Bartlet. *North Atlantic Triangle.* New Haven, 1945.

Brigham, Clarence S. *History and Bibliography of American Newspapers, 1690–1820.* 2 vols. Worcester, 1947.

Brown, Stuart G. *The First Republicans: Political Philosophy and Public Policy in the Party of Jefferson and Madison.* Syracuse, 1954.

Burns, Edward McNall. *James Madison: Philosopher of the Constitution.* New Brunswick, 1938.

Burt, Alfred Le Roy. *Guy Carleton, Lord Dorchester: An Estimate.* Canadian Historical Association Annual Report for 1935. Toronto, 1935.

――――. *A New Approach to the Problem of the Western Posts.* Canadian Historical Association Annual Report for 1931. Ottawa, 1931.

――――. *The United States, Great Britain, and British North America from the Revolution to the Establishment of Peace After the War of 1812.* New Haven, 1940.

Caldwell, Lynton K. *The Administrative Theories of Hamilton and Jefferson: Their Contribution to Thought on Public Administration.* Chicago, 1944.

Charles, Joseph. *The Origins of the American Party System.* New York, 1961.

Chinard, Gilbert. *Thomas Jefferson: The Apostle of Americanism.* Boston, 1929.

Clarfield, Gerard. "Postscript to the Jay Treaty: Timothy Pickering and Anglo-American Relations, 1795–1797." *William and Mary Quarterly,* Third Series, XXIII (January 1966), 106–120.

Clark, Mary Elizabeth. *Peter Porcupine in America: The Career of William Cobbett, 1792–1800*. Philadelphia, 1939.

Clauder, Anne Cornelia. *American Commerce as Affected by the Wars of the French Revolution and Napoleon, 1793–1812*. Philadelphia, 1932.

Cresson, W. P. *James Monroe*. Chapel Hill, 1946.

Cunningham, Noble E., Jr. *The Jeffersonian Republicans: The Formation of Party Organization, 1789–1801*. Chapel Hill, 1957.

Dangerfield, George. *Chancellor Robert R. Livingston of New York, 1746–1813*. New York, 1960.

Darling, Arthur Burr. *Our Rising Empire, 1763–1803*. New Haven, 1940.

Dauer, Manning J. *The Adams Federalists*. Baltimore, 1953.

DeConde, Alexander. *Entangling Alliance: Politics and Diplomacy Under George Washington*. Durham, 1958.

Destler, Chester McArthur. *Joshua Coit: American Federalist, 1758–1798*. Middletown, Conn., 1962.

Douglass, Elisha P. "The Adventurer Bowles." *William and Mary Quarterly*, Third Series, VI (1949), 3–23.

Dunbar, Louise B. *A Study of "Monarchical" Tendencies in the United States from 1776–1801*. University of Illinois Studies in the Social Sciences, Vol. X, No. 1. Urbana, 1922.

Earle, Edward Mead, ed. *Makers of Modern Strategy: Military Thought from Machiavelli to Hitler*. Princeton, 1943.

Elliott, Charles Burke. "The Doctrine of Continuous Voyages." *American Journal of International Law*, I (1907), 61–104.

Fay, Bernard. *The Revolutionary Spirit in France and America: A Study of Moral and Intellectual Relations. . . .* Translated by Ramon Guthrie. New York, 1927.

———. *The Two Franklins*. Boston, 1933.

Fee, Walter R. *The Transition from Aristocracy to Democracy in New Jersey, 1789–1829*. Somerville, N. J., 1933.

Feiling, Keith Grahame. *The Second Tory Party, 1714–1832*. London, 1938.

———. *Henry Dundas, First Viscount Melville*. London, 1931.

Fenwick, Charles G. *The Neutrality Laws of the United States*. Washington, 1913.

Ford, Henry J. *Timothy Pickering*. Vol. II, *The American Secretaries of State and Their Diplomacy*, edited by Samuel F. Bemis. New York, 1927.

Freeman, Douglas Southall, John Alexander Carroll, and Mary Wells Ashworth. *George Washington*. 7 vols. New York, 1948–1957.

Furber, Holden. "The Beginnings of American Trade with India, 1784–1812." *New England Quarterly*, XI (1938), 235–265.

Gibson, Edward, Lord Ashbourne. *Pitt: Some Chapters of His Life and Times*. London, 1898.

Gilbert, Felix. *To the Farewell Address: Ideas of Early American Foreign Policy*. Princeton, 1961.

Gilpatrick, Delbert Harold. *Jeffersonian Democracy in North Carolina, 1789–1816.* New York, 1931.

Graham, Gerald S. *Empire of the North Atlantic: The Maritime Struggle for North America.* Toronto, 1950.

———. *Sea Power and British North America, 1783–1820.* Cambridge, 1941.

———. "The Indian Menace and the Retention of the Western Posts." *Canadian Historical Review*, XV (1934), 46–48.

Graham, Malbone W. *American Diplomacy in the International Community.* Baltimore, 1948.

Griswold, Rufus Wilmot. *The Republican Court.* New York, 1855.

Gruver, Rebecca Brooks. "The Diplomacy of John Jay." Doctoral dissertation, University of California, 1964.

Hacker, Louis M. *Alexander Hamilton in the American Tradition.* New York, 1957.

Hamer, P. M. "The British in Canada and the Southern Indians, 1790–94." East Tennessee Historical Society Publications, II (1930), 107–134.

Handler, Edward. *America and Europe in the Political Thought of John Adams.* Cambridge, Mass., 1964.

Harlow, Vincent Todd. *The Founding of the Second British Empire, 1763–1793.* 2 vols. London, 1952.

Hayden, Ralston. *The Senate and Treaties, 1789–1817.* New York, 1920.

Hazen, Charles Downer. *Contemporary American Opinion of the French Revolution.* Johns Hopkins University Studies in Historical and Political Science, Extra Vol. XVI. Baltimore, 1897.

Higginson, Thomas Wentworth. *Life and Times of Stephen Higginson.* Boston, 1907.

Hill, William. *The First Stages of the Tariff Policy of the United States.* Publications of the American Economic Association, Vol. VIII, No. 6. Baltimore, 1893.

Hobhouse, Christopher. *Fox.* Boston, 1935.

Horsman, Reginald. "The British Indian Department and the Resistance to General Anthony Wayne, 1793–1795." *Mississippi Valley Historical Review,* XLIX (1962), 269–290.

Howe, John R. *The Changing Political Thought of John Adams.* Princeton, 1966.

Hutchins, John G. B. *The American Maritime Industries and Public Policy, 1789–1914.* Harvard Economic Studies, Vol. LXXI. Cambridge, 1941.

Hyneman, Charles S. *The First American Neutrality.* Illinois Studies in the Social Sciences, Vol. XX, Nos. 1–2. Urbana, 1934.

———. "Neutrality During the European Wars of 1792–1815." *American Journal of International Law,* XXIV (1930), 279–309.

Jay, William. *The Life of John Jay.* 2 vols. New York, 1833.

Johnson, Emory R., T. W. Van Metre, *et al. History of Domestic and Foreign Commerce of the United States.* 2 vols. Washington, 1915.

Jones, Howard Mumford. *America and French Culture, 1750–1848.* Chapel Hill, 1927.

Keith, Alice Barnwell. "John Gray and Thomas Blount, Merchants." *North Carolina Historical Review,* XXV (1948), 194–205.

————. "Relaxations in the British Restrictions on the American Trade with the British West Indies, 1783–1802." *Journal of Modern History,* XX (1948), 1–19.

Kenyon, Cecilia M. "Alexander Hamilton: Rousseau of the Right." *Political Science Quarterly,* LXXIII, No. 2 (1958).

Koch, Adrienne. *Jefferson and Madison: The Great Collaboration.* New York, 1964.

————. *The Philosophy of Thomas Jefferson.* New York, 1943.

————. *Power, Morals and the Founding Fathers.* Ithaca, 1961.

Krout, John A. and Dixon Ryan Fox. *The Completion of Independence, 1790–1830.* New York, 1944.

Kurtz, Stephen G. *The Presidency of John Adams.* Philadelphia, 1957.

Lingelbach, Anna L. "The Inception of the British Board of Trade." *American Historical Review,* XXX (1925), 701–727.

Link, Eugene Perry. *Democratic-Republican Societies, 1790–1800.* New York, 1942.

Lycan, Gilbert L. "Alexander Hamilton and the North Carolina Federalists." *North Carolina Historical Review,* XXV (1948), 442–465.

Mackintosh, William Archibald. "Canada and Vermont: A Study in Historical Geography." *Canadian Historical Review,* VIII (1927), 9–30.

Mahan, Captain Alfred Thayer. *The Influence of Sea Power upon the French Revolution and Empire, 1793–1812.* 2 vols. Boston, 1892.

Malone, Dumas. *Thomas Jefferson and His Times.* 3 vols. Boston, 1948—.

Manning, Helen Taft. *British Colonial Government After the American Revolution, 1782–1820.* New Haven, 1933.

Matheson, Cyril. *The Life of Henry Dundas, First Viscount Melville.* London, 1933.

Miller, John C. *Alexander Hamilton: Portrait in Paradox.* New York, 1959.

————. *The Federalist Era, 1789–1801.* New York, 1960.

Mitchell, Broadus. *Alexander Hamilton.* 2 vols. New York, 1957–1962.

Monaghan, Frank. *John Jay.* New York, 1935.

Morison, Samuel Eliot. *The Maritime History of Massachusetts, 1783–1860.* Sentry Edition. Boston, 1961.

Morris, Richard B. *John Jay, the Nation, and the Court.* Boston, 1967.

Newcomb, Josiah T. "New Light on Jay's Treaty." *American Journal of International Law,* XXVIII (1934), 685–692.

Ogg, Frederick Austin. *Jay's Treaty and the Slavery Interests of the United States.* American Historical Association Annual Report for 1901, Vol. 1. Washington, 1902.

Parkinson, C. N., ed. *The Trade Winds: A Study of British Overseas Trade During the French Wars, 1793–1815.* London, 1948.

Pellew, George. *John Jay.* Cambridge, 1890.

Perkins, Bradford. *The First Rapprochement: England and the United States, 1795–1805.* Philadelphia, 1955.

————, ed. "Lord Hawkesbury and the Jay-Grenville Negotiations." *Mississippi Valley Historical Review,* XL (1953–1954), 291–304.

Peterson, Merrill D. "Thomas Jefferson and Commercial Policy, 1783–1793." *William and Mary Quarterly,* Third Series, XXII (Oct. 1965), 584–610.

Phillips, Ulrich B. "The South Carolina Federalists." *American Historical Review,* XIV (1909), 529–543, 731–743, 776–790.

Phillips, W. Allison and Arthur H. Reede. *Neutrality: Its History, Economics and Law.* Vol. II, *The Napoleonic Period.* New York, 1936.

Pickering, Octavius and Charles W. Upham. *The Life of Timothy Pickering.* 4 vols. Boston, 1867–1873.

Pitkin, Timothy. *A Statistical View of the Commerce of the United States of America.* Second Edition. New York, 1817.

Ragatz, Lowell Joseph. *The Fall of the Planter Class in the British Caribbean, 1763–1833.* New York, 1928.

Rankin, R. R. *The Treaty of Amity, Commerce and Navigation Between Great Britain and the United States, 1794.* University of California Chronicles, Vol. IX, No. 2, supplement. Berkeley, 1907.

Robinson, William A. *Jeffersonian Democracy in New England.* New Haven, 1916.

Roosevelt, Theodore. *The Winning of the West.* 2 vols. New York, 1926.

Rose, John Holland. *Life of William Pitt.* 2 vols. London, 1911.

Russell, Nelson V. *The British Regime in Michigan and the Old Northwest, 1760–1796.* Northfield, Minn., 1939.

Savage, Carlton, ed. *Policy of the United States Toward Maritime Commerce in War.* 2 vols. Washington, 1934.

Savelle, Max. "The Appearance of an American Attitude Toward External Affairs, 1750–1775." *American Historical Review,* LII (1947), 655–666.

————. "Colonial Origins of American Diplomatic Principles," *Pacific Historical Review,* II (1934), 334–350.

————. *The Origins of American Diplomacy: The International History of Anglo-America, 1492–1763.* New York, 1967.

Schachner, Nathan. *Alexander Hamilton.* New York, 1946.

————. *The Founding Fathers.* New York, 1954.

Scott, Duncan Campbell. *John Graves Simcoe.* In *The Makers of Canada,* edited by Duncan Campbell Scott and Pelham Edgar. Toronto, 1905.

Sears, Louis M. *George Washington and the French Revolution.* Detroit, 1960.

————. "Jefferson and the Law of Nations." *American Political Science Review,* XIII (1919), 379–399.

Setser, Vernon G. *The Commercial Reciprocity Policy of the United States, 1774–1829*. Philadelphia, 1937.

Seybert, Adam. *Statistical Annals*. Philadelphia, 1818.

Smelser, Marshall. *The Congress Founds the Navy, 1787–1798*. Notre Dame, 1959.

Smith, Page. *John Adams*. 2 vols. Garden City, New York, 1962.

Sparks, Jared. *The Life of Gouverneur Morris*. 3 vols. Boston, 1832.

Stanwood, Edward. *American Tariff Controversies in the Nineteenth Century*. 2 vols. Boston, 1903.

Stone, William L. *Life of Joseph Brant. . . .* 2 vols. Albany, 1865.

Stourzh, Gerald. *Benjamin Franklin and American Foreign Policy*. Chicago, 1954.

Swanstrom, Roy. *The United States Senate, 1787–1801*. Washington, D. C., 1962.

Thomas, Charles M. *American Neutrality in 1793: A Study in Cabinet Government*. New York, 1931.

Tomline, George. *Memoirs of the Life of the Right Honorable William Pitt*. 3 vols. Second Edition. London, 1821.

Varg, Paul A. *Foreign Policies of the Founding Fathers*. Michigan State University, 1963.

Wagstaff, Henry McGilbert. *Federalism in North Carolina*. Chapel Hill, 1910.

Wallace, Paul A. W. *The Muhlenbergs of Pennsylvania*. Philadelphia, 1950.

Walters, Raymond, Jr. *Albert Gallatin: Jeffersonian Financier and Diplomat*. New York, 1957.

————. "Alexander James Dallas: Lawyer, Politician, Financier, 1759–1917." Manuscript copy, Library of Congress (n.d.).

Welch, Richard E. *Theodore Sedgwick, Federalist: A Political Portrait*. Middletown, Conn., 1965.

Whitaker, A. P. *The Spanish-American Frontier, 1783–1795*. Boston, 1927.

White, Leonard D. *The Federalists: A Study in Administrative History*. New York, 1948.

Williams, William Appleman. "The Age of Mercantilism: An Interpretation of the American Political Economy, 1763–1828." *William and Mary Quarterly*, Third Series, XV (1958), 419–437.

————. *The Contours of American History*. Cleveland, 1961.

Woolery, W. K. *The Relation of Thomas Jefferson to American Foreign Policy, 1783–1793*. Baltimore, 1927.

Zimmerman, James Fulton. *Impressment of American Seamen*. Columbia University Studies in History, Economics and Public Law, Vol. CXVIII, No. 1. New York, 1925.

INDEX